Extending Acrobat
Forms with
JAVASCRIPT

JOHN DEUBERT

Extending Acrobat Forms with JavaScript
John Deubert
Copyright © 2003 by John Deubert

This Adobe Press book is published by Peachpit Press.
For information on Adobe Press books, contact:
Peachpit Press
1249 Eighth Street
Berkeley, CA 94710
510/524-2178 (tel) / 510/524-2221 (fax)

To report errors, please send a note to errata@peachpit.com
Peachpit Press is a division of Pearson Education
For the latest on Adobe Press books go to
http://www.adobe.com/adobepress

Editor: Becky Morgan
Production Coordinator: Lisa Brazieal
Copyeditor: Sally Zahner
Compositor: Maureen Forys
Interior Design: Mimi Heft
Indexer: FireCrystal Communications
Cover Design: Hugh D'Andrade

ISBN 0-321-17238-8

9 8 7 6 5 4 3 2 1

Printed and bound in the United States of America

Dedication

For Barbara, always.

Acknowledgements

It takes a whole village to raise a book; the author gets to put his or her name on the cover, but it is everyone together who actually creates the creature of bound paper that sits on a bookshelf. I would like to thank several people who were part of the creation of this particular paper beast: in particular, my editor, Becky Morgan, who never, not once, boxed my ears for proposing radical changes to the book and asking when the deadline was. Production coordinator Lisa Brazieal, who made sure that the book was a pleasure to behold. There would also be no book without copyeditor Sally Zahner ("She of the Eagle Eye"), compositor Maureen Forys, and indexer Emily Glossbrenner. I also thank Hugh D'Andrade, who designed the beautiful cover.

There are many other people at Adobe and at Peachpit Press whose work went into this book and I thank them all.

Table of Contents

Introduction

Welcome to the Land of Acrobat JavaScript.

This book will teach you how to extend the abilities of your Acrobat forms by adding JavaScript programs to form fields, pages, and to the documents themselves. It is hard to exaggerate the extent to which JavaScript can enhance your forms' appearance, functionality, and interface; suffice it to say that even a basic knowledge of JavaScript opens a very wide range of capabilities to a form designer.

JavaScript is very fun, very powerful stuff. If you have already designed a range of forms and are looking to add such things as connection to databases, sophisticated user-interface features, automatic form-field formatting, and dynamically visible form fields, Acrobat JavaScript is the means by which you do this.

This book will show you how.

The Book

What this book is

This book is a non-programmer's guide to adding specific features to your Acrobat forms using JavaScript. If you are a form designer with good Acrobat experience, but have never written a line of JavaScript, C, or other programming code before (and were pretty sure you never wanted to do so), then this book is for you. We shall introduce programming concepts as we learn how to add specific enhancements to your forms; for example, we talk about arrays while adding a price table to a form, case statements while creating a pop-up menu, if...else commands while checking the version of the user's Acrobat viewer.

This book is not a complete reference to the JavaScript Language or to the JavaScript capabilities of Adobe Acrobat; it is a non-programmers introduction to both. Having read this book, you will be in an excellent position to read a more formal reference on the complete JavaScript language and to make use of Adobe's documentation on Acrobat JavaScript.

With one exception, all of the examples in this book will work with either the Mac or Windows version of Adobe Acrobat; the exception is database connectivity, which exists only in Acrobat for Windows. Illustrations are taken from both platforms; thankfully, the Acrobat user interface is nearly identical in the Mac and Windows versions.

Most of the scripts presented will work for either Acrobat 4 or Acrobat 5; some require the later version. Restrictions are noted when appropriate.

I am assuming you have reasonable experience in designing and creating Acrobat forms. We won't be discussing the mechanics of creating form fields or the differences among the different types of form fields. I also assume you are very comfortable with your computer environment.

How to use this book

The first two chapters of this book present basic information and terminology; and therefore must be read before you continue. Chapter 19 is a list of resources. The remaining chapters may be used in two ways:

- You can read Chapters 3 through 18 in order, proceeding as you would through any other book.

  Overall, this is probably the more effective way to approach the book, since chapters cannot help but refer to each other to some extent.

When you finish, you will have accumulated quite a sum of useful techniques and information for using JavaScript in Acrobat.

■ You can read Chapters 3 through 18 on a topic-by-topic basis, reading those chapters that apply to a specific feature you want to add to your forms.

Thus, if you need to add roll-over help to a form, you can skip ahead to Chapter 7 and see how to do it. The chapters have all been written to be somewhat autonomous; you don't need to read them sequentially to use the information. Some chapters will insist on being read as a unit (for example, Chapters 10, 11, and 12 on form field validation and formatting must be read as a set to be useful) and other chapters will send you elsewhere in the book for background information. By and large, however, the chapters are intended to be semi-independent parts.

All the chapters, however, assume you have read Chapters 1 and 2; start with those.

Online Resources

The Web site

Most chapters in this book are built around a sample form, to which we add JavaScripts that accomplish that chapter's goal. The form files for all the chapters are available free for the downloading on the *Extending Acrobat Forms* Web page: http://www.acumentraining.com/acrobatjs.html

Here you will find all the forms that appear in the book. Each form comes in two versions:

■ The complete form, with all JavaScripts in place and all the features working

■ A "raw" version of the form, with that chapter's JavaScripts missing

For example, for Chapter 3, you will find two form files: Ch03_Example1.pdf and Ch03_Example1_raw.pdf.

Each chapter gives step-by-step instructions for adding the JavaScripts to the raw version of the form. If you prefer to see the JavaScript already in place, just follow those same numbered steps with the complete file; when you get to the "type in the JavaScript" step, you will find the script already in place.

The *Acumen Journal*

You can find additional information on Acrobat JavaScript in my free, monthly newsletter, the *Acumen Journal.* Every month, the *Journal* has an article on Acrobat; every second month, that Acrobat article covers some topic in JavaScript that is specifically intended for readers of this book. The article presents information on how to do something useful in JavaScript or adds to your knowledge of the JavaScript language. These articles explicitly assume you have read this book. (Other people can also read the articles, of course; they will simply have to know as much as you will know upon finishing the book.)

The Acumen Journal is available at: http://www.acumentraining.com/ajournal.asp.

There is also a link to the *Journal* on the *Extending Acrobat Forms* Web page mentioned above.

Welcome to JavaScript!

Life is full of threshold phenomena.

Periodically in life, you learn something that broadens your world immeasurably, revealing an expanse of new experience, problems, opportunities, play, and work. Whole worlds that had invisibly surrounded you suddenly appear, providing a new space to explore. Reading, sex, driving, children, all bring with them concerns, interests, and interactions that had been previously inaccessible and unsuspected.

In its own small way, learning JavaScript will be just such a threshold event in your professional life. If you've been working with Acrobat for any length of time, you've probably gotten pretty good at it and have become quite comfortable at creating forms, adding music, creating slide shows, and all the other features Acrobat offers.

This book introduces the New World. A knowledge of JavaScript allows you to do things within Acrobat that far exceed what you've done so far: You can interface with databases; add your own pop-up menus; create forms with sophisticated, interactive interfaces; and implement form fields that can look up prices and other data. These are only a few of the things you can do within your Acrobat documents using JavaScript. The extent to which you can manipulate your Acrobat files is vastly greater with JavaScript skills than without.

Hence, this book.

Here you will learn how to accomplish a variety of useful tasks in Acrobat using JavaScript. Along the way, you will learn a great deal about JavaScript, programming, and Acrobat.

What You Should Know Already

This book assumes you have reasonably extensive experience in working with Acrobat and creating Acrobat forms. In particular, I assume you know how to create forms in Acrobat; you should be able to create a form field, set its properties, and assign actions to it. If you feel vaguely uneasy about any of these tasks, you may want to run right off and buy my earlier Adobe Press book, *Creating Adobe Acrobat Forms.* Buy two copies!

Beyond that, this book does not assume any knowledge of programming; you will learn the programming skills you need as we proceed through our examples.

What *Is* JavaScript?

JavaScript is a programming language. The term *programming language* often induces a case of jitters in newcomers, but, conceptually, it's not very scary: A programming language is a language that is used to describe the steps involved in carrying out some task. In Acrobat, these tasks include moving to a particular page of a document, sending data to a database, and calculating a form field value. Carrying out the steps described by a JavaScript is referred to as *executing* the program.

As a programming language, JavaScript's most significant characteristic is that it's sufficiently simple that many applications use it as their native scripting language. All Web browsers can interpret JavaScripts embedded in Web pages, and, particular to our topic, Acrobat can execute JavaScripts attached to form fields, pages, and PDF files.

Like any language, JavaScript has its own *vocabulary* (words that have meaning) and *syntax* (rules by which you make statements with those words). Learning JavaScript, therefore, has much in common with learning a human language, such as Spanish or German, only it's *much* easier. JavaScript is vastly simpler than any human language: There are no metaphors, no literally nonsensical idioms, no synonyms, no subtle shades of meaning. Just very precise statements telling Acrobat to do something specific.

JavaScript in Acrobat

Acrobat allows you to create four different kinds of JavaScripts:

- *Form Field JavaScripts* are attached to form fields. Acrobat executes the script when a particular event occurs in that form field, such as a button click. Most JavaScripts in Acrobat are attached to form fields.

- *Page JavaScripts* are executed when the user moves to or leaves a particular page in the Acrobat document.

- *Document Action JavaScripts* are executed when the user opens, closes, saves, or prints a document.

- *Document JavaScripts* are executed when the Acrobat document opens.

We shall talk about Page, Document Action, and Document JavaScripts in Chapter 2. For now, let's look at how you type in and use a Form Field JavaScript.

Our First JavaScript

(Files: Ch01.Example1.pdf, Ch01.Example1Raw.pdf)

Let's start exploring our new world by adding a simple JavaScript to the form field in **Figure 1.1**.

This form consists of a set of flash cards that are intended to be printed double-sided and then used to quiz students on vocabulary terms. Our PDF file has only a few flash cards; each card has a button that takes users to an order form they can use to purchase the complete set of cards. We are going to add a JavaScript to the Order Form button that takes the user to the order form, located on the last page of the Acrobat file (**Figure 1.2**).

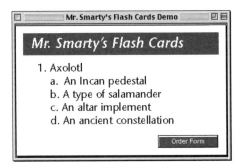

Figure 1.1 We shall add a JavaScript to this form, attached to the Order Form button's Mouse Up event.

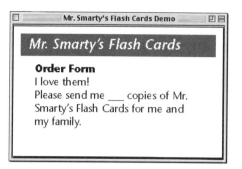

Figure 1.2   *The JavaScript associated with the Order Form button takes the viewer to the final page in the Acrobat document, which is an order page.*

As will be true throughout this book, there are two versions of this form on the book's Web page:

- Ch01.Example1.pdf is the full form, complete with all relevant JavaScripts.

- Ch01.Example1Raw.pdf, the "raw" version, lacks the chapter's JavaScripts so that you may type in the JavaScript yourself if you wish.

Attaching a JavaScript to a Form Field

As a reminder of something you probably already know, let's step through the process of attaching a JavaScript to a button, in this case our Order Form button.

To attach a JavaScript to a button:

Start with the form open in Adobe Acrobat.

1. Click on the Form tool 📋 .

Acrobat will display all of the form fields on the current page as a set of rectangles. Note that in our case, there's only one form field (**Figure 1.3**).

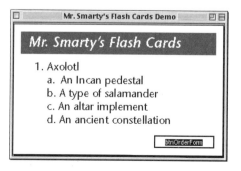

Figure 1.3   *Our flash card form has only one form field on each page: a button, btnOrderForm, that takes the user to the order form page.*

Form Field Events

As shown in Figure 1.4, there are six form field *events* to which you can attach an action:

- *Mouse Down* occurs when the user depresses the mouse button with the pointer in the form field.

- *Mouse Up* occurs when the user clicks on the field and then releases the mouse button with the mouse pointer still in the field.

- *Mouse Enter* occurs when the mouse pointer first enters the form field.

- *Mouse Exit* occurs when the mouse pointer leaves the form field.

- *On Focus* occurs when the user clicks on or tabs into the form field, so that it becomes the target for keyboard or other input.

- *On Blur* occurs when the user tabs out of a form field or clicks on some other form field, so that our field is no longer the target for user input. (*Blur* is the opposite of *Focus*, of course.)

The Field Properties dialog box, in Figure 1.4, lets you associate one or more Acrobat Actions (a JavaScript action, in our case) with any of these events.

2. Double-click the Order Form button.

Acrobat will present you with the Field Properties dialog box (**Figure 1.4**). Click the Actions tab. We want to attach a JavaScript action to the Mouse Up event for this button.

3. Select the Mouse Up action and click the Add button.

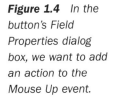

Figure 1.4 In the button's Field Properties dialog box, we want to add an action to the Mouse Up event.

You will now be looking at the Add an Action dialog box (**Figure 1.5**). Here is where we tell Acrobat what action we want to attach to the Mouse Up event.

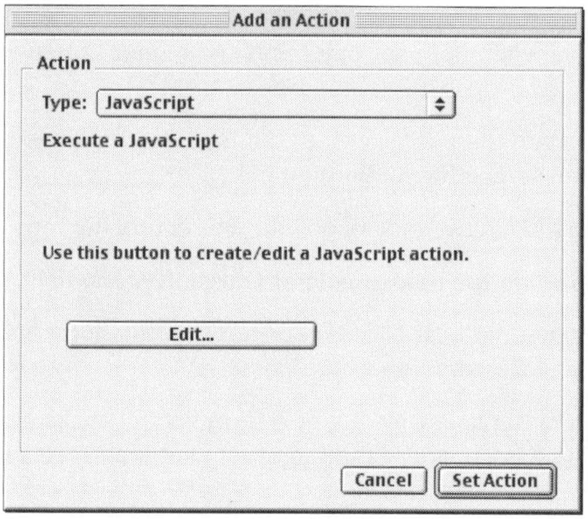

Add an Action

Action

Type: JavaScript

Execute a JavaScript

Use this button to create/edit a JavaScript action.

Edit...

Cancel   Set Action

Figure 1.5 *The Add an Action dialog box is where we attach Acrobat actions to events. We shall be attaching the JavaScript action to the Mouse Up event.*

4. In the Type pop-up menu, select JavaScript and then click the Edit button.

Acrobat will present you with the JavaScript Edit dialog box, which contains a simple text editor (**Figure 1.6**). This is where you type in the JavaScript that should be associated with the Order Form button.

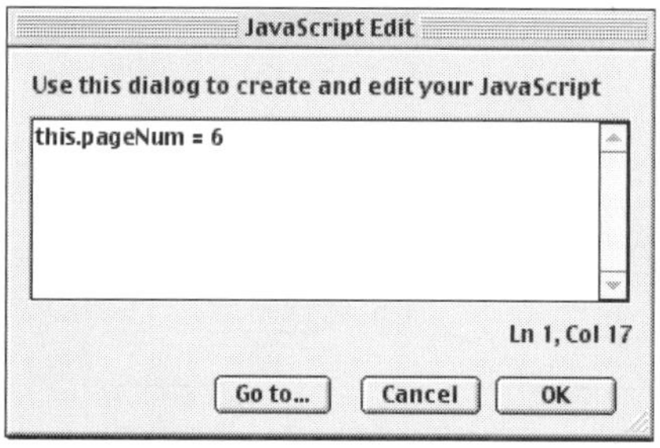

JavaScript Edit

Use this dialog to create and edit your JavaScript

this.pageNum = 6

Ln 1, Col 17

Go to...   Cancel   OK

Figure 1.6 *The JavaScript Edit dialog box provides a simple text-editing field into which you can type your JavaScript code.*

5. Type your JavaScript into the text field of this dialog box.

In the case of our order form, the JavaScript is a two-line program that moves the user's view of the document to the page containing the order form and then causes the user's computer to beep: Type these lines into the text-editing field exactly as above, making sure to match upper- and lowercase.

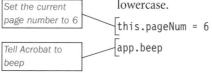

```
this.pageNum = 6
app.beep
```

Set the current page number to 6

Tell Acrobat to beep

The first line of code says, "In this document, set the current page number to 6." The second line tells the Acrobat application to beep.

6. Click the OK buttons of the JavaScript Edit, Add an Action, and Field Properties dialog boxes to return to the Acrobat form.

   You are now looking at the Acrobat flash card page with the Form tool still selected, as in **Figure 1.3**.

7. Click the Acrobat Hand tool .

   You are now back where you started.

8. Try it out: Click the Order Form button, and Acrobat will move to the order form page and then beep.

JavaScript Objects

Our two-line JavaScript makes use of two **JavaScript objects.** A JavaScript object is the representation of some piece of data within your JavaScript program. Before your program can manipulate or examine a form field, it must first create an object that represents that field. Most of the things you can manipulate in JavaScript (pages, signatures, database connections, and so on) are represented in your program as objects.

In our sample program, this refers to a **Doc object.** A Doc object represents an open Acrobat file to your JavaScript program; you use this object to change pages, save the document, and otherwise manipulate the document from within your program. The word this in our sample JavaScript refers particularly to the Acrobat document in which our JavaScript resides (the flash cards file, in our case); think of it as short for *this document.*

Program vs. Script vs. Code

Here are some closely related terms that we'll be using throughout this book.

- *Program* is a general term for a series of instructions that detail for a computer how to carry out a particular task. In general, a program is a stand-alone set of instructions, such as an application.

- A *Script* is a program that is intended to manipulate another program. JavaScript is a scripting language, because you use it to control the behavior of another program, such as Acrobat or Internet Explorer.

- *Code* is the term applied to the set of instructions that make up a program. Your JavaScript program is made up of JavaScript code.

The word app is an **App object,** a reference to the Acrobat application being used to view the current document. You use an App object to tell the Acrobat application to do something: open a file, put up an alert dialog box, or, in our case, beep.

Commonly used JavaScript object types include:

- *Annot* represents an annotation (for example, a "sticky note") in the current document.

- *App* represents the Acrobat application being used to view the current document.

- *Connection* represents a connection to an external database.

- *Doc* represents the current (frontmost) open Acrobat document.

- *Field* represents a form field.

- *Sound* represents a sound embedded in the current document.

Object properties

JavaScript objects are analogous to physical objects in the world around us, such as books, vases, and dogs. Every real-world object possesses a set of characteristics that define it (such as, for a dog, color, tail length, and number of fleas).

Which Acrobat?

There are currently three applications that are routinely used to view Acrobat files:

- *Adobe Acrobat Reader* is the free application that lets you view and print **PDF** files.

- *Adobe Acrobat Approval* is a relatively inexpensive product that lets a user view, print, and annotate PDF files and fully fill out Acrobat forms.

- *Adobe Acrobat* ("the full Acrobat") is what you use to add features to PDF files: rearrange pages, create form fields, specify start-up properties, and, specific to our purpose, attach JavaScripts to form fields.

Only with the full Acrobat can you create form fields and attach JavaScripts to form fields and pages. Most of the JavaScripts you write will work correctly with any of the three Acrobat viewer packages. There are exceptions (the Reader is particularly limited), but they are relatively few.

In this book, I will refer to all three of the Acrobat viewers as "Acrobat" except for cases where they behave differently.

The characteristics of a JavaScript object are referred to as that object's properties. These are elements of an object that our JavaScript programs can examine and change as needed. Each type of object has a set of properties that characterize it; for example, Doc objects have, among other things, a title, a current page number, an author, and a number of pages (see **Table 1.1**).

Table 1.1 Document Object Properties (Partial)

PROPERTY	DATA TYPE	DESCRIPTION
author	String	The author of the document
fileSize	Integer	The size of the PDF file, in bytes
numPages	Integer	The number of pages in the document
pageNum	Integer	The page number currently visible to the user
title	String	The name of the document

The phrase `this.pageNum` addresses the `pageNum` property of the Document object; this property is the page number the document is currently displaying to the user. Our program moves the user to the order form page by setting the current document's `pageNum` property to the order form's page number:

```
this.pageNum = 6
```

Data Types

The Data Type column of **Table 1.1** lists the type of information associated with each of the properties it lists. Computer programming, including JavaScript, uses special terms to precisely describe types of data. Here are the terms commonly used in JavaScript:

- *Integer* is a whole number, such as 1, 2, 87, or -6293.

- *Floating Point* is a number with a fractional part, such as 1.7, -842.9011, 1024.0. Note that the fractional part may be zero, as in 1024.0; in this case, the floating point number has the same value as an integer, though internally it is still a floating point number. Floating point numbers are often referred to as *floats*.

- *Boolean* is an entity that can have two values: true or false. Boolean data are used to describe characteristics that can have only two states. (For example, the *spayed* property in our dog object is a Boolean value; a dog either is or isn't.)

- *String* is text, that is, a "string of characters."

Some observations about this page number assignment:

- You address the property of an object by naming both the object and the property, joined by a period: *object-name.property-name.*

- The equal sign in the line of code above is an *assignment command*; it sets the value of something. In our case, it sets the current document's page number to 6.

- JavaScript is case-sensitive. Upper- and lowercases are distinct; our program would have failed if we had typed `This.PageNum`.

- Counterintuitively, Acrobat internally numbers pages in a document starting at zero; the seven pages in our Acrobat file are numbered zero through six. Thus, when our JavaScript set the `pageNum` property to 6, it was moving us to the last page in the document.

Object methods

A **method** is a command that is associated with a JavaScript object. Just as a dog can be given commands ("Sit," "Heel," "Spit that out this instant!"), JavaScript objects have commands that they can carry out. The set of commands is different for each type of object. For example, **Table 1.2** lists some of the commands the app object knows how to execute.

Table 1.2 *App Object Methods (Partial)*

METHOD	ARGUMENTS	DESCRIPTION
beep		Play the system's "beep" sound
alert	String	Put up an alert dialog box with the specified text
goBack		Go to the previous view
goForward		Go to the next view
newDoc		Open a new, blank Acrobat file
openDoc	String	Open an Acrobat file. The string argument contains the name of the file

In our Order Form JavaScript, we executed the app object's beep method:

```
app.beep
```

Note that we execute an object's method in the same way that we refer to one of its properties: the object name, a "dot," and the method name.

Some methods need additional information in order to carry out their task; for example, the openDoc method listed in **Table 1.2** needs to know the name of the file you want to open. Information handed to a method is called an **argument** to that method. The openDoc method takes a filename as its argument; this information, surrounded by parentheses, must follow the method name. An invocation of openDoc would look something like this:

```
app.openDoc("TermPaper.pdf")
```

The above JavaScript statement would open an Acrobat file named TermPaper.pdf.

Sometimes when you give a dog a command, you expect the dog to give you something back: the command, "Fetch the stick, boy!" should yield a stick in your hand. Similarly, many JavaScript methods have a **return value**, some piece of data they give back to the JavaScript program. The openDoc method we invoked above actually returns a Doc object representing the newly opened document, though our single-line use of openDoc just ignores it. We shall look at return values in much more detail in the next chapter.

JavaScript Program Syntax

Here we must discuss a couple of short topics regarding how JavaScript commands are put together into a program.

JavaScript statements

A JavaScript program—any computer program—consists of a series of statements, each of which carries out one step in the overall task. Our sample program consists of two statements:

```
this.pageNum = 6
app.beep
```

Usually, each line within a JavaScript program will contain a single JavaScript statement, as in our program above. You can put more than one statement on a line, separated by semicolons. Our two-line program could have been written on a single line:

```
this.pageNum = 6; app.beep
```

Why would you do this? Purely for esthetics; some people just prefer to combine very simple statements together. I recommend against this practice;

most programs are much easier to read if you have only one statement per line.

If you read other people's JavaScripts, you may notice that many programmers put semicolons at the end of every line in their program:

```
this.pageNum = 6;

app.beep;
```

This doesn't hurt anything, but it's quite unnecessary. Most of them do it out of habit; JavaScript looks very much like the programming languages C and C++, both of which require that all statements end with a semicolon. You can leave out the semicolons.

JavaScript text

JavaScript programs are simply text files; you can write them with any text editor or word processor and then copy and paste them into the Acrobat JavaScript Edit dialog box. In fact, the Windows version of Acrobat lets you specify an external editor that should be used for editing your JavaScripts; we'll discuss how to do this at the end of the chapter.

Space and tab characters within a JavaScript line have no particular meaning in JavaScript. You can use them as you wish to format your program. This is a purely visual issue; you want to format your JavaScript code so that it's easy to read.

Use whitespace characters lavishly! Reading program code is tedious at best; a program can be nearly undecipherable if the programmer has not formatted the code for easy reading. This is an important enough issue that I shall be providing formatting tips for many of the JavaScript constructs we use in this book.

JavaScript Errors

In the (ahem) rare event that you have an error in your JavaScript—you misspelled a variable name, miscopied a piece of code, and so on—Acrobat will present you with a dialog box called the JavaScript Console (**Figure 1.7**). The Console will display a message indicating the nature of the error; it will sometimes (but not always, alas) also indicate the line number within the script in which the error took place.

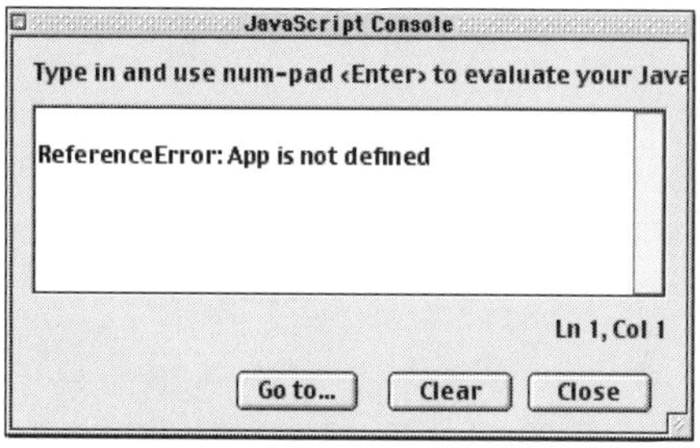

Figure 1.7 *The JavaScript Console is a dialog box used by Acrobat to display error messages that indicate a problem in your JavaScript code.*

Error messages can be somewhat cryptic at first, but with time and familiarity they become useful. The most common messages you are likely to see are the following:

- Reference Error: - XXX is not defined

  This indicates that you misspelled something; the name "XXX" (or whatever) is not one that JavaScript knows. Remember that JavaScript is case-sensitive; there is a difference between *app* (which JavaScript knows) and *App* (which it doesn't know).

- Syntax Error

  This means that JavaScript could not make sense of something in the code. This usually means you left something (a comma, a number, a close parenthesis) out of your script. An example of a syntax error would be

  ```
  app.alert("Hi, Mom", 3
  ```

  This line is missing its closing parenthesis.

The set of possible error messages is quite large, though most are pretty hard to provoke. Just sit tight, read the message, and carefully examine the suspect JavaScript code for misspellings and omissions.

JavaScript Comments

JavaScript code can be pretty cryptic. Puzzling over someone else's code (or even your own code from six months ago), trying to figure out exactly what it's doing, can be tedious. As a courtesy to others looking at your code and as an aid to your future self, it is very important to place comments in your JavaScript code.

A JavaScript *comment* is text in your code that is ignored by the JavaScript "machine." The purpose is to let you place your own notes in the text to be read by human beings examining the code.

JavaaScript recognizes (that is, ignores) two kinds of comments:

- *Single-line comments* start with a double slash (//) and extend to the end of the line in the JavaScript code. These are intended for brief comments.

```
//This is a single-line comment.
```

- *Block comments* start with a /* and end with a */. Between these two delimiters can be as much text as you wish, spread out over as many lines as you wish within the JavaScript file. This is for longer comments.

```
/* Here we have a block comment. This
   text will be completely ignored until
   we end the comment, right here. */
```

An example

Consider the following, uncommented JavaScript from later in this book:

```
var txtField = event.target
txtField.fillColor = color.red
txtField.textColor = color.white
```

Since we have not yet discussed these commands, the purpose of this script and how it carries out that purpose are very unclear.

On the other hand, if we include comments in the code, then it becomes possible for someone unfamiliar with the program to at least know what the intent of the program is and generally what it's doing:

```
/* This program changes the background and text color of
   a text field when the user tabs into or clicks in the
   field. */
var txtField = event.target      // Get a reference to the text field
txtField.fillColor = color.red    // Set the background to red
txtField.textColor = color.white // Set the text color to white
```

This version of the program is much clearer, even to someone new to the code.

Comments are a Force for Good in programming. Any script more complex than a couple of lines should include comments that describe what it does and how it works.

All of the examples in the rest of this book will be heavily commented to make them as comprehensible as possible.

Acrobat JavaScript Guide

This book is a nonprogrammer's introduction to using JavaScript within Adobe Acrobat. The full description of all of the things you can do with JavaScript in Acrobat is presented in a document distributed with the full Acrobat package: the *Acrobat JavaScript Object Specification* (AJOS) (**Figure 1.8**). This is the technical specification of all of the object types available to your JavaScript programs within Acrobat.

The AJOS is a technical specification, not a document you would read from one end to the other. It gives a detailed description of every JavaScript object type available in Acrobat and the properties and methods of each. Where the book you are reading presents a series of examples of how to carry out specific tasks in JavaScript, the AJOS describes *everything* you can do in Acrobat with JavaScript.

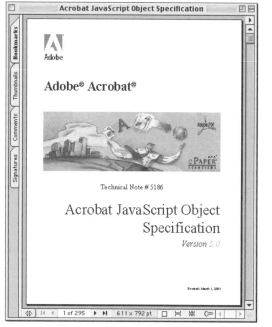

Figure 1.8 *The Acrobat JavaScript Object Specification describes, in detail, all the objects available to an Acrobat JavaScript, their properties, and their methods.*

To give you a bit of the flavor of the AJOS, **Figure 1.9** shows a screenshot of the complete description of the app object's beep method.

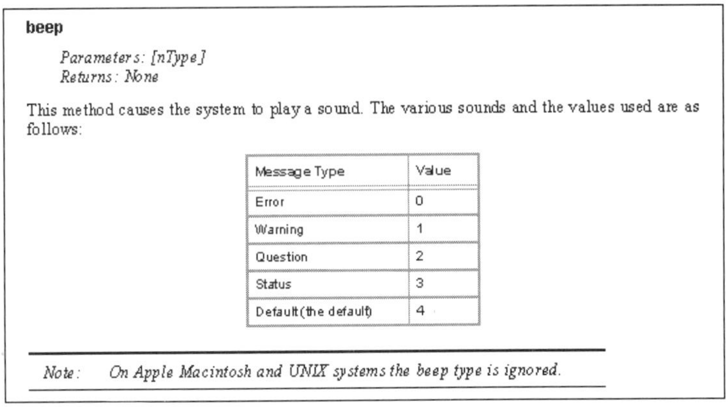

beep

> Parameters: [nType]
> Returns: None

This method causes the system to play a sound. The various sounds and the values used are as follows:

Message Type	Value
Error	0
Warning	1
Question	2
Status	3
Default (the default)	4

Note: On Apple Macintosh and UNIX systems the beep type is ignored.

Figure 1.9 *The description of the* app *object's* beep *method is a good example of the type of description provided for every object, method, and property in the Acrobat JavaScript Object Specification.*

I shall be making occasional references to the AJOS throughout this book.

You can open the AJOS directly from Acrobat by selecting Help > Acrobat JavaScript Guide.

Using Your Own Text Editor

The text editor built into Acrobat's JavaScript Edit dialog box (see Figure 1.6) is pretty minimal. It lets you type in your JavaScript, but it has no particularly fancy editing capabilities. For short JavaScripts, this is not important; when typing long, complex JavaScripts, however, you will miss having a fully featured text editor.

On the Macintosh, you can type your JavaScript into your own text editor and then copy and paste it into the JavaScript Edit dialog box. For what it's worth, my favorite free text editor on the Mac is BBEdit Lite, by Bare Bones Software (www.barebones.com).

The Windows version of Acrobat can automatically launch the text editor of your choice when you click on the Edit button in the Add an Action dialog box (see Figure 1.5). To set this up, you must specify in Acrobat's Preferences the editor you wish to use for editing JavaScripts.

To specify a text editor to use when editing JavaScripts:

Start with Acrobat open.

1. Select File > Preferences > General.

    Acrobat will present you with its Preferences dialog box.

2. Select JavaScript in the list of Preferences categories.

    The Preferences dialog box will display the controls that affect Acrobat's JavaScript support (**Figure 1.10**).

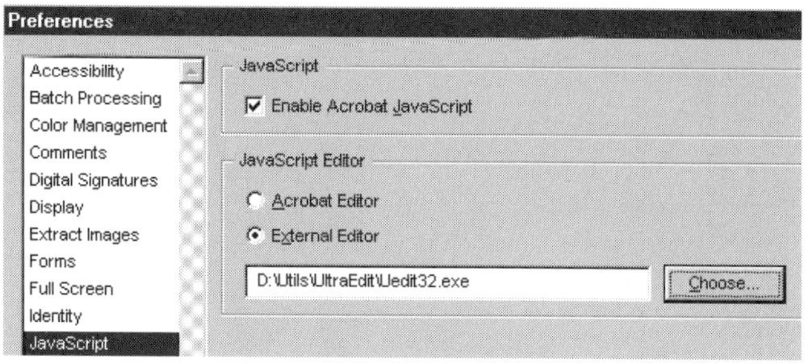

Figure 1.10 *The Acrobat Preferences dialog box allows you to use your favorite text editor to enter your JavaScript code. Alas, this is available only in the Windows version of Acrobat.*

3. Among the JavaScript Editor controls, select External Editor.

4. Click the Choose button and then navigate to the .exe file for the editor you want to use when editing JavaScripts.

5. Click the OK button.

That's all there is to it. Now, when you go to edit a JavaScript, Acrobat will automatically launch your text editor. Type your JavaScript code into the text editor's window, save the text, and then close the text editor. Your JavaScript will be automatically entered into Acrobat.

Among Windows text editors, I'm rather fond of TextPad (www.textpad.com) and UltraEdit (www.ultraedit.com); they are both relatively inexpensive shareware and well worth the money.

Page and Document JavaScripts

There are four broad types of JavaScripts in Acrobat, each differing in where it's used in the Acrobat document.

- *Form Field* JavaScripts are attached to form fields. As we saw in the previous chapter, Form Field scripts are associated with events that occur with a form field: Mouse Down, On Focus, and so on.

- *Document* JavaScripts are associated with the opening of the Acrobat file. Acrobat executes these when the document is first opened.

- *Document Action* JavaScripts are executed when one of a set of predefined events happens with the Acrobat file: the file closes, is saved, and so on.

- *Page* JavaScripts are associated with a particular page. You can provide scripts that Acrobat will execute when the user enters that page, leaves that page, or both.

We discussed Form Field JavaScripts in Chapter 1. In this chapter, we'll look at how to write the other three types of scripts.

The Project

(Files: Ch02_Example.pdf, Ch02_Example_raw.pdf)

Our sample file for this chapter is the pet store catalog pictured in **Figure** 2.1. In the course of our discussion, we'll add examples of Document, Document Action, and Page JavaScripts to this file.

Figure 2.1   *We will add several JavaScripts to this pet store catalog.*

Document JavaScripts

Document JavaScripts are attached to an Acrobat document and are executed by Acrobat upon opening that document. This is a convenient way to present the reader with an initial "splash screen" or to carry out some other start-up activity when the user opens your PDF file. You may attach as many Document JavaScripts to an Acrobat file as you wish.

As an example, we'll add a Document JavaScript to our catalog that displays a greeting when the reader opens our catalog document (**Figure** 2.2).

Figure 2.2   *We'll use a Document JavaScript to present this welcoming dialog box when our user opens the Acrobat file.*

To attach a Document JavaScript to an Acrobat document:

Start with the document open in Acrobat.

1. Select Tools > JavaScript > Document JavaScripts (**Figure 2.3**).

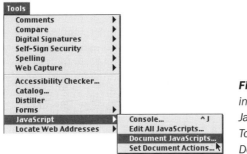

Figure 2.3 *The first step in creating a Document JavaScript is to select Tools > JavaScript > Document JavaScripts.*

Acrobat will display the JavaScript Functions dialog box (**Figure 2.4**).

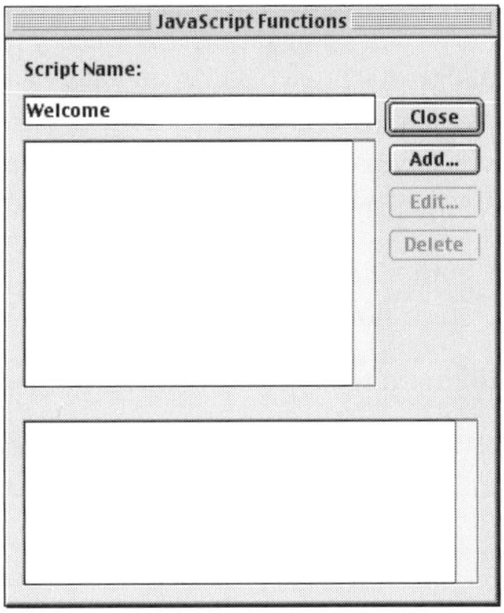

Figure 2.4 *The JavaScript Functions dialog box is where you add, edit, and delete Document JavaScripts.*

2. Type a name in the Script Name field of the JavaScript Functions dialog box.

Each Document JavaScript must have a name. Make it descriptive and short, and avoid using any tabs or spaces. In our case, let's use the name Welcome, since that's the purpose of this script.

3. Click the Add button.

Acrobat will present you with the JavaScript Edit dialog box (**Figure 2.5**). Note that this dialog box appears with some JavaScript code already entered into the text field. This code is the starting point for a JavaScript function definition; since we're not going to be defining a function, you can delete this initial code.

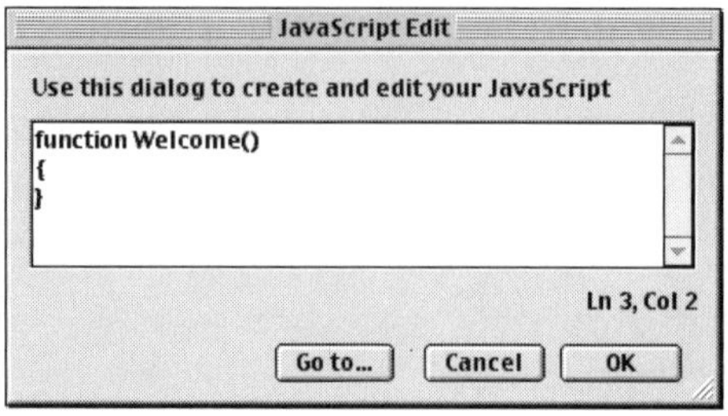

Figure 2.5 *Acrobat uses this same JavaScript Edit dialog box whenever it wants you to type some JavaScript code. In the case of Document JavaScripts, Acrobat supplies some initial JavaScript code, which we won't use; you should delete it.*

4. Type your own JavaScript in the Edit box. In our case, the JavaScript should be a single line:

```
app.alert("Welcome to the 1-Off Pets catalog!", 3)
```

This JavaScript displays the alert shown in **Figure 2.2**. The app object's alert method displays an alert with the specified text. The 3 indicates the kind of icon that should appear in the alert. We'll look at this method in more detail in Chapter 13. (You may recall we discussed the app object in Chapter 1.)

5. Click the OK button to return to the JavaScript Functions dialog box (**Figure 2.6**), which now lists our new Welcome script.

6. Click Close to return to the Acrobat file.

7. Try it out by saving the Acrobat file, closing it, and then reopening it. Acrobat should display the alert shown in **Figure 2.2**.

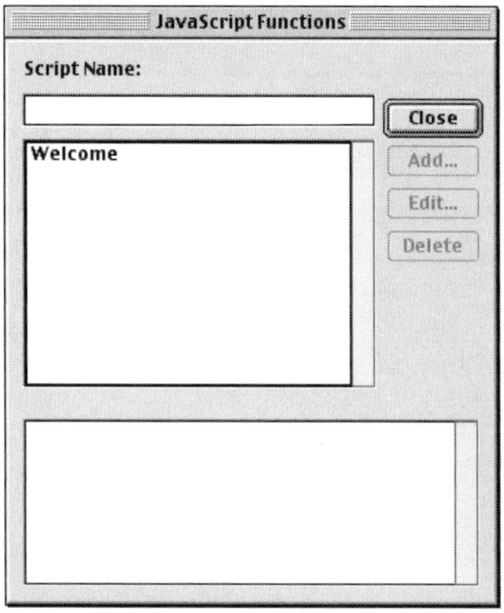

Figure 2.6 *The Welcome JavaScript now appears in the list of Document JavaScripts attached to this Acrobat file.*

Global Variables

One unobvious characteristic of Document JavaScripts is that any variables they create are visible to all the other JavaScripts in your document. For example, imagine you created a Document JavaScript with this line in it:

```
var iconType = 3
```

Here, we've created a variable named iconType whose value is 3. All the other scripts in our Acrobat document, of any sort (Document, Document Action, Page, Form Field) can use the variable iconType instead of the number 3.

```
app.alert("Welcome to the 1-Off Pets catalog!", iconType)
```

This can be very convenient. If you have, say, 50 scripts in your document that create alerts like the one above, changing the definition of iconType in your document script will change the icon displayed by all 50 of those alert JavaScripts.

Our iconType variable is referred to as a **global variable**; it is accessible by all scripts throughout the Acrobat document. We will be making use of global variables occasionally in this book's JavaScripts.

Document Action JavaScripts

A Document Action JavaScript is executed when a specific event occurs with the document. There are five events to which you can attach a JavaScript:

- *Document Will Close* means Acrobat is about to close the document.

- *Document Will Save* means Acrobat is about to save the document.

- *Document Did Save* means Acrobat has finished saving the document.

- *Document Will Print* means Acrobat is about to print the document.

- *Document Did Print* means Acrobat has finished printing the document.

To see how to attach a JavaScript to one of these events, let's make another change to our catalog. When the user closes the Acrobat file, let's thank the user for looking at our wares, as in **Figure 2.7**. We'll do this by attaching a JavaScript to the Document Will Close event.

Figure 2.7 *We'll use a Document Will Close JavaScript to present a farewell message to our user.*

To attach a Document Action JavaScript to a document:

1. Start with the document open in Acrobat. Select Tools > JavaScript > Set Document Actions (**Figure 2.8**).

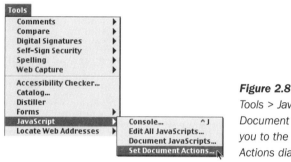

Figure 2.8 Selecting Tools > JavaScript > Set Document Actions takes you to the Document Actions dialog box

Acrobat will display the Document Actions dialog box (**Figure 2.9**).

2. Select Document Will Close, and click the Edit button.

Acrobat will display the JavaScript Edit dialog box.

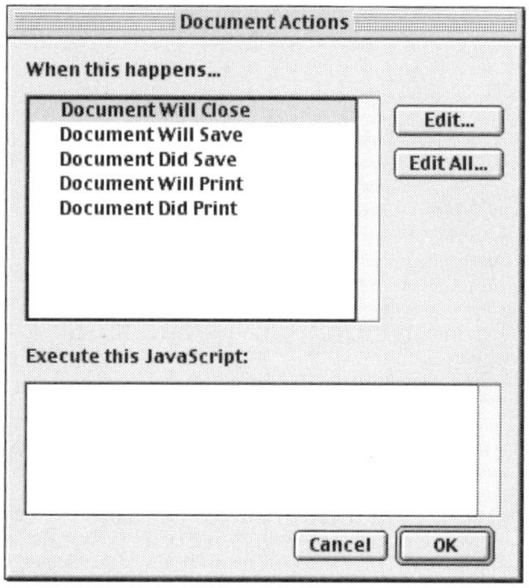

Figure 2.9 The Document Actions dialog box lets you attach a JavaScript to any one of five different events.

3. Type your JavaScript in the dialog box. For our purposes, the script should be:

```
app.alert("Thanks for looking at our catalog!", 3)
```

4. Click OK to back out of the JavaScript Edit and JavaScript Functions dialog boxes; you will now be back at your Acrobat page.

5. Try it out: Save the Acrobat document and then close it. Acrobat will present you with the Thanks alert, as shown in **Figure 2.7**.

Page Action JavaScripts

A Page Action is an Acrobat action that's associated with the opening or closing of a particular page. These can be any of the Action types that Acrobat knows: such as menu items, movie actions, sound actions—and in our case, of course, JavaScript actions. We'll attach a JavaScript action to our page.

There are two kinds of Page Actions in Acrobat:

- *Page Open* actions are executed when the user scrolls to the page (a Page Open event).

- *Page Close* actions are executed when the user leaves the page (a Page Close event).

As an example, we'll attach a Page Open action to the third page in our catalog to announce that 1-Off Pets is having a sale on pet croquet balls. Our Page Open action will display the alert shown in **Figure 2.10** when the user opens page 3.

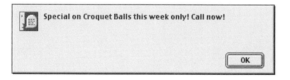

Figure 2.10 *We shall use a Page Open action attached to page 3 of our catalog to announce a sale on croquet balls.*

To attach a Page Action to a page in an Acrobat Document:

Start with the document open to the proper page; in our case, this is page 3.

1. Select Document > Set Page Action.

Acrobat will display the Page Actions dialog box (**Figure 2.11**).

2. Select the Page Open event and click the Add button.

Acrobat will present you with the Add an Action dialog box that we saw in the previous chapter (**Figure 2.12**).

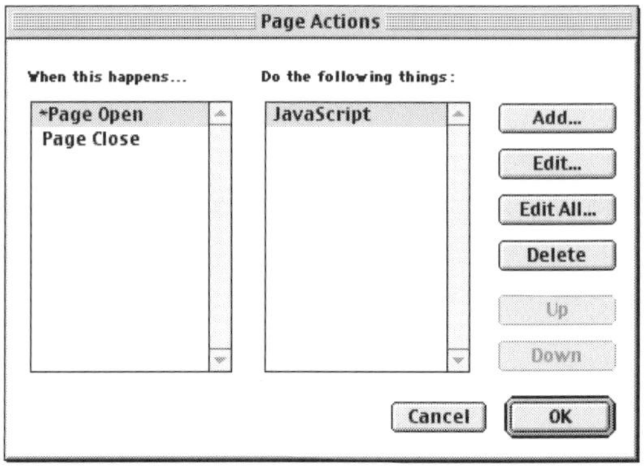

Figure 2.11 The Page Actions dialog box allows us to associate an action with each of two events: Page Open and Page Close.

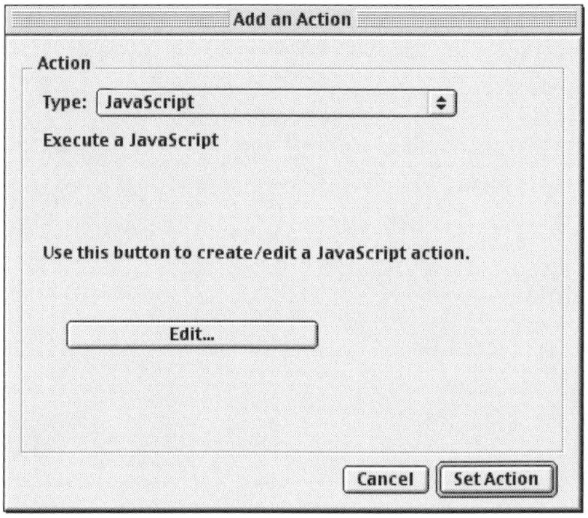

Figure 2.12 The Add an Action dialog box allows us to specify the details of the action associated with an event. Here, we are associating a JavaScript action with the Page Open event.

3. Select JavaScript for the action type and click the Edit button.

Acrobat will display the usual JavaScript Edit dialog box.

4. Type your JavaScript into the dialog box. In this case, use the following:

```
app.alert("Special on Croquet Balls this week only!
→ Call now!", 3)
```

5. Click Set Action and OK to back out of all the dialog boxes until you are again looking at the Acrobat file page.

6. Try it out by going to the previous page in the Catalog and then returning to page 3; you will see the alert that's pictured in **Figure 2.10**.

3

Form Field Highlighting

A recurring theme throughout this book is the importance of user feedback in forms. It should be clear to a user at every moment exactly what he or she is expected to do and what part of your form is expecting information.

In this chapter, we shall look at one useful way of doing this; we shall create a form whose text fields exhibit *colored entry highlighting*—that is, they change color when the user clicks on them or tabs into them.

The Project

(Files: Ch3_Start.pdf, Ch3_End.pdf)

We shall add colored entry highlighting to the order form in **Figure 3.1**. This Acrobat file starts out as an entirely unremarkable form a user would fill out to order a copy of his or her records. As you can see from **Figure 3.2**, this form contains a handful of text fields and a single Submit button.

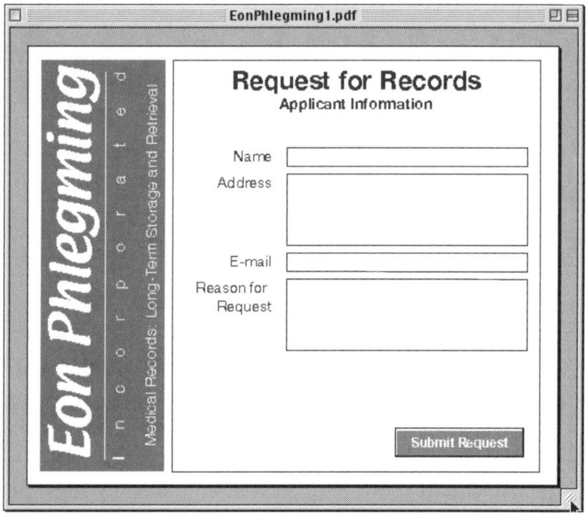

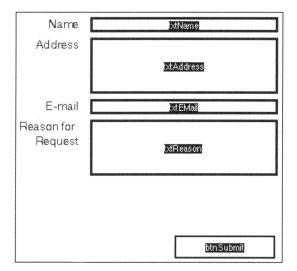

Figure 3.1 _We shall add entry highlighting to this form._

Figure 3.2 _Our form contains four text fields for collecting data from the user and a single button that submits data to the company._

Because of the colored entry highlighting, when the user clicks in a text field, the field will turn red, indicating that it's the active field (**Figure 3.3**).

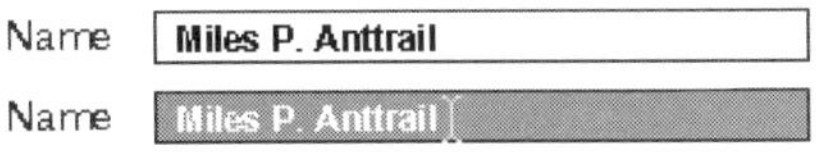

Name | Miles P. Anttrail |

Name | Miles P. Anttrail |

*Figure **3.3*** *When the user clicks in a text field, the field's contents will be highlighted, displaying white text against a red background.*

The JavaScript

Normally, text fields contain black text displayed against a white or transparent background. We are going to modify the text fields so that when the user clicks on a field (or tabs into it), the field turns into white text against a red background, indicating that the field is ready to receive keyboard input (see **Figure 3.3**).

Approaching the Problem

To implement entry highlighting, we shall attach JavaScripts to the On Focus and On Blur events for each text field in our form (**Figure 3.4**). *On Focus* events occur whenever a form field becomes the target for data entry, usually because the user clicked on the field or tabbed into it. *On Blur* events occur when a form field loses the focus—that is, when some other form field becomes the target for data entry. (If the name *On Blur* seems a bit peculiar for this event, what single word would *you* use to describe the opposite of *focus?*)

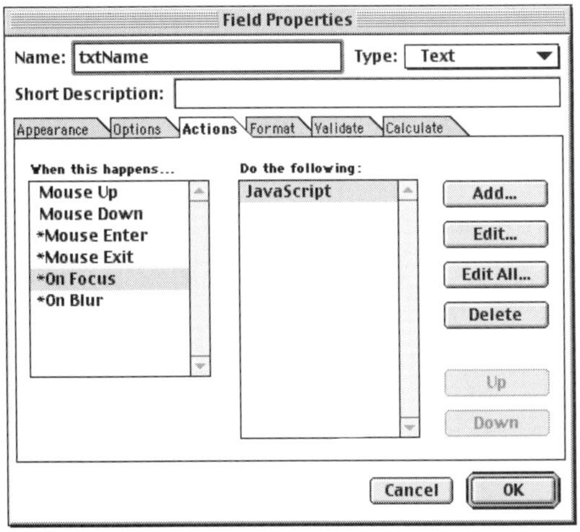

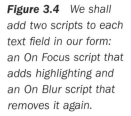

*Figure **3.4*** *We shall add two scripts to each text field in our form: an On Focus script that adds highlighting and an On Blur script that removes it again.*

Our On Focus JavaScript will set the form field's background color to red and turn the text color to white. The On Blur script will set the background and text colors back to transparent and black, respectively. We will need to add these JavaScripts to all of the text fields in which the user may enter data.

By the way, the On Focus and On Blur events were added in Acrobat 5, so our highlighting won't work if the form is viewed with earlier versions of Acrobat. (Nothing will break if the form is viewed with Acrobat 4; the user just won't see the highlighting.)

The Code

Step 1: The On Focus JavaScript

The following JavaScript is intended for the On Focus event of each of the text fields in this form (see **Figure 3.2**).

Get a reference to our text field.

```
// This is the On Focus JavaScript
var txtField = event.target
```

Change the color of the background and text.

```
txtField.fillColor = color.red
txtField.textColor = color.white
```

The code in detail:

```
var txtField = event.target
```

This first line gets the field that caused the On Focus event to occur (the *target* of the event) and assigns it to a named reference (a *variable*) whose name is txtField. This is the name by which we will refer to our text field in the remainder of the JavaScript.

```
txtField.fillColor = color.red
txtField.textColor = color.white
```

Having gotten a reference to our text field, we set two of its properties:

- fillColor is the background color of the form field. We set it to red.

- textColor is the color of the text in the form field. We set it to white.

Notice that we specify our colors as `color.red` and `color.white`. Acrobat provides a set of predefined names for common colors, as follows:

- color.transparent
- color.green
- color.yellow
- color.black
- color.blue
- color.dkGray

- color.white
- color.cyan
- color.gray
- color.red
- color.magenta
- color.ltGray

Step 2: The On Blur JavaScript

Our On Blur script is identical to the On Focus script—only different. We set the `textColor` and `fillColor` properties back to their original values:

```
var txtField = event.target
txtField.fillColor = color.transparent
txtField.textColor = color.black
```

Similarly to step 1, we get a reference to the text field that caused the On Blur event and then change the colors of the background (transparent) and text (black). `color.transparent` is a valid color in this context.

That's all you need to do. Once you add both of these JavaScripts to each text field in your form, your form will have colored entry highlighting and your users will be very impressed.

Customization Notes

There is nothing too difficult about customizing this JavaScript to your own purposes; in fact, the JavaScripts we use here can be used, unmodified, for any text field in any form.

The only sensible bit of customization you may want to do is select other colors for your text fields. You can highlight your text field with any combination of `fillColor` and `textColor` you wish. The list at the end of step 1 shows the standard, named colors that Acrobat recognizes; you can, however, set the colors to any RGB, CMYK, or gray values you wish, using a format such as this:

```
txtField.fillColor = ["RGB", .5, 1, .5 ]
```

The values for the color components—R, G, and B, in our case—must each be a number between 0 and 1.

Finally, if you set both a field's fillColor and textColor to color.transparent, the field effectively disappears. You could use this to dynamically hide a form field; however, we'll look at another, better way to do this in Chapter 8.

Checking
Acrobat Version

Prior to Acrobat 4, support for forms in Acrobat was practically nonexistent. Acrobat 4 introduced robust support for forms into Acrobat, and Acrobat 5 enriched the capabilities of the form mechanism still further. Unfortunately, as a form designer, you have no control over what version of the Acrobat viewer your user may have, and this creates a challenge in form design.

Inevitably, you must make an assumption as to what version of Acrobat is being used to view your form. If a user has version of Acrobat earlier than this, you must detect the fact and handle the situation gracefully.

This is what we shall discuss in this chapter. We shall see how to determine the version of Acrobat our user has and how to automatically close the document if the user's program is too primitive to present it properly.

The Project

(Files: Ch04_Example1.pdf, Ch04_Example1_Raw.pdf)

Figure 4.1 shows a form that uses *colored entry highlighting* to change a form field's color when the user selects it. (Chapter 3 shows you how to do this, by the way.) This form implements the highlighting by attaching JavaScripts to the On Focus and On Blur events for each text field. Because these two events were added in Acrobat 5, our form will not work properly with versions of Acrobat earlier than 5.

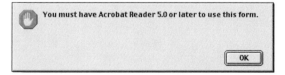

Figure 4.1 *This form depends on form field events that were added in Acrobat 5. We shall add a Document JavaScript that checks the current user's Acrobat version and present an alert if the version isn't sufficiently recent.*

In this chapter, we shall further modify this form, looking at the user's Acrobat version number. If the version number is less than 5, we shall first put up an alert (**Figure 4.2**) announcing the fact and then close the form.

Figure 4.2 *We shall display this alert if the user's version of Reader is not recent enough.*

The JavaScript

Checking for the proper version of Acrobat is something you would want to do when the user first opens the document. For this reason, we shall use a Document JavaScript, which Acrobat will execute when the user first opens the document.

Approaching the Problem

This script is relatively simple. We shall look at the user's Acrobat version and compare it to the minimum version of Acrobat we need (Acrobat 5, in our case). If the version is less than 5, we'll post the alert shown in **Figure 4.2** and then close the Acrobat file. We can easily determine the version number by examining the app object's `viewerVersion` property, whose value is the version number of the current Acrobat viewer.

The Code

This JavaScript needs to be entered as a Document JavaScript. (Refer to Chapter 2 for a reminder of how to attach a Document JavaScript a document.) Remember that Document JavaScripts must always have a name. I'm going to name our script CheckVersion (**Figure 4.3**)—descriptive, if unimaginative.

Is the viewer version less than 5?

```
if (app.viewerVersion < 5)  {
```

Display an alert with this text.

```
    app.alert("You must have Acrobat Reader 5.0 or later to use
    → this form.")

    this.closeDoc(true)
}
```

The code in detail

This program is built around a call to the JavaScript `if` command. This command compares two things (in our case, the Acrobat version and the number 5) and executes a block of code if the comparison is true. The `if` command and its cohort, `else`, are ubiquitous in JavaScript; we shall be seeing them quite a lot throughout this book. Anytime your JavaScript needs

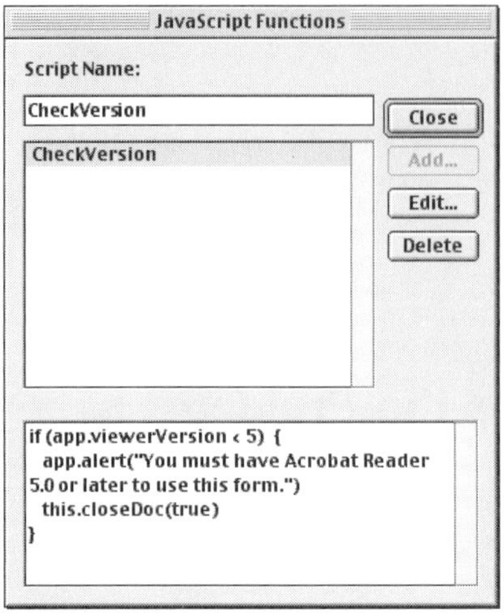

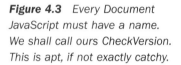

Figure 4.3 *Every Document JavaScript must have a name. We shall call ours CheckVersion. This is apt, if not exactly catchy.*

to do one thing in some circumstances and something else otherwise, these are the programming tools you use.

```
if (app.viewerVersion < 5)
```

Here is where we look to see if our Acrobat version is less than 5; change the numeral to reflect your minimum required version of Acrobat. (We are examining the viewerVersion property of the app object.) Most professional forms should make sure the user has at least Acrobat 4.

The JavaScript code that should be executed if the comparison is true (in other words, if the version of the viewer is less than 5) appears between the braces that immediately follow the comparison. In our case, there are two lines within this "conditional block":

```
app.alert("You must have Acrobat Reader 5.0 or later to use this
→ form.")
```

Here is where we tell the app object to display an alert, as in **Figure 4.2**. The text in the parentheses is the text that should appear in the alert; you can change this to anything you wish.

```
this.closeDoc(true)
```

Finally, having informed the user of the problem, we tell the current document to close itself. Remember that "this" refers to the current document (that is, "this document"). The Boolean true indicates that the user should *not* be given a chance to save the document before it closes. If you change the Boolean to false, Acrobat will present the user with a standard "Do you want to save first" dialog box (**Figure 4.4**). This would allow the user to save the Acrobat file before it was closed. (For example, you might want to use `false` if you are using the `closeDoc` method in a Close Form button you put in your form; it would give the user the opportunity to save whatever changes he or she has made to the form.)

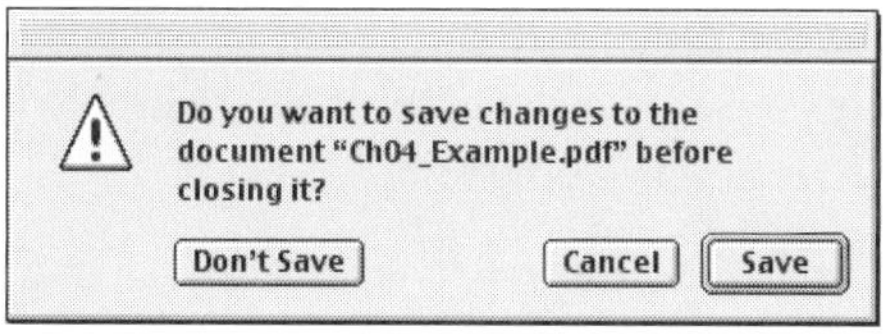

Figure 4.4 *If you supply a* `false` *to the* `closeDoc` *method, Acrobat will give the user a chance to save the Acrobat file before closing it. This can be useful, preventing the user from accidentally losing form field entries.*

As a convenience, you may leave out the Boolean value if you do want a "save" dialog box; in this case, your call to `closeDoc` would look like this:

```
this.closeDoc()
```

This saves you from having to type "false", but is otherwise no different from our original version.

Testing the Code

Testing this program—to make sure you haven't mistyped something, for example—is a bit tricky if you're using Acrobat 5 to create your form. Since our comparison (`app.versionNumber < 5`) never comes up false (our own version of Acrobat is never less than 5), our calls to `app.alert` and `this.closeDoc` will never be executed; if you have misspelled one of these, you won't know it until you (or a user!) try to open the document with an earlier version of Acrobat.

One way you can test this script is to temporarily modify it by placing `true` in the `if` operator's comparison clause:

```
If (true)    {
    app.alert("You must have Acrobat Reader 5.0 or later to use
    → this form.")
    this.closeDoc(true)
}
```

This forces the code in braces to be executed, letting you see if there are any errors hidden in there.

Customization Notes

The obvious opportunities for customization are:

- Change the version number in the `if` line to whatever minimum Acrobat version you want. Again, most forms should at minimum check that the version is 4 or greater.

- Change the text in the alert to whatever you wish to have appear on screen.

Following are some less-obvious changes you can make to this program.

Testing for Viewer Type

Finally, you can easily modify this chapter's JavaScript code to see which Acrobat program your user is using to look at your form: Acrobat Reader or the full Acrobat. The app object has a property named `viewerType` that will have one of two string values, `"Reader"` or `"Exchange"`, depending on which type of viewing software the user has. If your form needs the capabilities of the full Acrobat package (perhaps your form lets the user save the form data to disk, something only available in the full Acrobat), you could modify this chapter's Document JavaScript to read as follows:

"==" means "is equal to"

```
if (app.viewerType == "Reader")  {
    app.alert("You must have the full Acrobat to use this form.")
    this.closeDoc(true)
}
```

This will warn the user and then close the document if he or she looks at your form with the Acrobat Reader.

Alert icons

The alert that we are displaying in this chapter's program displays a Halt icon, indicating that something has gone so wrong that we're going to stop what we're doing.

Sometimes, however, you don't want quite so emphatic an icon in your alert. The `app.alert` method allows you to specify, in addition to the text that should go into your alert, the icon that should appear. See Chapter 13 for a full discussion of how to specify the icon used in your alerts.

Calculating Form Fields

Calculation is fundamental to so much of what we do in the computer world. Spreadsheets, statistical analysis, accounting information—even unobvious things like word processing and page layout—all depend on a computer's ability to perform calculations, saving delicate little human brains for more lofty pursuits. Because it runs on a computer, Acrobat can also calculate, allowing you to specify that a form field's value should be calculated, rather than typed in by the user. You do this using either a JavaScript or one of Acrobat's predefined calculations; here we shall learn how to create calculated form fields that use both methods.

The Project

(Files: Ch05_Example_2.pdf, Ch05_Example_2_Raw.pdf)

In this chapter, we shall add calculations to the purchase order form in **Figure 5.1**. This form is used by employees of a small business to order office supplies or other necessary items. For each item users want to buy, they supply a description and the price and quantity they need. The form automatically fills in the subtotal, tax, and total purchase price.

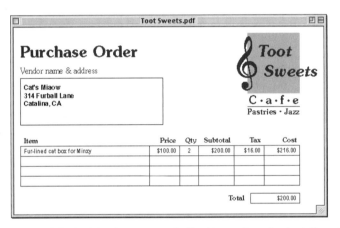

Figure 5.1 *In this chapter, we shall add a series of calculations to the fields in this form so that the fields for item cost, subtotal, tax, and total cost are automatically filled in.*

Looking at **Figure 5.2**, we can see that the form is made up of text fields arranged in six columns for the item name, price, quantity, subtotal, tax amount, and final cost of that item. We also have a final total amount at the bottom of the form. If this were a form you made for your company, it would also need a Submit button and, perhaps, a Clear Form button; I omitted those here for the sake of compactness.

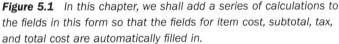

Figure 5.2 *Here are the form fields in our sample form. We shall turn the fields in the txtSubtotal, txtTaxAmt, and txtCost columns and the txtTotal field into calculated fields.*

The calculations we need to put into this form are as follows:

For each purchased item:

■ Subtotal = price x quantity

■ Tax = tax rate x subtotal

■ Item cost = subtotal + tax

Finally,

■ Total = sum of the item costs

Let's see how to add these calculations to our form.

The JavaScript

Creating a Calculated Field

You may remember that a text field can be declared to be a calculated field. Acrobat will automatically recalculate the value of this field as needed; all we need to do is tell Acrobat exactly what calculation to perform. We do this from the Field Properties dialog box (**Figure 5.3**).

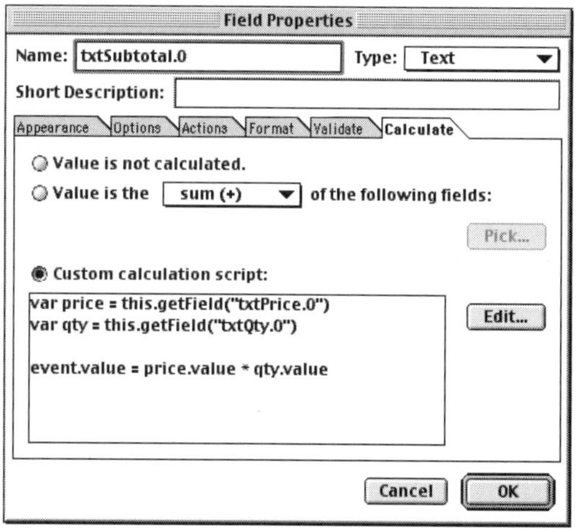

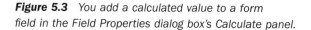

Figure 5.3 *You add a calculated value to a form field in the Field Properties dialog box's Calculate panel.*

Numeric Calculations with a Text Field?

The value of a text field is the text that field contains. If that text is a valid number, then the field's value can be used in a JavaScript calculation, as we are doing here. If a text field's value is not a valid number (if the field contained "Mooseberries", for example), then the value may still be used in a calculation, but the value will be interpreted as 0.

The easiest way to ensure that a text field contains only valid numbers is to set its format to *Number;* Acrobat will then reject any keystrokes that are not part of a numeric value. (You also need to do this if you want to use the Acrobat predefined calculations.)

To set a text field's format to Number:

Start with the text field selected with the Acrobat Form tool.

1. Double-click on the text field to gain access to its properties.

2. Go to the Format panel (**Figure 5.4**).

3. Select Number from the list of available formats.

4. Select other options (currency symbol, and so on) if they seem useful.

5. Click the OK button.

This form field will now accept only numbers, a decimal point, and an initial plus or minus sign.

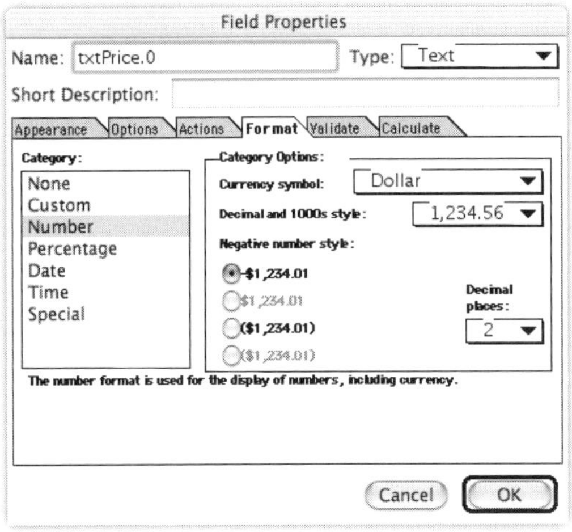

Figure 5.4 *To ensure that a text field contains only a valid numeric value, set its format to Number.*

To attach a calculation to a text field:

1. Double-click the text field.

You will now be looking at the Field Properties dialog box for that text field.

2. Click the Calculate tab.

You are now looking at the controls that let you specify a calculation for the value of the text field.

3. For a simple calculation, click the second radio button ("Value is the…") and select from the pop-up menu of predefined calculations. If you don't see this second radio button, that means that the field's format isn't set to Number.

4. If you need a more complex calculation, click the third radio button ("Custom calculation script") and then click the Edit button to enter a JavaScript.

Predefined calculations

There are five calculations that are built in to Acrobat. Without writing a speck of JavaScript, you can set the value of a text field to the sum, product, average, minimum, or maximum of two or more other form fields. This is the meaning of the second radio button in the Field Properties dialog box's Calculate panel.

Again, these predefined calculations are available only if you have explicitly set the format of the text field to Number.

To use one of the predefined calculations:

Start in the Field Properties dialog box's Calculate panel.

1. Select the radio button that "turns on" the predefined calculations (**Figure 5.5**).

Figure 5.5 *The second radio button lets you perform simple calculations on two or more fields.*

2. From the pop-up menu (**Figure 5.6**), select the calculation you want.

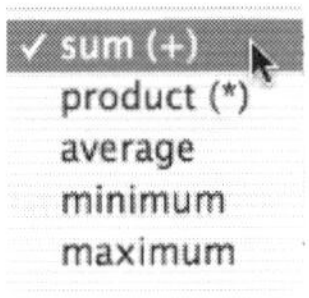

Figure 5.6 *Acrobat lets you choose one of five predefined calculations.*

3. Either type into the text field the names of the text fields that supply the data for the calculation.

or

To save typing, click the Pick button and choose from the resulting list (**Figure 5.7**) the data fields the calculation should use.

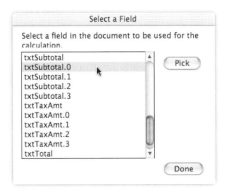

Figure 5.7 *Clicking the Pick button presents you with the Select a Field dialog box, which lets you choose the form fields whose values should be used in a predefined calculation.*

It is far more convenient to select among the predefined calculations than to write the equivalent JavaScript code. In our Purchase Order form, we shall use the predefined calculations for the Cost field (whose value is the sum of the subtotal and tax) and the Total field (the sum of all the items' costs) (**Figure 5.8**). The calculation of the tax requires multiplication by a constant value (our tax rate), and so cannot be done using a predefined calculation. (Predefined calculations can multiply two or more form fields together, but can't multiply a form field by a fixed number.) We shall write a JavaScript for the Tax field.

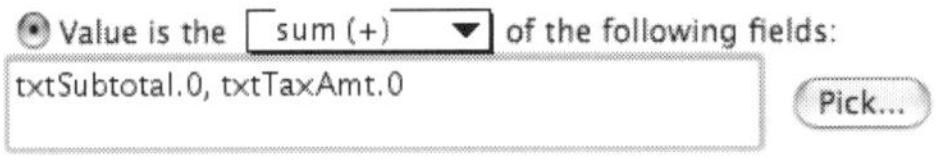

⦿ Value is the [sum (+) ▼] of the following fields:

txtSubtotal.0, txtTaxAmt.0   (Pick...)

Figure 5.8 *The calculated value of our txtCost.0 field will be the sum of the associated subtotal and tax amount.*

We could also use a predefined calculation for the Subtotal field (it's the product of the price and quantity). Nonetheless, we shall do the subtotal with a JavaScript; the reason for this will become clear when we see the enhancements at the end of this chapter.

The Item Calculations

Let's add the calculations that apply to the individual purchase items in our form. We need to apply calculated values to the fields txtTaxAmt, txtSubtotal, and txtCost for each item. Note that the names we have applied to these fields conform to the Adobe Hierarchical Naming Convention (see sidebar); thus, as we go down the Tax column, for example, the names of the fields are txtTaxAmt.0, txtTaxAmt.1, and so on. This naming convention makes the field names easy to remember and can be useful when using a predefined calculation, as we shall see when we discuss the txtTotal field.

In our discussion of the item-related calculations, we shall look at the JavaScripts that apply to item 0, the first row of form fields. For the full form, you will need to repeat these calculations for items 1, 2, and 3, changing the field names as appropriate.

Adobe Hierarchical Naming Convention

We have picked a consistent naming strategy for our text fields. The text fields associated with the purchase items are named txtItem.0, txtItem.1, and so on. The fields that hold all the other item-by-item information are named similarly (txtCost.0, txtCost.1; txtQty.0, txtQty.1; and so forth).

These names adhere to the Adobe Hierarchical Naming Convention. This is a set of loose rules that specify how to assign names to related fields. These names are similar to the URLs (Web addresses) that identify Web sites. A "dot" is used to separate different parts of each name; related fields should share the first parts of their names to indicate their relationship. Thus, txtCost.1 and txtCost.2 are both text fields that contain a cost.

This makes it easy to see the relationship among your text fields. Also, as we shall see in calculating the Total field, the Hierarchical Naming Convention makes it possible to refer to an entire set of form fields just by using the first part of their names. That is, in a predefined calculation, "txtPrice" is a shorthand reference to all fields that start with this name: txtPrice.0, txtPrice.1, and so on. See "Calculating txtTotal" below to see a concrete example.

Calculating *txtSubtotal.0*

The subtotal for an item is the price per item multiplied by the number of items you are buying. In terms of our form, this means that the value of txtSubtotal.0 should be the product of txtPrice.0 times txtQty.0. This could be done using an Acrobat predefined calculation, but we shall nonetheless do this as a JavaScript. Two reasons:

- I want to make it clear that the predefined calculations are doing nothing magical; anything the predefined calculations can do, you can easily do in JavaScript.

- Among the enhancements we discuss at the end of the chapter, we shall see a good reason for doing all calculations as JavaScript. It has to do with the appearance of fields in which the value is zero. But we'll come back to this.

To attach this calculation to txtSubtotal.0, start by opening the Calculate panel of the Field Properties dialog box (**Figure 5.9**). (Follow steps 1–2 under "To attach a calculation to a text field" on page 43 to reach this panel.)

Click the "Custom calculation script" radio button and then click the Edit button. Acrobat will present you with the JavaScript Edit dialog box (**Figure 5.10**); type in the following JavaScript and click OK.

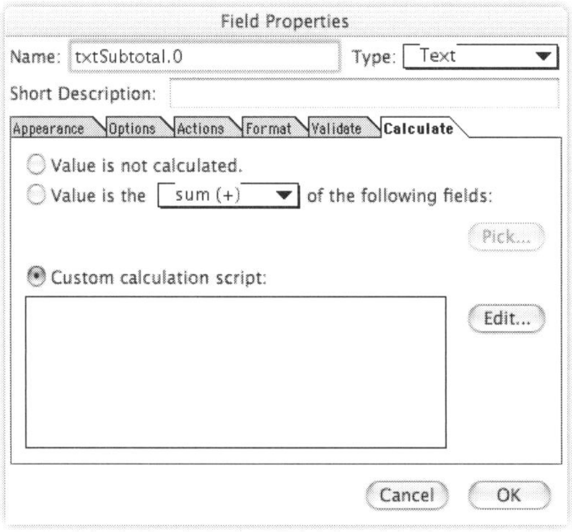

Figure 5.9 *To calculate a form field's value using a JavaScript, you start by clicking the "Custom calculation script" radio button and then clicking the Edit button.*

Figure 5.10 *You type your calculation JavaScript into the standard JavaScript Edit dialog box.*

Remember that double-slashed lines indicate JavaScript comments, which are ignored by Acrobat and JavaScript. You can omit these, if you wish, although I recommend typing them in, as well. (They will help you remember what's happening when you return to the code later.)

```
// Get references to the price and quantity fields
var price = this.getField("txtPrice.0")
var qty = this.getField("txtQty.0")
```

Get the form fields we need for the calculation

```
/* Set the value of our text field to
the product of price and quantity.*/

event.value = price.value * qty.value
```

Multiply the fields' values

This short script is reasonably straightforward. We create variables `price` and `qty` that hold references to the txtPrice and txtQty form fields. We then multiply the values of those two fields and assign the resulting product to something called `event.value`.

The only unobvious part of this script is our use of the term `event.value`. In a calculation script, event refers to an **Event object**; this object contains a variety of information associated with the *calculation event* that provoked the execution of the script. In particular, `event.value` is a reference to the value of the text field that is the target of the calculation. This is a convenience; if we hadn't used the event object, we would have had to explicitly obtain a reference to the txtSubtotal.0 field and used that in our calculation:

```
var subtotal = this.getField("txtSubtotal.0")

subtotal.value = price.value * qty.value
```

There's nothing wrong with this way of doing things; it just takes a bit more typing. (Minor laziness is a virtue in programming.)

At this point, we have calculated our subtotal, multiplying the price by the quantity. Now, we are ready to calculate the tax amount.

Calculating txtTaxAmt.0

The tax on an item is the subtotal for that item multiplied by your local sales tax rate. In my area, the tax rate is 8 percent (those of you in states without sales tax just keep quiet); so the amount of tax owed on each item is the subtotal times .08.

As before, go to the Calculate panel for the txtTaxAmt.0 field (**Figure 5.11**). Select the "Custom calculation script" radio button and click the Edit button. Type the following JavaScript into the JavaScript Edit dialog box:

```
var subtotal = this.getField("txtSubtotal.0")

event.value = .08 * subtotal.value
```

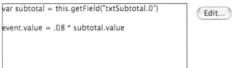

Figure 5.11 *The JavaScript for the txtTaxAmt.0 field sets the field's value to the value of txtSubtotal.0 multiplied by the tax rate—in this case .08.*

Here, too, our code is pretty easy: Get a reference to the txtSubtotal.0 field and set `event.value` to the subtotal's value times .08.

There is an enhancement we can add to all of our txtTaxAmt fields, but I'll defer that until later in the chapter (see "'Global' Tax Rate," below).

Calculation Syntax

JavaScript calculations use the standard characters to denote basic arithmetic. You have no doubt seen these characters in use throughout your computer experience: "+," "-," "*," and "/" correspond to addition, subtraction, multiplication, and division.

In addition, you can use parentheses to cause some parts of the calculation to happen before others: The parts of your calculation that are in parentheses will be executed before parts that are outside the parentheses. Thus, if you wanted to calculate the average of two variables `price1` and `price2`, you would express it this way:

```
var avg = (price1 + price2) / 2
```

We must first add the two prices together, then divide the sum by 2.

Calculating *txtCost.0*

The final cost of each item in our Purchase Order form is the sum of that item's subtotal and its tax. Because summation is one of Acrobat's predefined calculations, we shall use that mechanism, rather than a JavaScript, to calculate the cost. (Don't hesitate to *not* use a JavaScript if Acrobat provides a convenient alternative; always use the simplest way to achieve your goal.)

As before, double-click the txtClick.0 field and go to the Calculate panel. This time, specify a predefined calculation by doing the following:

1. Click the middle radio button ("Value is the…").

2. Select Sum in the pop-up menu.

3. Type into the text box the names txtSubtotal.0 and txtTaxAmt.0.

 As an alternative, you can click the Pick button and choose those two fields from the resulting list.

We have now calculated all of the information we need for item 0: its subtotal, tax, and cost. We have two more things to do: set up the same calculations for items 1 through 3 and then calculate the total cost of the order.

Calculating items 1 through 3

The calculated fields for items 1, 2, and 3 are identical to those for item 0. Repeat the same JavaScripts and predefined calculations but simply change the number ".0" to ".1," ".2," or ".3," to match the item number. (I always just copy and paste the earlier script into my new field and then modify the item numbers.)

Thus, the JavaScript for txtSubtotal.1 would be:

```
var price = this.getField("txtPrice.1")
var qty = this.getField("txtQty.1")


event.value = price.value * qty.value
```

Calculating *txtTotal*

Finally, we need to calculate the total amount of money owed—the sum of all four items' costs. This, too, is a summation; therefore, we can use the predefined Sum calculation. Go to the Calculate panel for the txtTotal field and, following the same procedure as for the txtCost fields, set the calculated value for this field equal to the sum of the four txtCost fields, as in **Figure 5.12**.

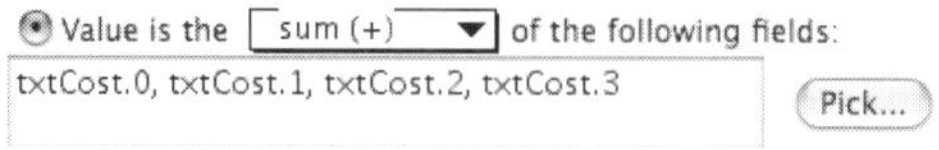

> ◉ Value is the [sum (+) ▼] of the following fields:
>
> txtCost.0, txtCost.1, txtCost.2, txtCost.3
>
> (Pick...)

Figure 5.12 *The total cost of the purchase will be the sum of the costs of the individual items. We can use a predefined calculation for this.*

Figure 5.12 shows all four txtCost field names typed into the calculation text box. However, because the Cost fields have names that conform to the Adobe Hierarchical Naming Convention, we can take a shortcut in specifying the txtTotal calculation. If we enter the name txtCost into the calculation text box (**Figure 5.13**), Acrobat will take this as shorthand for all the fields whose names start with txtCost-dot-*something*. This is a real benefit of using the Hierarchical Naming Convention: You can refer to whole families of fields by the initial part of their names. There's no good reason not to use this shortcut when the opportunity presents itself.

> ◉ Value is the [sum (+) ▼] of the following fields:
>
> txtCost
>
> (Pick...)

Figure 5.13 *Because we used the Adobe Hierarchical Naming Convention to name our txtCost form fields (txtCost.0, txtCost.1, and so on), we can specify a predefined calculation as being the sum of txtCost.*

We're done! We now have a functioning order form that, given the price and quantity, automatically fills out all the other information. Try it out. Type in some numbers. Give the items imaginative and amusing names!

Calculation Order

The order in which our calculations take place in a form is important. We must calculate the subtotal before we calculate the tax amount, the subtotal and the tax amount before the item cost, and so on.

Sometimes you will find that the calculations in your Acrobat form seem to be happening in the wrong order. You can specify the order in which your form fields are calculated by selecting Tools > Forms > Set Field Calculation Order (**Figure 5.14**).

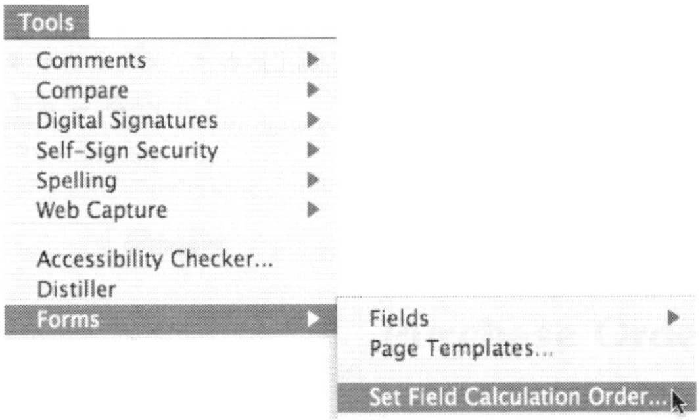

Figure 5.14 *To change the order in which your form fields are calculated, select Tools > Forms > Set Field Calculation Order.*

Acrobat will present you with the Calculated Fields dialog box (**Figure 5.15**), which contains a scrolling list of all the calculated form fields in the current Acrobat file; the order in which the fields appear in this list is the order in which they are calculated.

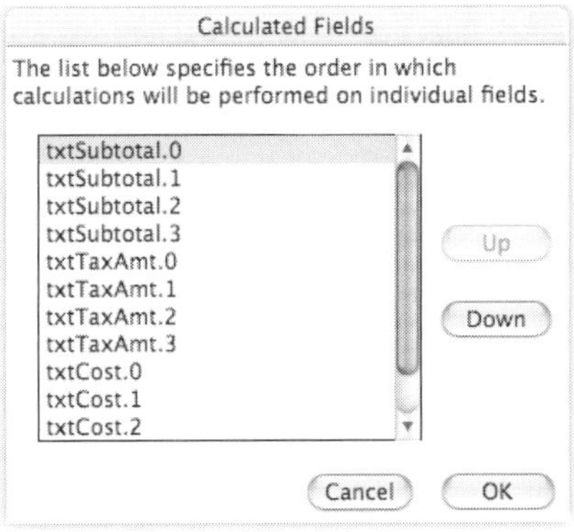

Figure 5.15 *The Calculated Fields dialog box lists all of the calculated fields in your Acrobat file in the order in which they are calculated. You may change the position of the fields in this list using the Up and Down buttons.*

To change the position in the list of one of the form fields, simply select it and click the Up or Down button as appropriate.

The fields should finally be in this list in calculation order. You must calculate the subtotal before you can calculate the tax; you must calculate the tax before you can calculate the cost of the item; and you must calculate the cost of all the items before you can calculate the total cost. Therefore, in the list, Subtotal must be above Tax, which must be above Cost, which must be above Total.

If you ever find your form is presenting blatantly incorrect results and you can find nothing wrong with any of the individual field calculations, check to make sure none of the fields are being calculated out of order.

Enhancements

There are a couple of enhancements we can add to our form. These are strictly optional but will pay off in the long run. If you want to see them in action, they have been applied to the file Ch05_Example1_B&W.pdf in the chapter's samples. (*B&W*, here, is short for *Bells and Whistles*.)

Hiding Zeros

In our form so far, there is one significant visual difference between the form as we've been constructing it and the one pictured in **Figure 5.1**. In our version of the form, all the calculated fields associated with "empty" rows have zeros in them, the results of the calculations they perform (**Figure 5.16**). Although this is technically correct, it is esthetically annoying. If we haven't specified an item to be purchased, its associated form fields would be better left blank, rather than displaying explicit zeros.

To eliminate this visual clutter, we need to change the calculation associated with the txtSubtotal and txtTaxAmt fields. They should perform their calculations only if the corresponding txtQty has a nonzero value; if txtQty has a zero value (which will be the case if that field is blank), then our subtotal and tax fields should be blank—that is, they should have values of "".

Item	Price	Qty	Subtotal	Tax	Cost
Fur-lined cat box for Minxy	$100.00	4	$400.00	$32.00	$432.00
			$0.00	$0.00	$0.00
			$0.00	$0.00	$0.00
			$0.00	$0.00	$0.00

Total $432.00

Figure 5.16 *Unless we do something special, our calculated fields will all show unsightly 0 values when there is no item purchased in a particular row. It would look better if these were blank.*

Here is the new calculation JavaScript for txtSubtotal.0:

```
// Get the two fields we'll need
// for our calculation
var price = this.getField("txtPrice.0")
var qty = this.getField("txtQty.0")
```

If qty is not zero...	`if (qty.value != 0)        // != means "not equal to"`
...do this	`event.value = price.value * qty.value`
Otherwise...	`else`
...do this	`event.value = ""`

Remember how the JavaScript if...else commands work: The if command is followed by a comparison in parentheses; in our case, we compare qty.value and 0, testing to see if they are *not* equal. The comparison, in turn, is followed by one or more lines of JavaScript that should be executed if the comparison is true; in our case, the single line that should be conditionally executed carries out our subtotal calculation.

The else command, if supplied (it's optional), is followed by one or more lines of JavaScript that should be executed if the if comparison is *not* true; in our case, if the comparison is false (that is, if qty.value is equal to 0), then we shall set our text field's value to an empty string: "".

The net result of this change is that if the quantity field for an item is empty (giving it a value of zero), then the txtSubtotal.0 field will be blank.

To apply the same effect to the txtTaxAmt fields, you should change their value calculations to this:

```
var subtotal = this.getField("txtSubtotal.0")


if (subtotal.value != 0)
    event.value = gTaxRate * subtotal.value
else
    event.value = ""
```

This embodies exactly the same reasoning as the txtSubtotal.0 field, except that we check to see if the value of txtSubtotal.0 is zero to decide whether to put a blank into our tax field.

You should add the if...else block to all four of the txtSubtotal and txtTaxAmt fields.

Predefined calculations

Unfortunately, any field that uses one of the predefined calculations, such as our txtCost fields, will continue to be "0.0" if its value is *0*. This is probably the only reason to use a JavaScript when a predefined calculation would do. If we want our txtCost.0 field to properly blank itself when it's zero, we need to calculate its value with a JavaScript, rather than the predefined sum:

```
var subtotal = this.getField("txtSubtotal.0")

var tax = this.getField("txtTaxAmt.0")
```

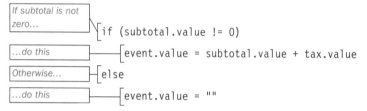

```
if (subtotal.value != 0)

    event.value = subtotal.value + tax.value

else

    event.value = ""
```

This is a little more work than using the predefined calculation, but it does give us the esthetic improvement of having zero-value totals appear blank.

"Global" Tax Rate

Let's say that, long after you have designed this form, the tax rate changes in your locale. In our form, we use the tax rate (.08) to calculate the value of the txtTaxAmt fields:

```
event.value = .08 * subtotal.value
```

Our form has four of these fields; in other forms, the tax rate could conceivably be used dozens of times, in fields scattered throughout a complex form.

Chasing down all of these references to the tax rate and replacing .08 with, say, .09 would be tedious at best.

As it happens, it's easy to initially design your form to make changing all the references to the tax rate easy. We shall add a Document JavaScript to our form that does just one thing: It defines a variable that contains our tax rate.

You may remember from Chapter 2 that variables defined in a Document JavaScript can be used by any JavaScript in the Acrobat document. This being so, any JavaScript in our form that needs to refer to the tax rate can use the name of the tax rate variable, rather than using the numeric value directly. If we later modify the Document JavaScript, changing the value assigned to the tax rate variable, *all* JavaScripts that use that variable will use the new tax rate. In one blow, we will change the tax rate used throughout our form.

Variables, such as our tax rate, that can be used throughout an Acrobat file are referred to as **global variables**. Anything you define in a Document JavaScript is global, that is, available to all the JavaScripts in the document.

Creating the Document JavaScript

You may want to review Chapter 2 for a detailed description of the behavior and creation of Document JavaScripts in general. Here, we'll simply list the steps for creating our specific JavaScript.

To create a Tax Rate JavaScript:

Start with the Acrobat document open and the Hand tool selected.

1. In Acrobat, select Tools > JavaScript > Document JavaScript.

Acrobat will present you with the JavaScript Functions dialog box.

2. In the Script Name text box, type TaxRate or some other descriptive label (**Figure** 5.17).

3. Click the Add button.

Acrobat will present the standard JavaScript Edit dialog box with some preliminary (and useless to our purposes) code already entered.

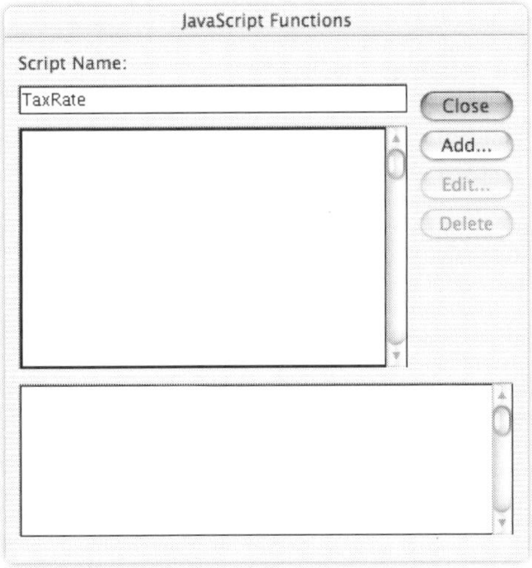

Figure 5.17 We are going to add a Document JavaScript called TaxRate to our document. This script will define a variable, gTaxRate, that holds the tax rate to be used by all the other JavaScripts in our Acrobat file.

4. Delete the default code in the JavaScript Edit dialog box and type the following:

```
var gTaxRate = .08
```

This one-line JavaScript creates a variable named gTaxRate and assigns it the value .08 (**Figure 5.18**). (I always precede global variable names with a lowercase *g*; this way, I know that when I see the variable name used in other JavaScripts that it's a global variable, defined in a Document JavaScript.)

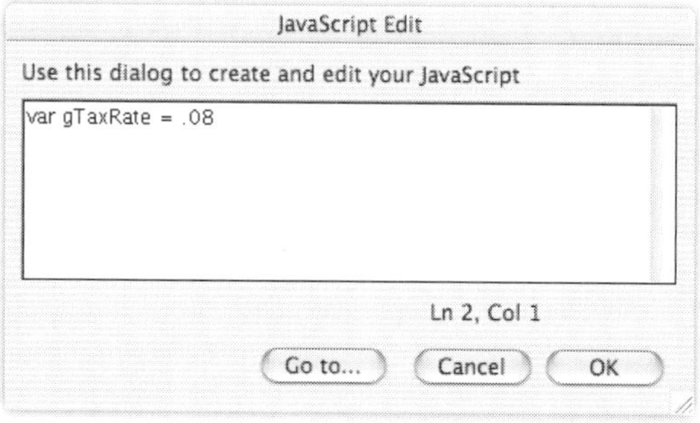

Figure 5.18 *Our Document JavaScript is quite short. It simply defines a single variable named* gTaxRate.

5. Close all dialog boxes until you are back to the Acrobat document.

We have now created a Document JavaScript that creates our global variable gTaxRate.

Using the global variable

Now we need to modify our four txtTaxAmt calculations so that they use gTaxRate, instead of directly using the number .8.

As usual, I'll step us through changing txtTaxAmt.0 and let you modify the other three txtTaxAmt fields.

To apply the new global variable:

Start with the form open in Acrobat and the Form tool selected.

1. Double-click on txtTaxAmt.0 to get to the Field Properties dialog box.

2. Go to the Calculate panel.

3. Click the Edit button next to the Calculation JavaScript.

You will now be looking at the JavaScript Edit dialog box displaying our current JavaScript. This JavaScript defines the calculation as:

```
event.value = .08 * subtotal.value
```

4. Replace the .08 in the calculation with the name gTaxRate.

Your calculation line should now look like this (**Figure 5.19**):

```
event.value = gTaxRate * subtotal.value
```

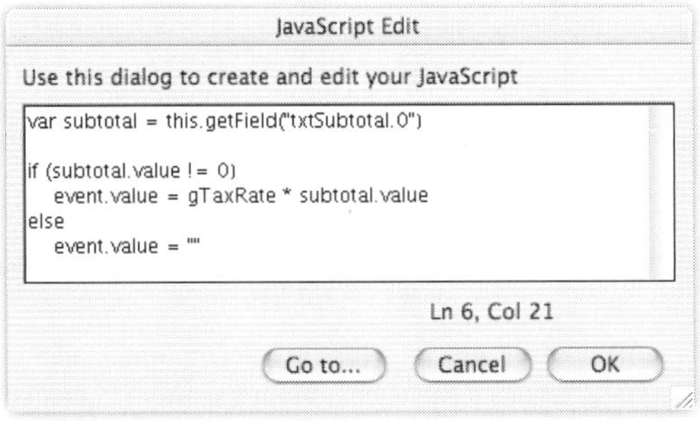

Figure 5.19 *In our form field JavaScripts, we must use the name of our global variable,* gTaxRate, *instead of the actual numeric value. If we later change the value of* gTaxRate *in our Document JavaScript, this will automatically change the tax rate used in all our calculated form fields.*

5. Close all dialog boxes until you are back to the Acrobat document.

You should make the above change to all four of the txtTaxAmt calculation JavaScripts.

Having done so, you will see no immediate change. After all, our tax rate hasn't changed; we are simply getting to it from a variable rather than using the number directly.

Change the tax rate

To see why this change has been a useful thing to do, suppose that your area has had a tax rate change (an increase, presumably). To make all the necessary changes at once, you need only change the value of gTaxRate in the Document JavaScript.

To change the tax calculation for all the items in the form:

1. Select Tools > JavaScript > Document JavaScripts.

You will be looking at the JavaScript Functions dialog box.

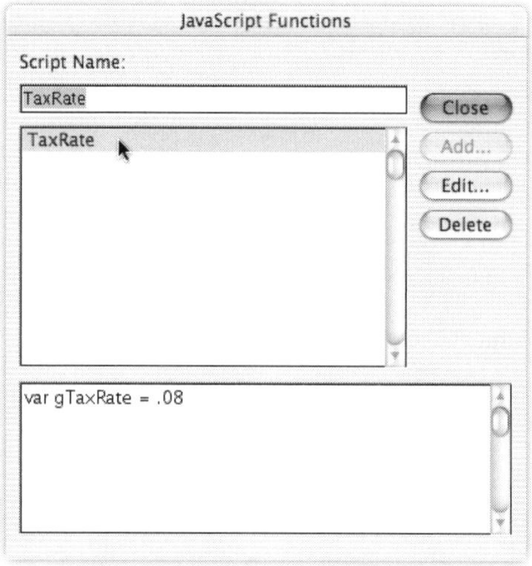

Figure 5.20 *If you later want to change the tax rate used throughout your form, simply go to the JavaScript Functions dialog box, click on the TaxRate script, and click Edit. You can then change the value assigned to the* gTaxRate *variable.*

2. Select the TaxRate JavaScript in the list (as we have in **Figure 5.20**) and click the Edit button.

3. In the JavaScript Edit dialog box, change the tax rate to .09, or whatever other number appeals to you:

```
Var gTaxRate = .09
```

4. Exit all dialog boxes until you are at your Acrobat document.

5. Examine the tax amount fields; all four of them will now contain calculated values that reflect the new tax rate.

By changing the single tax rate value in the Document JavaScript, we updated the tax rate used by *all* JavaScripts throughout our form. In this case, there were only four such JavaScripts; in a larger form, there could be many dozens.

6

Auto-Entering Form Data

One of the beauties of electronic forms is their ability to supply information that the user would otherwise need to type in. For example, when the user selects a product to buy in an electronic order form, the form should be able to fill in the proper price per item and calculate the total cost.

For this to happen, the form must contain a table of products and their prices. Each time the user chooses a product, the form must look up that item in the table and obtain the price of that item.

This is what we shall learn in this chapter: how to build a table of items and prices in a form and then fetch information from that table to automatically fill in form fields.

The Project

(Files: Ch06_Example_1.pdf, Ch01_Example_1_Raw.pdf)

In this chapter, we shall link the combo box (**Figure 6.1**) in our order form to the Price/ml field in the same form. When the user selects a new product from the combo box's menu, the form will change the price per milliliter to reflect the chosen product and then recalculate the total cost (**Figure 6.2**).

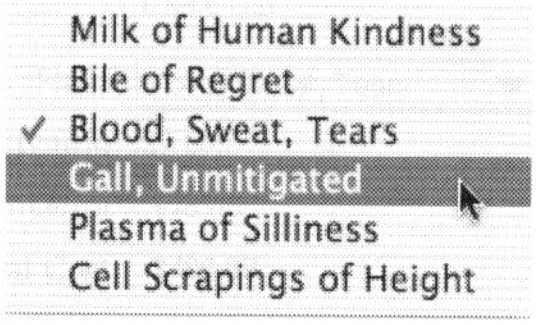

Figure 6.1 *The form contains a list of prices for all the items that appear in this combo box.*

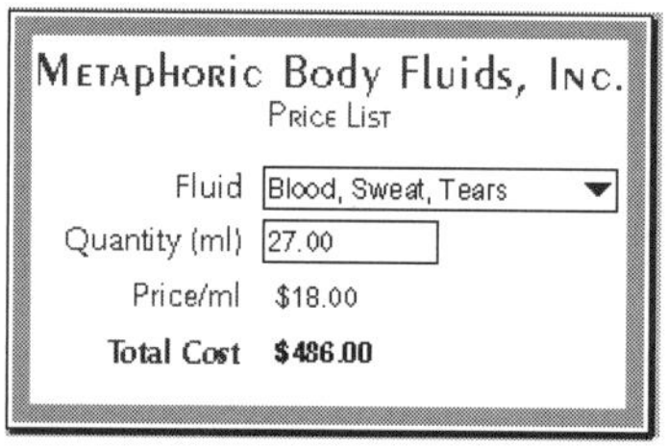

Figure 6.2 *The Price/ml and Total Cost fields always reflect the item currently selected in the combo box. When the user picks a new item, the price per milliliter and the total cost change to reflect the new item*

Looking at **Figure 6.3**, we can see that this form has four fields: a combo box *(cboFluid)* and three text fields (txtQuantity, txtRate, and txtTotal*)*. The field we most care about is the combo box; we shall be adding a JavaScript to this field that changes the txtRate and txtTotal fields to reflect the user's choice of fluid. Specifically, this field must do three things when we pick an item from its menu:

- Look up the price of that item.

- Set the value of txtRate to the item's price.

- Recalculate the value of txtTotal.

Let's see how to do it.

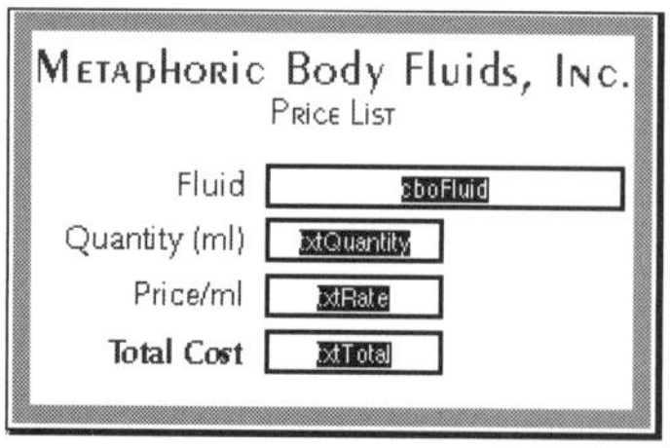

Figure 6.3 *Our form has four fields in it: a combo box and three text fields.*

The JavaScript

The Approach

In this program, we need to build a table of prices for the items in the combo box menu. We shall do this with a JavaScript Array object. An Array object represents a list—in our case, a list of prices. Each item in the list can be looked up by its position in the list or by a keyword, a string that we have associated with that value in the list. In our case, we shall use the *export value* (see next section) of each item in the combo box as the keyword we use to fetch that item's price.

We need to write two JavaScripts for our form:

- A Document JavaScript that creates our table of prices. This script will create an Array object and then load it up with pairs of export values and associated prices.

- A JavaScript attached to our combo box that looks up the current export value in the price table and uses the resulting price to set the values of the txtRate and txtTotal fields.

Combo Box Export Values

Each item in a combo box's menu has two pieces of text associated with it:

- The *item text* that actually appears in the pop-up menu.

- The *export value* that represents the combo box's selected value when the form data is exported to a file or submitted for processing.

The text and export value of each item in the combo box is set by the form designer in the Field Properties dialog box (**Figure 6.4**).

If you examine the properties of our combo box, you will find there are six items in the menu, with the following export values: MHK, BST, PS, BR, GU, CSH. There is nothing magic about these values; I picked them just to be rough abbreviations of the menu item text. (Thus, "MHK" is the export value for "Milk of Human Kindness.")

Our JavaScripts will associate each of these export values with the price per milliliter of the corresponding product.

Figure 6.4 *Each menu item in a combo box has two strings associated with it: the item text that appears in the menu and the export value that is used to report the user's selection when the combo box's data is processed.*

Creating the Price List Array

Our first JavaScript is a Document script that creates our price list. This will be an Array object containing paired export values and prices. Refer to Chapter 2 for a full discussion of Document JavaScripts.

To create the Document Script:

Start with the form file open in Acrobat.

1. Select Tools > JavaScript > Document JavaScripts.

Acrobat will present you with the JavaScript Functions dialog box (**Figure 6.5**).

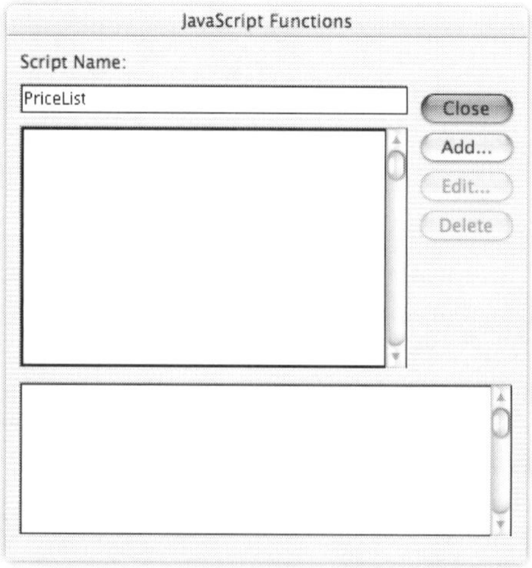

Figure 6.5 *The Java-Script Functions dialog box is where you create a Document JavaScript. Type in a name for the JavaScript ("PriceList," in this example) and click the Add button.*

2. In the Script Name box, type the name "PriceList" or something similarly descriptive.

3. Click the Add button.

Acrobat will present you with the usual JavaScript Edit dialog box containing some initial JavaScript code.

4. Remove the default JavaScript code and type in the following JavaScript (**Figure 6.6**):

This array will contain our price list

```
var gPriceList = new Array    // Create a reference to a new array


// Load the array up with prices for the products:
gPriceList["MHK"] = 16       // MHK's price is $16/ml
gPriceList["BR"] = 12        // ...etc.
gPriceList["BST"] = 18
gPriceList["GU"] = 6
gPriceList["PS"] = 4
gPriceList["CSH"] = 72.50
```

Here we associate export values with prices

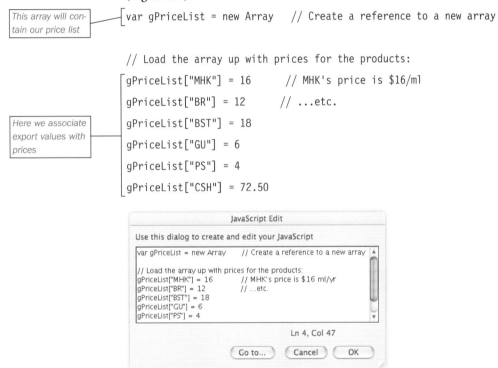

Figure 6.6 *You type your Document JavaScript into the JavaScript Edit dialog box.*

5. Click OK to exit all the dialog boxes until you are back at the Acrobat page.

You won't see anything different in your form at this point. Our new JavaScript creates a price list array, but we haven't yet used it to do anything.

The code in detail

```
var gPriceList= new Array
```

The JavaScript new command creates a new object, in this case, a new Array object. We assign the newly created Array object to a global variable, gPriceList, (created by the var command). Since this is taking place within a Document JavaScript, gPriceList will be usable within any JavaScript in our Acrobat file.

```
gPriceList["MHK"] = 16
```

Here we associate prices with the export values in our combo box. An array name (gPriceList) followed by a pair of square brackets enclosing a value indicates one of the entries in the list. Inside the square brackets there may be a number specifying the sequential position within the list of the particular item we want, or a string in quotes indicating the keyword associated with the desired item.

In our case, we are assigning a value to the MHK entry in the list. The above line of JavaScript, translated into English, says, "In the array gPriceList assign the number 16 to the keyword MHK."

We repeat this for all six of the export values in our combo box.

Formatting Your Code

JavaScript is pretty forgiving about letting you add spaces or tabs to make your code readable. You can indent your JavaScript any way you wish to improve how well the eye scans it. For example, I usually indent the statements that follow if commands to emphasize the fact that they will be executed only if the comparison is true:

```
if (event.changeEx in gPriceList)
    rateFld.value = gPriceList[event.changeEx]
```

Similarly, I usually use some combination of tabs and spaces to separate my comments from the executable JavaScript code; I also try to make them line up:

```
gPriceList["MHK"] = 16      // MHK's price is $16/mljyr
gPriceList["BR"] = 12       // ...etc.
```

This makes them more readable and is, to my eye, more esthetically pleasing.

You may double-space your JavaScript statements and add spaces and tabs as you wish. Your goal should be to make your programs as readable as possible. This is a service not only to other people, but to yourself when you return to your programs months later.

Creating the Combo Box Script

Now we need to teach our combo box how to look up export values and do something useful with them.

We are going to attach a **keystroke JavaScript** to our combo box. This is a JavaScript that is executed every time the user types a character into the combo box. Surprisingly, this script also gets called anytime the user picks an item from the combo box's menu.

So when the user picks an item from the combo box menu, Acrobat will execute our keystroke JavaScript, which will do our table lookup, change the value of txtRate, and, finally, calculate a new value for txtTotal.

To attach the keystroke JavaScript to our combo box:

Start with the form open and the Form tool selected.

1. Double-click the combo box to get to its properties.

Acrobat will present you with the Field Properties dialog box (**Figure 6.7**).

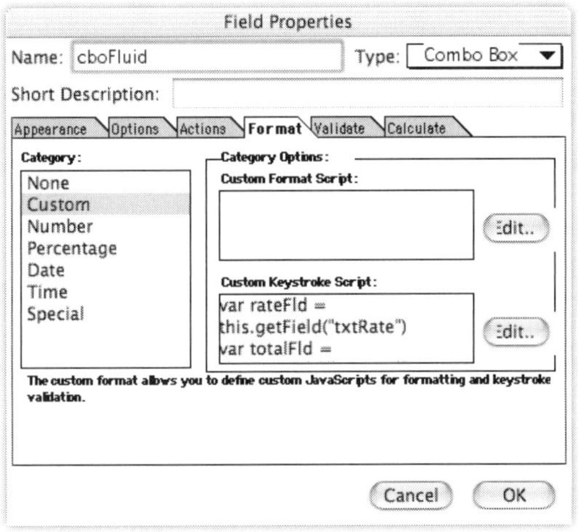

Figure 6.7 *You create a keystroke JavaScript by double-clicking the combo box and then going to the Format panel in the resulting Field Properties dialog box.*

2. Go to the Format panel.

3. Select Custom in the Category list.

4. Click on the Edit button next to the Custom Keystroke Script text box. You will now be looking at the JavaScript Edit dialog box (**Figure 6.8**).

5. Type in the following script:

```
// Get references to our form fields.
```

Get references to all three of the text fields

```
var rateFld = this.getField("txtRate")

var totalFld = this.getField("txtTotal")

var quantityFld = this.getField("txtQuantity")
```

```
// Is the new export value a keyword in our price list?
```

Is our export value a keyword?

```
if (event.changeEx in gPriceList)
        rateFld.value = gPriceList[event.changeEx]
// Now calculate a new value for the total price
```

If so, get the price

```
totalFld.value = quantityFld.value * rateFld.value
```

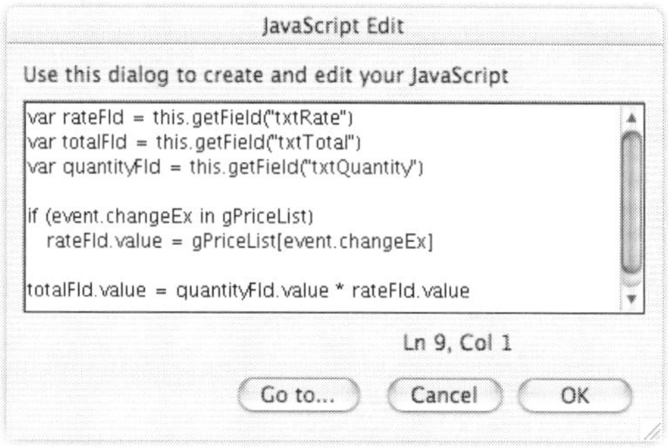

Figure 6.8 *Type your keystroke JavaScript into the JavaScript Edit dialog box, as usual.*

6. Click OK to close all dialog boxes.

7. Try it out: Select various items from the pop-up menu and watch the price per milliliter and total cost fields change value.

The code in detail

```
var rateFld = this.getField("txtRate")

var totalFld = this.getField("txtTotal")

var quantityFld = this.getField("txtQuantity")
```

This script starts by getting references to the three text fields we need to access, placing those references in appropriately named variables.

```
if (event.changeEx in gPriceList)
```

We are here executing a JavaScript `if` command that checks to see if the new export value is a valid keyword in our `gPriceList` array. In a keystroke JavaScript for a combo box, `event.changeEx` refers to the export value of the newly selected menu item. The phrase (`Event.changeEx in gPriceList`) translates into: "Is there a keyword matching our export value in the `Array` object `gPriceList`?"

```
rateFld.value = gPriceList[event.changeEx]
```

This is the line of JavaScript that `if` executes if `event.changeEx` is a keyword in `gPriceList`.

The phrase `gPriceList[event.changeEx]` fetches the value in the `gPriceList` array that is associated with the export value. Put differently, the phrase gives us the price of the item currently selected in the combo box. We set the value of the txtRate field to this number. The txtRate field will immediately display the new price per milliliter.

```
totalFld.value = quantityFld.value * rateFld.value
```

Finally, we change the value of the txtTotal field (residing in the `totalFld` variable) to the product of the quantity and rate. The latter two numbers we obtain from the txtQuantity and txtRate fields.

Roll-Over Help

Every well-designed form needs some mechanism by which it prompts the user on how to fill out the form. The most common way of doing this in Acrobat is via the *tool-tip* help that is built in to the Acrobat form mechanism. (Any text you enter into the Short Description field in the Field Properties dialog box becomes tool-tip text for that field.) In this chapter, we shall see how to implement an alternative: *roll-over* help. This is text that automatically appears when the mouse pointer enters a form field; there is no half-second pause, as with tool-tip help. The use of roll-over help, rather than tool-tip help, is purely an esthetic decision, based on how you want your form to "feel" to the person who fills it out.

The Project

(Files: Ch07_Example_1.pdf, Ch07_Example_1_raw.pdf)

We are going to add roll-over help to the text fields in the form in **Figure 7.1**. Whenever the mouse pointer moves over one of the text fields, a bit of help text will appear in the large blue area at the bottom of the form, as in **Figure 7.2**.

Figure 7.1 We are going to add roll-over help to the text fields in this form.

Figure 7.2 When the mouse pointer moves over a text field (top), descriptive text will appear in the blue area at the bottom of the form (shown below).

There are five text fields in this form (**Figure 7.3**). The top four collect data: the name, address, nickname, and email address of the applicant; the bottom field, txtHelp, is an invisible text field perched over the blue rectangle that is part of the form design.

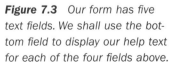

Figure 7.3 Our form has five text fields. We shall use the bottom field to display our help text for each of the four fields above.

The txtHelp field is invisible not because the Hidden attribute is selected in the Field Properties dialog box, but because it has no background or border color (**Figure 7.4**) and no initial text in it. It will become visible only when it has text to display.

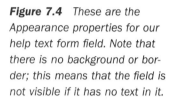

Figure 7.4 *These are the Appearance properties for our help text form field. Note that there is no background or border; this means that the field is not visible if it has no text in it.*

To make our roll-over help, whenever the mouse pointer enters one of the four data-gathering text fields, a JavaScript in that field will place appropriate help text into the txtHelp field. When the pointer leaves the text field, that field's JavaScript will remove the text from txtHelp.

The JavaScript

The Approach

We are going to need two JavaScripts for each of the four text fields:

- A JavaScript attached to the field's Mouse Enter event that puts appropriate help text into the txtHelp field

    Remember that the Mouse Enter event occurs when the mouse pointer passes into the boundary of a form field.

- A JavaScript attached to the field's Mouse Exit event that removes the text from txtHelp

    Remember that the Mouse Exit event occurs when the mouse pointer passes out of the form field again.

The Code

Here we shall attach the JavaScripts to the txtName field. To complete the form, you will need to carry out these same steps for each of the remaining data-gathering fields.

Start with the form open in Acrobat and the Form tool [icon] selected.

1. Double-click the txtName field to gain access to its properties (**Figure 7.5**); go to the Actions panel of the Field Properties dialog box.

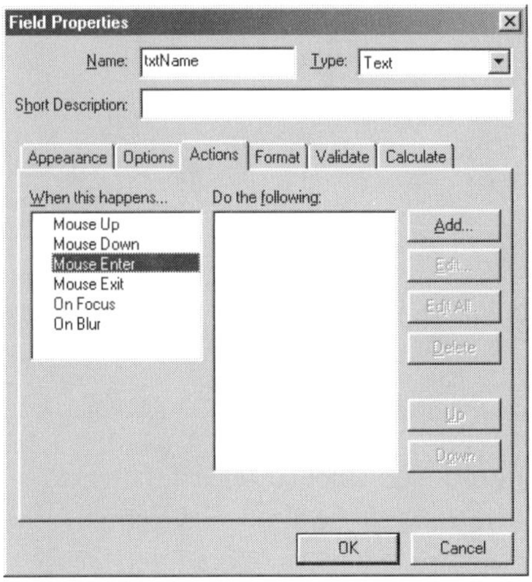

Figure 7.5 The Actions panel of the Field Properties dialog box is where you attach a JavaScript to a text field.

2. In the "When this happens" box, select Mouse Enter and then click the Add button.

    Acrobat will present you with the Add an Action dialog box (**Figure 7.6**).

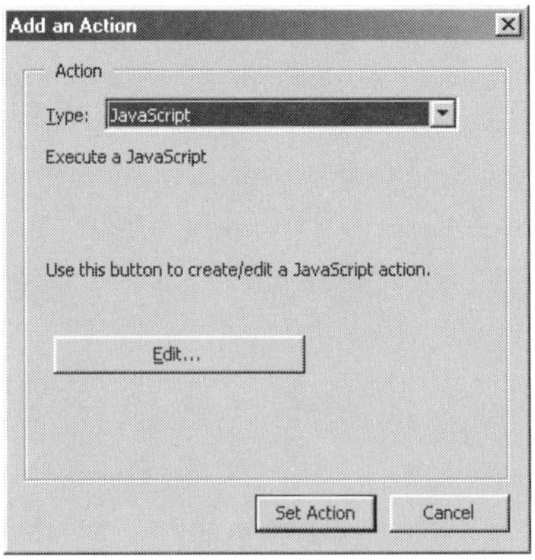

Figure 7.6 The Add an Action dialog box lets you attach an action to a form field. Our action will create a JavaScript to add help text to the Name field.

3. Select JavaScript in the pop-up menu and then click the Edit button.

Acrobat will present you with the JavaScript Edit dialog box (**Figure 7.7**).

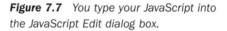

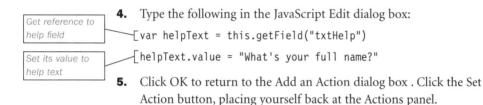

Figure 7.7 *You type your JavaScript into the JavaScript Edit dialog box.*

4. Type the following in the JavaScript Edit dialog box:

Get reference to help field

```
var helpText = this.getField("txtHelp")
```

Set its value to help text

```
helpText.value = "What's your full name?"
```

5. Click OK to return to the Add an Action dialog box . Click the Set Action button, placing yourself back at the Actions panel.

There is now a bullet next to the Mouse Enter event, indicating there's an action associated with that event (**Figure 7.8**).

Figure 7.8 *When you return to the Actions panel, there will be a bullet by the Mouse Event, indicating that this event has an action assigned to it.*

6. Repeat steps 2 through 5 for the Mouse Exit event, typing this JavaScript into the JavaScript Edit dialog box:

```
var helpText = this.getField("txtHelp")
```

```
helpText.value = ""
```

7. Close all dialog boxes until you are back at the Acrobat page.

8. Try it out: Click the Hand tool, then pass the mouse pointer over the Name field; you should see your help text appear in the blue box.

You will want to repeat these steps for the txtAddress, txtNickname, and txtEmail fields, using appropriate help text for each.

The code in detail

Let's look first at the Mouse Enter JavaScript:

```
var helpText = this.getField("txtHelp")
```

We start by getting a reference to our help text field, txtHelp. We assign this reference to the variable helpText.

```
helpText.value = "What's your full name?"
```

We now set the value of the helpText field to our help text, "What's your full name?" The value of a text field is the text that it displays to the user. When we set the field's value, we cause it to immediately display that text. In our case, this script causes the help text to appear when the mouse pointer enters the txtName field.

The Mouse Exit JavaScript is almost identical to the Mouse Enter script:

```
var helpText = this.getField("txtHelp")
helpText.value = ""
```

It gets a reference to the txtHelp field but this time sets its value to "". Open and close quotes together, with nothing in between, indicates "no text." The txtHelp field displays no text and, therefore, effectively disappears again when then mouse pointer leaves txtName.

Enhancement

(Files: Ch07_Example2.pdf, Ch07_Example2_raw.pdf)

Our roll-over help in its current state works very well. If there is anything to complain about, it would be that our bits and snippets of help text are distributed among all of our text fields; if we wanted to rewrite the help entries—say, to translate them into Spanish—we would have to chase them down and change them one by one.

It would be helpful if we could collect all of the help text strings in one place, for ease of maintenance and modification. We can do this by placing them all in a JavaScript Array object. You may remember from Chapter 6 that an Array object embodies a list in your JavaScript code—in our case, a list of help text strings.

We shall create our array of help text in a Document JavaScript so that it will be usable from within every other JavaScript in our document. In particular, our Form Field JavaScripts will be able to use strings from the array, rather than have the text in quotes within the Field script itself.

We need to do two things to implement this new method:

■ Write a Document JavaScript that creates an Array object containing all the appropriate help text.

■ Modify the Mouse Enter JavaScripts in all of our form fields so that they use help text from this global array ("global" because the array is accessible throughout our form).

This modification is completely optional, but it pays off in the long run, particularly with large, complex forms that have lots of roll-over help text.

The Document JavaScript

To create the new Document JavaScript, start with the form file open in Acrobat and do the following:

1. Select Tools > JavaScript > Document JavaScripts.

Acrobat will present you with the JavaScript Functions dialog box (**Figure 7.9**).

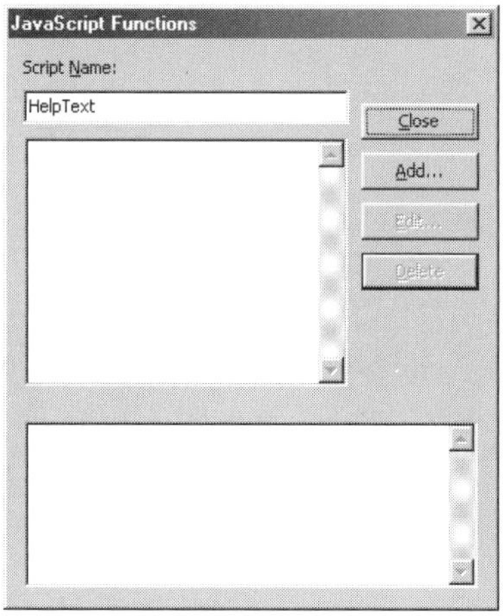

Figure 7.9 *The JavaScript Functions dialog box is where you create a Document JavaScript. Type in a name for the JavaScript ("HelpText," above) and click the Add button.*

2. In the Script Name box, type the name "HelpText" or something similarly descriptive.

Remember that all Document JavaScripts must have names.

3. Click the Add button.

Acrobat will present you with the usual JavaScript Edit dialog box (**Figure 7.10**) containing some initial JavaScript code.

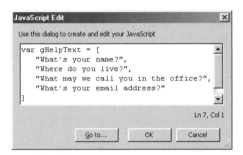

Figure 7.10 *You type your Document JavaScript into the JavaScript Edit dialog box.*

4. Replace the default JavaScript code with the following JavaScript; this script creates an array and loads it up with strings all at once; we'll discuss it in more detail in a moment:

```
var gHelpText = [            // Create a variable, gHelpText

    "What's your name?",                  // String #0

    "Where do you live?",                 // String #1

    "What may we call you in the office?", // String #2

    "What's your email address?"          // String #3

]
```

5. Click OK to exit dialog boxes until you are back at the Acrobat page.

You won't see anything different in your form at this point. Our new JavaScript creates a list of help text strings, but the form doesn't yet do anything with it. We'll teach our form to use the new array in a moment, but first, a look under the hood of our JavaScript.

The code in detail

```
var gHelpText = [...]
```

Although it's not immediately obvious, this Document JavaScript has only one JavaScript statement in it: the statement that creates an array and loads it up with a list of values. The var command creates a variable, as usual—in this case, named gHelpText. (The initial *g* in the name indicates this is a globally accessible variable; that's my own naming convention, not a JavaScript requirement.)

When the name of the variable is followed by a pair of square brackets, as in this case, the var command creates the variable as an array and places into the array the list of items it finds inside the brackets:

```
[

    "What's your name?",

    "Where do you live?",

    "What may we call you in the office?",

    "What's your email address?"

]
```

In this case, the array is filled with a list of strings, each a little piece of help text for one of our form fields.

This is all our Document JavaScript needs to do. The gHelpText array is now a repository for all our help text. Other JavaScripts can get to these strings using the following syntax:

```
gHelpText[2]
```

The number in the brackets is the sequential position within the array gHelpText of the string that we want. Items within an array are numbered from zero, so that gHelpText[0] will refer to the string "What's your name?" in our list.

New Form Field JavaScript

Now that we have created a globally available array of help text, we need to teach our form field scripts to use it. Specifically, in each of our text fields, we need to change the script we associated with the Mouse Enter event.

Here is the new version of the Mouse Enter JavaScript for the txtName field:

```
var helpText = this.getField("txtHelp")
helpText.value = gHelpText[0]
```

This is identical to our earlier Mouse Enter script, but for one change: In the second line of code, we set the value of the text field to string number 0 in the gHelpText array ("What's your name?"), rather than having the string directly in this script in quotes, as we did earlier.

We need to change each of the Mouse Enter JavaScripts in our text fields, using the appropriate numeric position for each field's help text.

To a user, our form will look no different than it did before. However, making future changes to our help text (to support other languages, for example) will be much easier, since all of the text resides in one place in our form.

Trust me, for a complex form, you'll find this technique *very* useful.

Dynamic Form Fields

One of the most common "special effects" in Acrobat forms is the revealing and hiding of form fields based on responses to other form fields. For example, click on a check box marked "self-employed," and a series of text fields may appear, asking for your business name, federal taxpayer ID, and other related information; if you uncheck the box, the text fields all disappear.

I refer to this effect as the **progressive display** of the form's fields. The fields are not all initially visible; the hidden fields are revealed to the user only as he or she selects choices from the visible controls.

In this chapter and the next, we are going to see how to do this. This chapter will present a technique for toggling the visibility of a relatively small number of form fields. In the next chapter, we shall see how to make whole pages of form fields appear on command.

Project 1: Attaching the JavaScript to a check box

(Files: Ch08_Example1.pdf, Ch08_Example1_raw.pdf)

We are going to add progressive display to the form pictured in **Figure 8.1**. Initially, the only control visible to the user is the check box. When the user selects the check box, two combo boxes and a button are revealed, allowing the user to specify a genre and a movie and submit the request (**Figure 8.2**). If the user deselects the check box, then the combo boxes and the button disappear again.

Figure 8.1 We are going to add progressive display of the form fields in this Acrobat document. Initially, the only form field visible is the check box.

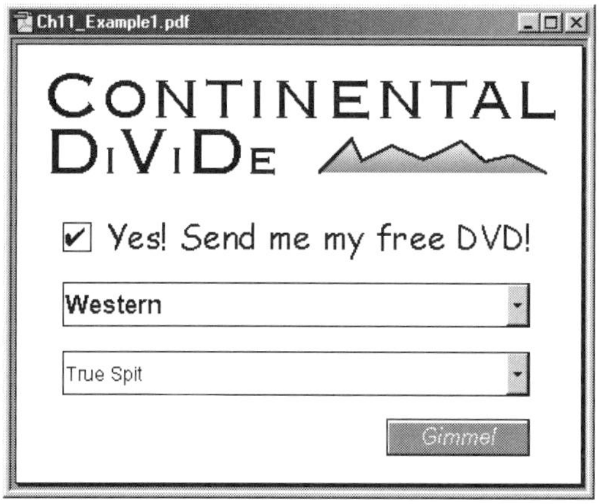

Figure 8.2 When the user clicks on the check box, a JavaScript attached to that control makes the other fields in the form visible.

Figure 8.3 shows the form fields in our Acrobat file. There are four of them:

- *chkYes* is the check box that lets the user declare a desire for a free DVD.

- *cboGenre* is a combo box from which the user can select a genre.

- *cboTitle* is a combo box from which the user can select a title.

- *btnSubmit* is a standard submit-data button.

Of these, only chkYes is visible when the document is first opened; the others all have their visibilities set to hidden (in the Field Properties dialog box). The other fields will become visible as a result of JavaScripts we shall write.

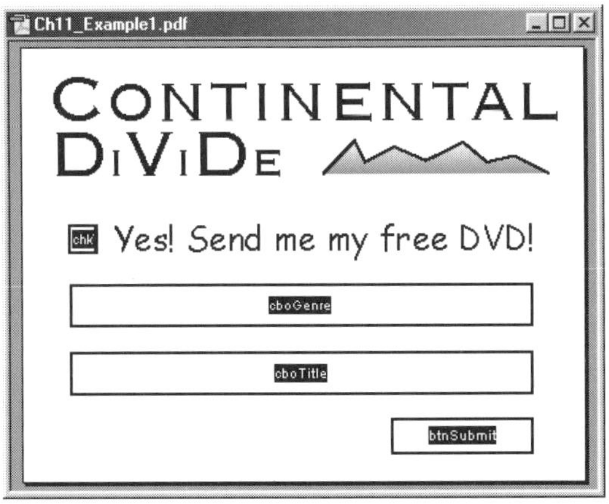

Figure 8.3 *Our sample form has four fields, of which only the check box is initially visible.*

The JavaScript

Approaching the Problem

Conceptually, this is a pretty easy problem. Every form field has a Boolean (true/false) property named hidden that determines whether that field is visible or not; if the hidden property is set to true, then the field is not visible to the user.

We need to write a JavaScript that toggles the hidden attribute of the two combo boxes and the button. We shall attach this JavaScript to the Mouse Up event for the check box field. The JavaScript will look to see if the check box has been selected or deselected. If the check box is selected, then the JavaScript will set the other fields' hidden attribute to false, making them visible to the user; otherwise, the script will set the `hidden` attribute to `true`, hiding the other fields.

How can our JavaScript tell if the check box is selected or not? We can look at the export value of that field. (The export value of a check box is the value that the field has if the check box is selected.) When I created this form, I set up the check box so that its export value is the string "Yes" (**Figure 8.4**). Our JavaScript has only to look at the check box's `value` property to see if it is "Yes" and then set the other fields' `hidden` property appropriately.

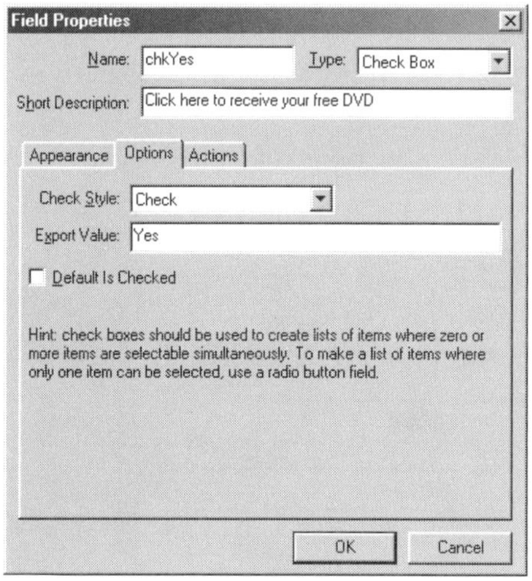

Figure 8.4 *The check box has an export value of "Yes"; this is part of the design of the form when I first created it.*

The check box script

To attach the JavaScript to the check box:

Start by going to the Actions panel of the Field Properties dialog box (**Figure 8.5**) for chkYes check box. (See Chapter 1 for a reminder of how to get there.)

1. Select the Mouse Up event and click the Add button.

   You will now be looking at the Add an Action dialog box.

2. Select the JavaScript option in the pop-up menu and click the Edit button.

   Acrobat will present you with the usual JavaScript Edit dialog box.

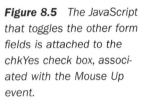

Figure 8.5 *The JavaScript that toggles the other form fields is attached to the chkYes check box, associated with the Mouse Up event.*

3. Type the following script into the JavaScript Edit dialog box (**Figure 8.6**):

Get references to the form fields
```
var genreFld = this.getField("cboGenre")
var titleFld = this.getField("cboTitle")
var submitBtn = this.getField("btnSubmit")
```

If the check box is selected, make the form fields visible
```
if (event.target.value == "Yes")     {
    genreFld.hidden = false
    titleFld.hidden = false
    submitBtn.hidden = false
}
```

Otherwise, hide the fields
```
else    {
    genreFld.hidden = true
    titleFld.hidden = true
    submitBtn.hidden = true
}
```

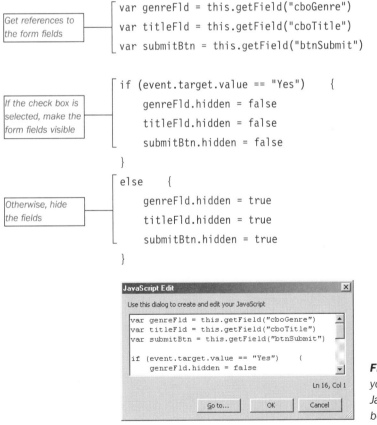

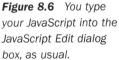

Figure 8.6 *You type your JavaScript into the JavaScript Edit dialog box, as usual.*

4. Exit from all the dialog boxes until you are once again looking at your Acrobat page.

5. Try it out: Return to the Hand tool and click on the check box; all the other form fields should appear on the page. Uncheck the box, and the other fields will disappear.

The code in detail

```
var genreFld = this.getField("cboGenre")
var titleFld = this.getField("cboTitle")
var submitBtn = this.getField("btnSubmit")
```

We start by getting named references to the three form fields whose visibilities we are going to manipulate. We need these references in order to gain access to their hidden properties.

Remember that you can make up whatever names you wish for variables. I made up the names genreFld, titleFld, submitBtn; to me they're descriptive and yet reasonably short. You can choose any names you wish, as long as the names don't already have meaning to JavaScript. (Naming a variable if, for example, would not work; JavaScript would interpret it as part of an if-else statement.)

```
if (event.target.value == "Yes")    {
```

We execute the if command, which looks to see if the value of our check box is "Yes." If so, then if executes the JavaScript lines in the braces following the parenthetical comparison. (Remember that double equals signs (==) mean *is equal to*.)

The phrase event.target.value may look odd at first, but it becomes clear if you nibble at it left to right. You may remember from earlier chapters that event.target is a reference to whatever form field triggered this JavaScript; in this case, the target of the event is our check box. Since event.target is our check box, event.target.value is the value of our check box. This value will be "Yes" (the check box's export value) if the check box is selected.

```
genreFld.hidden = false
titleFld.hidden = false
submitBtn.hidden = false
```

Here's where we make our two combo boxes and the Submit button visible; we do this by setting their hidden attributes to false. (Since they're not hidden, they must be visible, no?)

```
else    {
    genreFld.hidden = true
    titleFld.hidden = true
    submitBtn.hidden = true
}
```

The else command specifies what should happen if the earlier if comparison was *not* true; in our case, this would be if the check box is not checked. If the earlier comparison is not true, then else executes the JavaScript lines in braces, setting the fields' hidden properties to true, making them disappear.

Project 2: Attaching the JavaScript to a combo box

(Files: Ch08_Example2.pdf, Ch08_Example2_raw.pdf)

In this chapter's second project, we are going to see how to use a combo box to display and hide other form fields.

If you look at the file Ch08_Example2.pdf, you will see it looks much like our earlier example; I saved this file with the check box already selected, so that when you open the file, it will look like **Figure 8.2**. In this project, we'll examine how the items in the lower combo box change according to the genre you select in the top combo box (**Figure 8.7**). If you pick Westerns in the top combo box, the lower one presents you with three Westerns from which to choose.

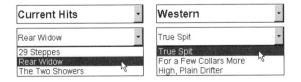

Figure 8.7 *In our second project, the movies shown in the lower combo box will change according to the genre the user selects in the upper combo box.*

Figure 8.8 shows our combo boxes as they appear with the Acrobat Form tool selected. The upper combo box, cboGenre, has three items in its menu: Current Hits, Music DVD, and Westerns; when I created this control, I gave these items the export values CH, MS, and WS, respectively. (You create a combo box's menu items and export values in the Options panel of the Field Properties dialog box.)

Figure 8.8   *The lower combo box in our form is really three combo boxes—only one of which is visible— stacked atop one another.*

The name of the lower combo box looks a bit jumbled in **Figure 8.8**; this is because it actually consists of three combo boxes placed on top of one another, one for each of the genres. Only one of these will be visible at any time; the other two will have their visibility controls set to hidden in the Field Properties dialog box. These combo boxes have the names cboTitleHit, cboMusic, and cboTitleWesterns.

When the user makes a selection from cboGenre, that control will determine which item the user chose and then change the visibilities of the three stacked combo boxes so that the corresponding control is visible and the other two are hidden. For example, if the user chooses Westerns for the genre, then the JavaScript attached to the cboGenre control will make cboWesterns visible and hide the other two combo boxes.

The JavaScript

We shall attach our JavaScript to the cboGenre field as a keystroke JavaScript; Acrobat will execute this script every time the user types a keystroke into the field. In a combo box, a keystroke JavaScript is also executed whenever a user selects an item from the combo box's menu; this is what makes the keystroke JavaScript the perfect place to put our "enable proper movie list" script.

In a keystroke JavaScript for a combo box, the event.changeEx property holds the export value of the menu item the user selected. We are going to compare event.changeEx with each of cboGenre's export values in turn; when we find a match, we shall then set the hidden property of the other three combo boxes.

The combo box script

To attach the keystroke JavaScript to the combo box:

Start with the Form tool selected and the Field Properties dialog box displaying the Format panel for cboGenre. (See Chapter 1 for a reminder of how to get to the Field Properties dialog box.)

1. Click the Edit button for the Custom Keyboard Script (**Figure 8.9**).

Acrobat will present you with the JavaScript Edit dialog box.

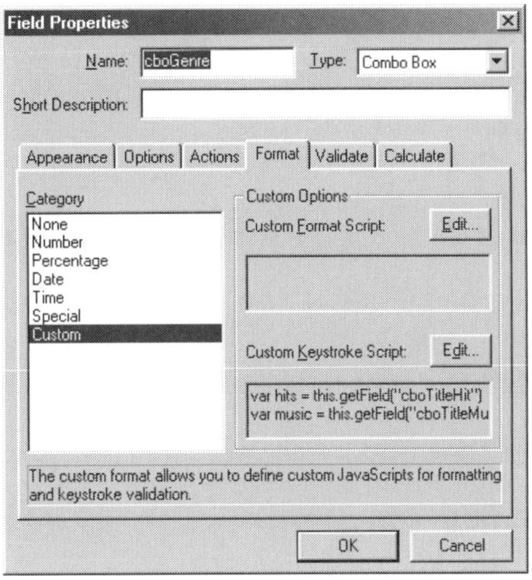

Figure 8.9 For a combo box, you want your JavaScript to be a keystroke JavaScript. Acrobat will execute this script every time the user picks an item from the combo box's menu.

2. Type the following script into the JavaScript Edit dialog box.

```
// Get references to our three combo boxes
var hits = this.getField("cboTitleHit")
var music = this.getField("cboTitleMusic")
var westerns = this.getField("cboTitleWesterns")

// Has the use selected "Current Hits?"
if (event.changeEx == "CH")     {
    hits.hidden = false
    music.hidden = true
    westerns.hidden = true
}
```

```
    // Has the user selected "Music DVDs?"
    else if (event.changeEx == "MS")    {
        hits.hidden = true
        music.hidden = false
        westerns.hidden = true
    }
    // Has the user selected "Westerns?"
    else if (event.changeEx == "WS")    {
        hits.hidden = true
        music.hidden = true
        westerns.hidden = false
    }
```

3. Exit out of all the dialog boxes until you are once more at the Acrobat page.

4. Try it out: Using the Hand tool, select different genres from the top combo box; the second combo box will change with each genre.

Let's look at what we've done here.

The code in detail

```
var hits = this.getField("cboTitleHit")
var music = this.getField("cboTitleMusic")
var westerns = this.getField("cboTitleWesterns")
```

We start by getting references to the three combo boxes whose visibility we want to control. We assign each combo box object to an appropriately named variable. (Again, I picked these variable names myself; there's nothing special about these names.)

```
if (event.changeEx == "CH")    {
```

Here we have a call to the if command that compares event.changeEx, which contains the export value of the item the user selected in cboGenre, with the string "CH", which is the export value for the Current Hits menu item. As always, if the comparison is true, then if will execute the JavaScript lines in braces.

```
hits.hidden = false
music.hidden = true
westerns.hidden = true
```

If the `if` comparison is true—that is, if the user selected Current Hits in the Genre combo box—then we will make the `hits` object (the cboTitleHit combo box) visible by setting its `hidden` attribute to `false`. We shall also set the `hidden` attribute of the other two combo boxes to `true`, hiding them from view.

```
else if (event.changeEx == "MS")    {
    hits.hidden = true
    music.hidden = false
    westerns.hidden = true
}
```

If the first `if` comparison is false—if the user didn't select Current Hits—then we shall check to see if they selected Music DVD; we compare `event.changeEx` with "MS," the export value for the Music DVD item in our Genre combo box. As before, if the comparison is true, then we make visible the Music DVD combo box, cboTitleMusic, and hide the other two.

```
else if (event.changeEx == "WS")    {
    hits.hidden = true
    music.hidden = true
    westerns.hidden = false
}
```

Finally, we check to see if the user selected Westerns as their genre, showing the cboTitleWesterns combo box and hiding the others.

JavaScripts for Other Control Types

As you can see, the principle behind creating a small number of dynamically visible form fields is pretty straightforward: You attach a JavaScript to the controlling form field that sets the `hidden` attribute for the fields you wish to manipulate. The JavaScript may need to determine the value of the controlling field in order to decide which controls to make visible and which to hide, as we did with our combo box.

Our two examples attached controlling JavaScripts to a check box and a combo box. We shall finish this chapter by briefly reviewing how to use other form types as the controlling field. We shall not step through any of these in detail, but an example of each is among this chapter's sample files.

List Box

Using a list box field to control other fields' visibility is nearly identical to using a combo box. In fact, the JavaScript for a list is identical to the JavaScript you would use in a combo box. In both cases, the event.changeEx property will contain the export value of the item the user selected; we can examine this property and then alter other fields' visibility accordingly.

The difference is that the JavaScript for a list box field must be attached to the field's Selection Change event, rather than being a keystroke JavaScript. The Selection Change JavaScript is accessible through a panel in the list box field's Field Properties dialog box (**Figure 8.10**). Select the "This script executes…" radio button, click the Edit button, and type your JavaScript into the resulting JavaScript Edit dialog box.

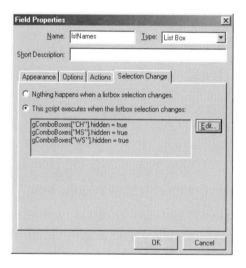

Figure 8.10 *The JavaScript for a list box field should be attached to the list's Selection Change event, which is accessible in the Field Properties dialog box.*

The file Ch08_Example3.pdf demonstrates how to use a list box field to control the visibility of other fields. This is our same order-a-movie form, but the user picks a genre from a list (**Figure 8.11**).

Radio Buttons

The JavaScript that controls fields' visibility from within a set of radio buttons is nearly identical to that we used with our original check box. You will attach a JavaScript to the Mouse Up event for each radio button in a set; the script for each radio button is responsible for making visible and hiding the controls associated with the choice that button represents.

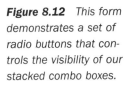

Figure 8.11 *Here is a list box field that controls the visibility of our stacked combo boxes.*

For example, **Figure 8.12** shows our form, now changed so that the user picks a genre from among a series of radio buttons. (This file is Ch08_Example4.pdf in this chapter's sample files.)

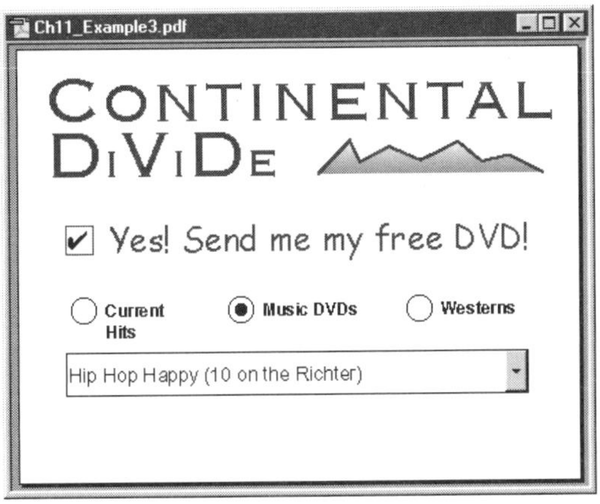

Figure 8.12 *This form demonstrates a set of radio buttons that controls the visibility of our stacked combo boxes.*

The script attached to the radio button labeled Westerns makes the cboTitleWesterns combo box visible and hides the others:

```
var hits = this.getField("cboTitleHit")

var music = this.getField("cboTitleMusic")

var westerns = this.getField("cboTitleWesterns")


hits.hidden = true

music.hidden = true

westerns.hidden = false
```

Buttons and Text Fields

If you use a button field to control other fields' visibility, as in **Figure 8.13**, you will set up the button exactly as we did the radio buttons. You will attach a Mouse Up JavaScript to the button that sets the hidden property of whichever form fields the button must control. Examine the file Ch08_Example5.pdf to see **Figure 8.13**'s form in action.

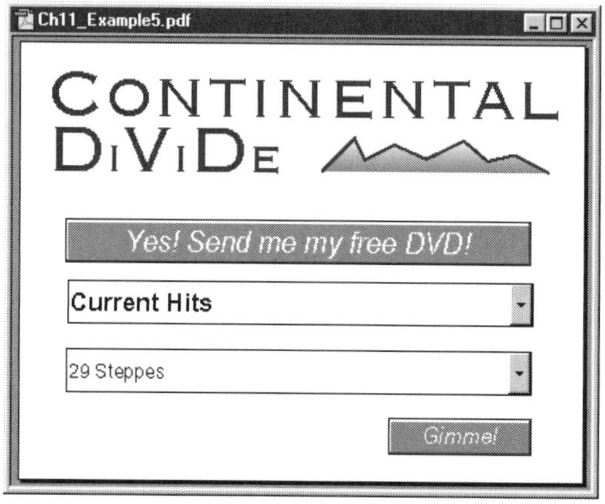

Figure 8.13 *The button in this form controls the visibility of all the other controls in the form.*

Text fields are usually inappropriate for use as a controlling form field. Although you can attach a JavaScript to the field's On Blur event that alters the hidden property of other fields, the fact that a text field allows the user to type in anything they wish usually makes for difficult script writing. You need to accommodate any random input, and the code for this can get messy. Usually, you want to limit the user's input to a set of known entries (Current Hits, Westerns, and so on), and for this a combo box works much better than a text field.

Dynamic Controls with Templates

In Chapter 8, we saw how to make a set of form fields appear as the result of some user action: clicking a check box, selecting an item from a combo box, and so on. We did this with a JavaScript that directly manipulated the fields' hidden property. This technique is appropriate if we're managing the visibility of a small number of controls, but it becomes burdensome if we need to manipulate a large number.

Acrobat provides a mechanism specifically for dynamically adding controls and even entire pages to an Acrobat form: templates. A template is a page in an Acrobat file whose contents—form fields, text, graphics—can be added by a JavaScript either to an existing page in the file or to a new page that's inserted in the document. The process of adding a template's contents to a document, either as a new page or as an addition to an existing page, is referred to as spawning the template.

A template page can be made so that it's initially invisible; the template items will appear to the user only when the template is spawned.

Using templates to create dynamic forms has two advantages over directly setting the dynamic fields' hidden properties, as we did in the previous chapter:

■ A template can have as many form fields on it as needed; spawning a crowded, full template is no harder than spawning one with just a few items. This makes templates more appropriate for managing a large number of dynamic fields.

■ Spawning a template adds *everything* on the template page to the document, including artwork, text, labels, and images, as well as form fields. We couldn't do that with the last chapter's technique, since only form fields have a hidden property.

What do we lose by using a template? Once you have spawned a template, there is no easy way to remove those items again; there is no "unspawn" feature. With templates, as elsewhere in life, spawning works in one direction only.

In this chapter, we shall see how to create templates and add their contents to a form.

The Project

(Files: Ch09_Example1.pdf, Ch09_Example1_Raw.pdf)

In this chapter, we shall be working with the three-page PDF file in **Figure 9.1**. We are going to convert pages 2 and 3 into invisible templates; when the user first opens the file, it will look like a single-page file consisting of only page 1.

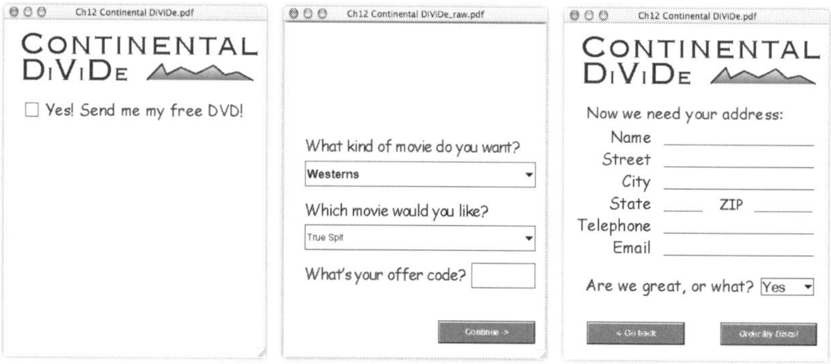

Figure 9.1 *Our sample document for this chapter has three pages. We're going to turn the second and third pages into templates whose contents will become visible only when the user clicks on the first page's check box.*

When the user clicks the Yes! check box, a JavaScript attached to that control does two things:

- It spawns the page 2 template, adding its contents to page 1 of the form.

- It spawns the page 3 template as a new page added to the end of the form.

What the user sees is that, upon selecting the Yes! check box, two combo boxes, a text field, a button, and their labels appear on the current page (**Figure 9.2**) and a second page suddenly appears that gathers shipping information. Try this out with the sample file Ch09_Example1.pdf; it's fun to watch.

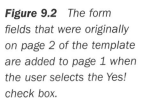

Figure 9.2 *The form fields that were originally on page 2 of the template are added to page 1 when the user selects the Yes! check box.*

The JavaScript

We shall add a Mouse Up JavaScript to the check box on page 1 that spawns two templates, as described above. Before we can do this, however, we need to create those templates; this entails going to pages 2 and 3, one at a time, and telling Acrobat that these pages should be treated as templates.

You may find it particularly useful in this chapter to open the file Ch09_Example1_Raw.pdf and follow along with the instructions as we first create the templates and then attach our JavaScript to the check box.

Creating the Templates

We want to turn both pages 2 and 3 in Ch09_Example1_Raw.pdf into templates. Let's start with page 2.

To turn page 2 into a template:

Start with the Acrobat file turned to page 2.

1. Select Tools > Forms > Page Templates.

    Acrobat will display the Page Templates dialog box (**Figure 9.3**). This dialog box lists all templates defined in the Acrobat file. The list initially will be blank.

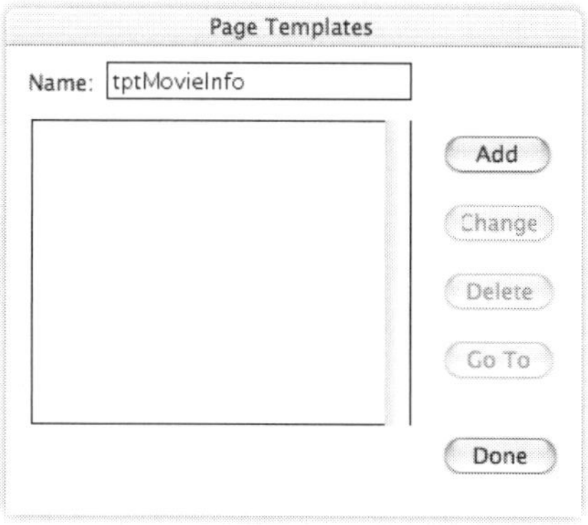

Figure 9.3 *The Page Templates dialog box lets you create, modify, and otherwise manage the list of templates in the current Acrobat document.*

2. Type a name into the Name field at the top of the dialog box.

    This will become the name of the page 2 template within the document. Pick something descriptive of the template's contents. (I chose tptMovieInfo; the "tpt" prefix will remind me later that this is the name of a template.)

3. Click the Add button and then click Yes in the resulting confirmation dialog box.

    Acrobat will turn this page into a template with the specified name; the name will now appear in the Page Templates list (**Figure 9.4**). There will be a bullet to the left of the name; this indicates whether the template initially will be visible in the form. If you click the bullet, it will toggle between a bullet, indicating the template is visible, and a minus sign, meaning it's invisible.

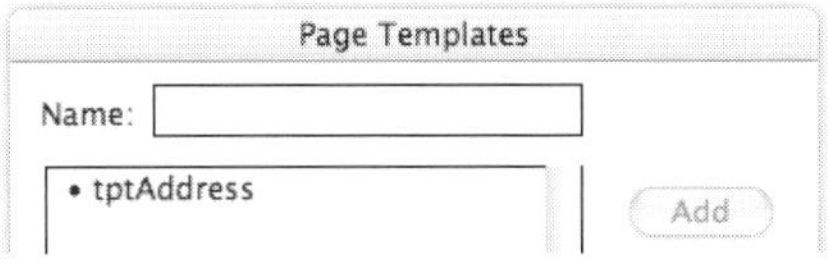

Figure 9.4 *When you create a template, it's added to the list in the Page Templates dialog box. The bullet to the left of the template name indicates whether the template is initially visible (·) or invisible (-).*

4. Click the bullet, setting it to a minus sign.

As soon as you change the bullet to a minus sign, page 2 disappears from your document. It's actually still there; it's just become an invisible template within the PDF file. (You will notice that even the status bar at the bottom of the page now reports one less page in the document; to Acrobat, templates do not count as pages unless they're visible.)

Usually, you'll want your templates to be invisible initially. You would leave them visible if you always wanted a page with those contents as part of the form; in that case, spawning the template would add another instance of a page that already exists. For example, in an expense report form, you would always want to have a page with expense items on it; your template would allow you to spawn another page with additional expense items.

5. Click the Done button, returning to your PDF document.

Turn to page 3 (now apparently page 2) in your Acrobat file and repeat steps 1 through 5, turning that page into a template. I named this second template tptAddress, but you may give it any name you choose. As always, something short and descriptive is best.

The Check Box JavaScript

Having created our templates, we need to add a JavaScript to our check box that will spawn the templates. We shall attach this JavaScript to the Mouse Up event for our check box field, chkYes. (Note that this check box is the only control visible to the user when the form first opens.)

Our JavaScript must carry out two steps for each template we want to spawn:

1. Create a `Template` **object** that represents that template.

A `Template` object is a JavaScript object that represents a particular template within your JavaScript program. You create `Template` objects with a call to the current document's getTemplate method. The phrase this.getTemplate("tptAddress") creates a Template object representing the template, tptAddress. (Remember that this in a JavaScript refers to the current document.)

2. Call the Template object's spawn method.

The spawn method creates a duplicate of the template's contents, adding the contents either to an existing page or to a new page that's inserted into the document. (We'll see how to specify exactly where the contents go in a moment.)

Our Mouse Up JavaScript will need to carry out these two steps for each of the two templates in our form.

To attach the JavaScript to our check box:

Start with the check box's Field Properties dialog box displaying the Actions panel, as shown in **Figure 9.5**. (See Chapter 1 for a reminder of how to get here.)

1. Select the Mouse Up event and click the Add button.

The Add an Action dialog box appears.

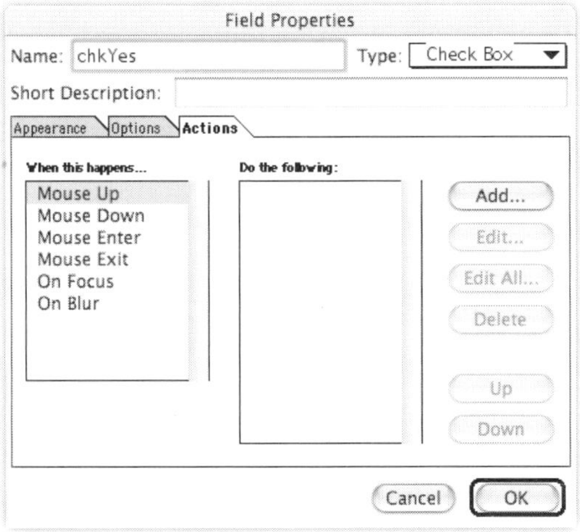

Figure 9.5 *We're going to attach our template-spawning JavaScript to the check box's Mouse Up event.*

2. In the Add an Action dialog box, select JavaScript in the pop-up menu and click the Edit button.

Acrobat will present you with the usual JavaScript Edit dialog box.

3. Type the following script into the JavaScript Edit dialog box (**Figure 9.6**):

Get Template objects

```
var orderInfoTemplate = this.getTemplate("tptMovieInfo")
var addressTemplate = this.getTemplate("tptAddress")
```

```
if (this.numPages == 1)    {
```

Spawn them

```
    orderInfoTemplate.spawn(0, false, true)
    addressTemplate.spawn(1, false, false)
}
```

4. Exit from all the dialog boxes until you are once again looking at your Acrobat page.

5. Try it out: With the Hand tool, click the check box; the other form fields and the second page will all appear.

Figure 9.6 *We type our JavaScript into the JavaScript Edit dialog box.*

The code in detail

```
var orderInfoTemplate = this.getTemplate("tptMovieInfo")
var addressTemplate = this.getTemplate("tptAddress")
```

These two lines make calls to the getTemplate method, obtaining Template objects for both of the templates in this form. The first line gets the tptMovieInfo template (which originally was page 2 in our Acrobat document) and assigns it to a variable named orderInfoTemplate. The second line gets our page 3 template and assigns it to the variable addressTemplate.

```
if (this.numPages == 1)    {
```

This call to the if command receives, in parentheses, a comparison that checks to see if the current page number is 1. If so, if executes the JavaScript lines in the braces; these lines spawn our two templates. The Doc property numPages is the number of pages in the Acrobat document.

We are doing this test because we want to spawn our templates only once, when the user first clicks the check box. If the user repeatedly clicks chkYes, we don't want each Mouse Up to add another set of spawned controls to the Acrobat document, one on top of another.

Since the tptAddress template will add a new page to our Acrobat form, our JavaScript can look at the number of pages currently in the form to determine whether or not we have already spawned the templates. If our document has only one page (that is, if this.numPages == 1), then we have not yet spawned any new pages and we can add the new controls and page to our document.

```
orderInfoTemplate.spawn(0, false, true)
```

Here we spawn our page 2 template, adding that template's contents to the current page in our form (**Figure 9.7**). The Template object's spawn method takes three *arguments* (that is, three values that must be passed in parentheses when we call the method): a page number and a pair of Boolean values. Depending on the arguments you give it, spawn duplicates the template's contents onto either a currently existing page or a new page in the Acrobat document.

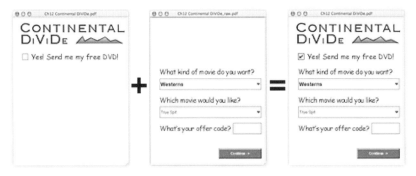

Figure 9.7 *The template that was originally page 2 in our document is overlaid onto the first page (in other words, page number 0) of our form.*

Let's discuss the arguments in some detail:

- *Page Number*—The first argument is a page number within the Acrobat document. This specifies where the newly spawned items should go. Its exact meaning is determined by the final Boolean argument to the spawn method, described below.

  Remember that, within a JavaScript, document pages are numbered starting with 0; if a document has 16 pages, they will be numbered 0 through 15. Thus, the 0 in our JavaScript line refers to the first page in the Acrobat file.

- *Rename Fields Boolean*—The second argument is a Boolean value that specifies whether form fields in the template contents should be renamed or retain their original names. A true value tells Acrobat to assign new names to the template's form fields; false specifies that the fields should retain their original names.

  In our JavaScript line, we set this argument to false, so that all the fields in the template will retain the names we originally gave them. We shall discuss in a moment why you would want to rename the template's form fields and how Acrobat chooses new names.

- *AddToPage Boolean*—This is the Boolean that specifies the meaning of the page number argument. If it's true, the template contents will be placed on that numbered page; if the argument is false, the template contents will be placed on a new page, which will be inserted into the document immediately before the numbered page.

  In our line of JavaScript, this argument is false, so we are adding the contents of orderInfoTemplate to the first page of our form, as in **Figure 9.7**.

```
addressTemplate.spawn(1, false, false)
```

Here we spawn the page 3 template, adding its contents to a new page, which is inserted at the end of the file (**Figure 9.8**); the page's fields collect the user's name, address, and other delivery information.

The page number specified here is 1, indicating the new page should be inserted in front of page 1. Since this form starts out with only one visible page, numbered 0, placing a page in front of page 1 places the page at the end of the document.

The second argument, a Boolean, is false, telling Acrobat to not rename the form fields on this template. The final Boolean argument is also false, which tells Acrobat to add a new page to the document rather than adding the template contents to an existing page.

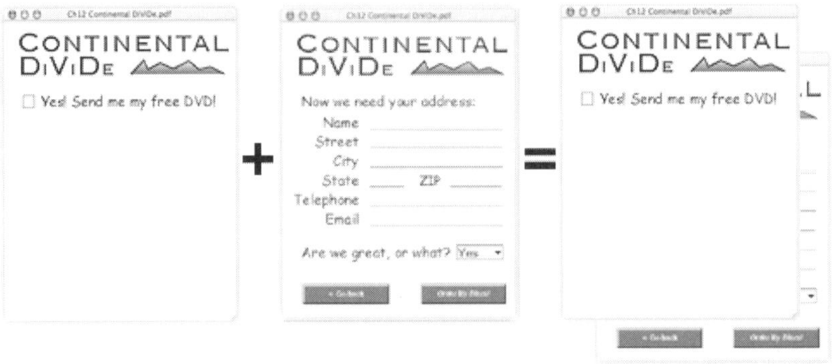

Figure 9.8 *The template that was originally page 3 in our document is added to the end of our form as a new page. The resulting Acrobat file now has two pages: the original page 1 and a new second page that was formerly the template.*

Automatically renamed fields

In most of the cases where you spawn a template to add dynamic fields to a form, you'll have Acrobat leave the form field names untouched. (You specify this by using a value of false for the spawn method's second argument.) This will preserve the names that you originally gave those fields.

Adding a Page to the End of the Document

Spawned pages are commonly added to the end of the current Acrobat document. This is easy if you know how many pages the document contains: Simply specify a page number that's one greater than the last page number in the document.

However, you don't always know, when you write the JavaScript that spawns a template, how many pages there will be in the document when the script is executed. There may be several templates in your form, all of which spawn new pages, which the user may trigger in any order.

The way around this is to make use of the Doc object's numPages property; this.numPages will always be the number of pages in the document. This number will also always be one greater than the last page number in the document, exactly the number we need to spawn a new page at the document's end. Simply use this.numPages for the page number in your call to the spawn method:

```
addressTemplate.spawn(this.numPages, false, false)
```

This guarantees the spawned page will be appended at the end of the Acrobat file.

However, there are cases where a form may need to repeatedly spawn a particular template. For example, an expense account form may let the user add as many pages of new expense items as needed. If we don't let spawn rename the fields, then the name of each field on a spawned page will be identical to the name of the corresponding field on all the other spawned pages. If you enter a number into one of the fields, that number will immediately become the value of all the other, identically named fields.

The form fields on repeatedly spawned pages almost certainly need to have unique names, since the information the user enters will usually be different from one page to the next.

In this case, you'll want to have Acrobat automatically rename the form fields on the template page. You specify this by setting the second argument to true when you call the spawn method:

```
addressTemplate.spawn(this.numPages, true, false)
```

The new name given to each form field on the newly spawned page will be derived from the original name that field had in the template. The name will consist of the following:

- the letter *P*, plus…

- the page number of the new page, plus…

- a dot followed by the template's name, plus…

- a dot followed by the original field name.

So if a template named tptNewItems were spawned into a form as page 6 and had a form field originally named txtCost, the name of the corresponding field on the new page would be P6.tptNewItems.txtCost.

Not pretty, but very probably unique.

10

Keystroke Checking

One user interface nicety common to forms is checking the keystrokes that you type into a field and rejecting the "illegal" ones. For example, a form field that collects a quantity will usually not accept any characters other than 0 through 9; a JavaScript attached to the form field examines each character as the user types it into the field, determines whether it's a numeral or something else, and accepts or rejects it accordingly.

JavaScript provides an extremely powerful mechanism called regular expressions that can be used to examine keystrokes (and other strings) to see if they conform to a desired pattern. A *regular expression* is a concise, precise description of a pattern that a sequence of characters should follow. Should a string start with a number, be followed by six alphabetic characters, and then end with an exclamation point? You can express this sequence using a regular expression. (Regular, here, means conforming to a pattern, predictable.)

However, with power comes complexity; even a light discussion of regular expressions spans multiple chapters. This chapter and the two that follow will explore some of the tasks made possible by the use of regular expressions. This chapter will start with a simple case: looking at a one-character string to see if it is "legal" for a particular form field.

The Project

(Files: Ch010_Example1.pdf, Ch010_Example1_raw.pdf)

We are going to add to the form pictured in **Figure 10.1** a JavaScript that prevents the user from typing any nonalphanumeric characters into the Validation Key field. (Alphanumeric characters are a–z, A–Z, and 0–9.) Our form contains three form fields, as you can seen in **Figure 10.2**: a combo box from which the user can pick his or her response to the poll's question; a text field, into which the user types a validation code, indicating his or her membership as an official eReferenda data source; and a Submit button that sends the response to eReferenda Central.

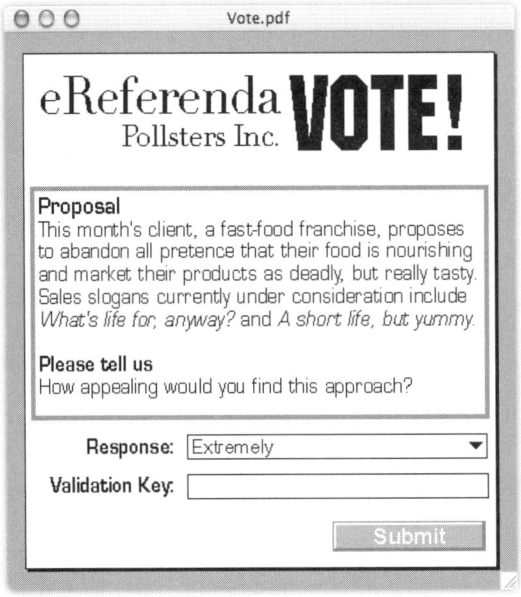

Figure 10.1 We shall add a keystroke JavaScript to this form's Validation Key field that will restrict the user's keyboard entry to alphanumeric characters. Any other characters will be ignored.

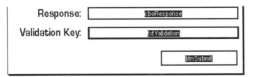

Figure 10.2 Our form has three fields in it: a combo box, a text field, and a button. This chapter's example adds a keystroke JavaScript to the text field.

eReferenda validation codes are all alphanumeric text sequences, so we are going to ignore any nonalphanumeric characters the user types into this field. We shall do this by attaching a keystroke JavaScript to the form field. A *keystroke JavaScript* is executed every time the user types a character into a form field to which the script is attached. The JavaScript can examine the character that was typed and tell Acrobat to reject it if it does not pass whatever test the JavaScript applies. In our case, we shall check whether the character the user enters is alphanumeric and reject it if it is not.

Before we can look at the keystroke JavaScript for this field, however, we must learn something about JavaScript regular expressions and how they work.

RegExp Objects

A RegExp object is a JavaScript object that contains a regular expression describing a pattern of characters. You can use this object to test whether or not a particular string conforms to or contains that pattern. Does the string contain the characters *Peachpit*? Is it entirely numeric? Does it have any numbers in it at all? Does it begin with a capital letter? Is it a valid telephone number? The regular-expression syntax is astonishingly rich; there are virtually no limits to what you can test for within a string.

The Submit Button

Notice that the Submit button is disabled and grayed out by default. If you type in a known validation code (such as *holmes, Watson, lestrade,* or *Mycroft*), it will become enabled (**Figure 10.3**). How to accomplish that is outside this chapter's scope, but if you're curious, you should first read Chapter 6 to see how JavaScript Array objects work, and then examine the On Blur JavaScript of the txtValidation field and the Document JavaScript for this Acrobat file.

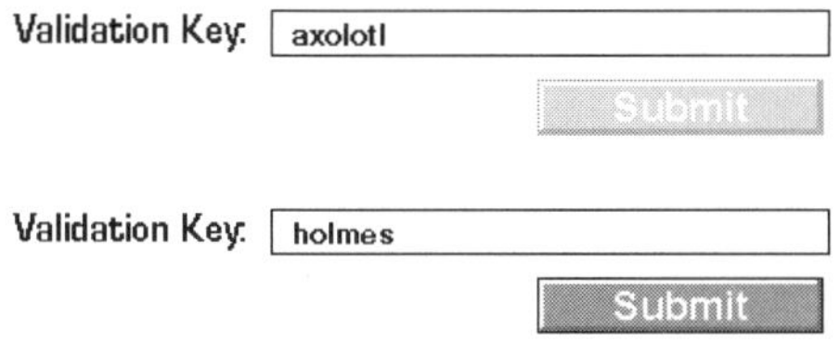

Validation Key: `axolotl`

Submit

Validation Key: `holmes`

Submit

Figure 10.3 *In this form, the Submit button is initially disabled (top). If you enter a known validation code, it becomes enabled (bottom).*

You specify the regular expression's character pattern using a "language" that qualifies as the most cryptic-looking syntax in JavaScript; it takes some getting used to. Once you know how to interpret it, however, the regular-expression syntax is no more difficult than reading. You just need to take it a little bit at a time.

Our First Regular Expression

Let's start by looking at the regular expression we shall use in this chapter's example: the pattern that specifies a single-character, alphanumeric string:

```
var re = /^\w$/
```

This is a decidedly strange line of code. We can immediately see that it's defining a variable named re (for *regular expression*), but the stuff to the right of the equals sign looks, at first, like a prank. The variable re is a RegExp object, an object that represents a regular expression; the bizarre text we have assigned to it is actually a regular expression describing a character pattern. Let's examine this regular expression.

A regular expression consists of a series of individual character specifications, one after another, that indicates which characters should occur within a string. Each item within the expression is either a specific character to be matched or a **metacharacter** that indicates a set of characters to be matched. In programming terminology, a *metacharacter* is a code, appearing in a string, that stands for another character. (For example, in many programming languages, the two-character code \t stands for a tab character.) This may sound confusing, but that's because it's much more easily demonstrated than explained.

We'll look in detail at the regular expression above to see how it works.

```
/^\w$/
```

Regular expressions begin and end with slash characters. These provide unambiguous markers as to where the expression begins and ends in the JavaScript code.

```
/^\w$/
```

The caret character indicates the beginning of the string. Including a caret at the beginning of the expression says that the set of characters described by this regular expression must occur at the beginning of whatever string we are testing.

```
/^\w$/
```

The \w combination is a metacharacter that matches any single alphanumeric character in the string we are testing: a–z, A–Z, or 0–9. What we have discussed so far, /^\w, would match any string that starts with an alphanumeric character.

/^\w$/

Finally, the dollar sign is a code that indicates the end of the string. This means that, to be a match for the regular expression, our single alphanumeric character must be immediately followed by the end of the string.

So, our regular expression describes the following character sequence:

- The beginning of the string (^)

- A single alphanumeric character (\w)

- The end of the string ($)

Simply put, this describes a one-character string.

Using the Regular Expression

The variable, re, that we created contains a description of a one-character alphanumeric string of text. We can use this object to test whether any particular JavaScript string matches that description. We do this using the test method of the RegExp object:

```
re.test("a")      // Returns true
re.test("abcd")   // Returns false; too many characters
re.test("-")      // Returns false; not alphanumeric
```

The test method takes a string as its argument, compares the string to the regular expression, and returns a Boolean (true/false) value if the string matches the pattern. In the above three JavaScript statements, only the first example is a match, the string being a one-character, alphanumeric string.

Keystroke JavaScripts

A keystroke JavaScript is executed every time the user types a character into a text field to which it's attached; it lets you examine the just-typed character and reject it if it doesn't pass some test applied by the JavaScript itself. The Acrobat event object contains fields that provide information useful to the keystroke JavaScript:

- event.change is a string that contains the character most recently typed by the user.

- `event.value` is a string containing the contents of the text field excluding the newly typed character.

- `event.rc` is a Boolean that the keystroke JavaScript can set to `false` to indicate that the character typed in by the user should be rejected. If the JavaScript rejects a character in this way, Acrobat will discard the character; it will be as though the user never pressed that key.

Something I've ignored up to now is that a keystroke JavaScript attached to a text field is actually executed in *two* circumstances, only one of which we've discussed so far:

- When the user types a character into the text field

  This lets you examine each character typed by the user, as we've been describing.

- When the user leaves the text field by tabbing out of it or clicking elsewhere in the form

  This lets you examine the field as a whole, to accommodate cases where you can't establish the validity of the user's input by examining just one character at a time. (For example, you may want to reject field contents that don't look like a valid date.) This type of keystroke JavaScript serves much the same purpose as the validation scripts we shall discuss in Chapter 11; validation scripts, as we shall see, are a more appropriate way to examine the contents of an entire form field.

A JavaScript can determine which of the two circumstances caused it to be executed by examining the `event.willCommit` property. This Boolean property has a value of `true` if the user has tabbed out of the text field; a `false` value indicates that the user pressed a key. (By the way, the property is called `willCommit` because the user is about to "commit" to the field's current value.)

As a result, a keystroke JavaScript that wants to check the validity of a single, newly typed character must contain an `if` statement that checks `event.willCommit` and executes its character-checking statements only if that Boolean is `false`:

```
if (event.willCommit == false)   {

    ... examine the character in event.change ...

}
```

Remember that the JavaScript if command is followed by a true-false state-ment in parentheses and then by a set of JavaScript commands in braces ({}) that should be carried out if the statement is true. (If there is only one command to be carried out, you may omit the braces.)

The JavaScript

In our form, we shall use a keystroke JavaScript with our re object, defined as above, to test the characters our user types into the field, one by one. If the character typed by the user is not alphanumeric, then we shall tell Acrobat to beep and ignore the keystroke.

To create the keystroke JavaScript:

Start with the Form tool selected and do the following:

1. Double-click the txtValidation field to get to its properties.

    The Field Properties dialog box opens.

2. Go to the Format panel (**Figure 10.4**).

3. Select Custom in the Category list.

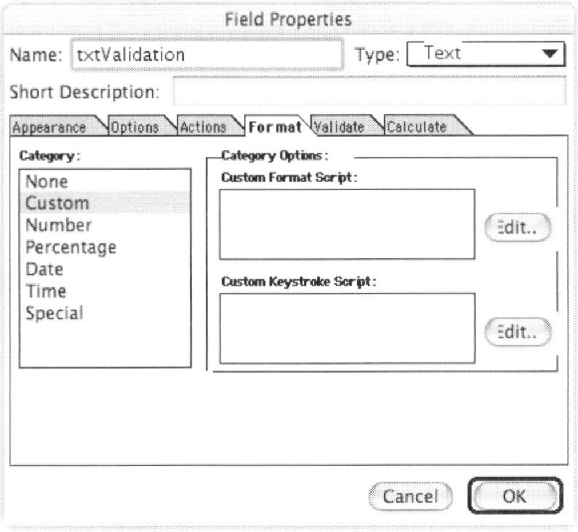

Figure 10.4 *You create a keystroke JavaScript by double-clicking the text field and then going to the Format panel in the resulting Field Properties dialog box.*

4. Click the Edit button next to the Custom Keystroke Script text box.

The JavaScript Edit dialog box opens (**Figure 10.5**).

Figure 10.5 *Type your keystroke JavaScript into the JavaScript Edit dialog box, as usual.*

5. Type in the following script:

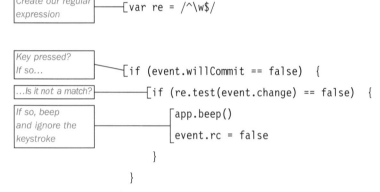

```
var re = /^\w$/

if (event.willCommit == false) {
    if (re.test(event.change) == false) {
        app.beep()
        event.rc = false
    }
}
```

Create our regular expression

Key pressed? If so...

...Is it not a match?

If so, beep and ignore the keystroke

6. Close all dialog boxes.

7. Try it out: Select the Hand tool and type some characters into the Validation Key text field.

If you try typing any nonalphanumeric characters, Acrobat will beep and ignore the key.

The code in detail

```
var re = /^\w$/
```

This is our definition of the RegExp object, re, as we discussed earlier. This object's regular expression will match any single-character alphanumeric string. We haven't done anything with this regular expression, yet; we've just defined it for later use.

```
if (event.willCommit == false)   {
```

As we said earlier, the property `event.willCommit` will be true if our keystroke JavaScript is being executed because the user is exiting the form field. In this case, we want to do nothing. We want to use our regular expression only if the `willCommit` property is *not* true, that is, if the user has pressed a key. Hence, our `if` operation.

We are looking to see if `event.willCommit` is false, meaning the user has pressed a key. (Double equals signs (==) mean *is equal to* in JavaScript.) If so, we execute the set of JavaScript statements in braces; these will check to see if the current keystroke is a match for our regular expression.

```
if (re.test(event.change) == false)   {
```

Inside the first `if` command's braces, we have another `if` command. This second, nested `if` command tests the current keystroke to see if it is a match for our regular expression, `re`.

Remember that `re.test` examines a string to see whether it matches the regular expression. The string in our case is `event.change`; for a keystroke script, `event.change` is a string that contains the character that the user pressed. Our `if` comparison checks to see if our regular-expression test returns false, that is, if the key pressed by the user does *not* match the regular expression. The `if` operator will therefore execute the JavaScript statements in braces if the user presses something other than an alphanumeric character.

```
app.beep()
```

```
event.rc = false
```

Finally, in the second, nested set of braces, we have the two lines of JavaScript code that will be executed if our user presses something other than an alphanumeric key.

The first of these two lines tells Acrobat (represented by the `app` object) to beep.

The second line is a bit less obvious: It sets the `rc` property of the `event` object to `false`. Here, `rc` stands for *return code*; this is a Boolean value that tells Acrobat whether or not to accept the user's keystroke. If a keystroke JavaScript sets `event.rc` to `false`, as we have done here, then Acrobat will ignore the keystroke.

Additional Regular-Expression Metacharacters

The set of metacharacters that a regular expression can contain is rich; **Table 10.1** presents a sample of the metacharacters that are most applicable to testing individual characters in a string. We shall see some more codes in the next two chapters, appropriate to those chapters' tasks. Appendix B presents a complete list of regular-expression metacharacters.

Table 10.1 *Some Regular-Expression Metacharacters*

CODE	MEANING
\w	Matches a single alphanumeric character. Thus, \w would be a match if the test string were *X*, but not if it were "™".
\W	Matches a single *non*alphanumeric character.
[xyz]	Matches any one of the characters in the brackets. You can use a hyphen to indicate a range of characters. Thus, [afbt] would match *a, f, b,* or *t*, but not *m*. Similarly, [a-c] would match *a, b,* or *c*.
[^xyz]	Matches any character except those in the brackets. Thus, [^afbt] would match *m*, but not *a, f, b,* or *t*. Note that this is a different use of the caret character than we used in our sample script.
\d	Matches a single-digit character, 0 through 9.
\D	Matches any nondigit character.
\s	Matches a single whitespace character—that is, a single space, tab, carriage return, or linefeed character.
\S	Matches a single nonwhitespace character—that is, any character except a space, tab, carriage return, or linefeed.

11

Field Validation

One experience common to everyone who uses computers is typing in a long, complex serial number and then having the application kick it back, saying it's not a valid number. In this chapter, we shall see how to do this ourselves. We are going to look at the technique of *field validation*—examining the contents of a form field to see if it matches a particular pattern.

In discussing this, we are going to build on the discussion of regular expressions that we started in Chapter 10. *Regular expressions* are an extremely powerful tool for matching a string (such as the contents of a text field) to a particular pattern. However, with power comes complexity; even a light discussion of regular patterns extends across multiple chapters in this book. This is all to say that you should read Chapter 10 before attempting this one.

The Project

In this chapter, we are going to add validation to two of the text fields in the form pictured in **Figure 11.1**. The fields in this form are pictured in **Figure 11.2**; we shall add validation scripts to the following:

- txtName—We shall make sure that the text is a valid *first-name-space-last-name* combination.

- txtSN—We shall verify that the input is a valid serial number. The format I've chosen here is typical of software serial numbers; the sequence A6BF-479X-2139 will be a valid account number.

Figure 11.1 We shall check the text the user types into two of the text fields in this form to make sure it's valid.

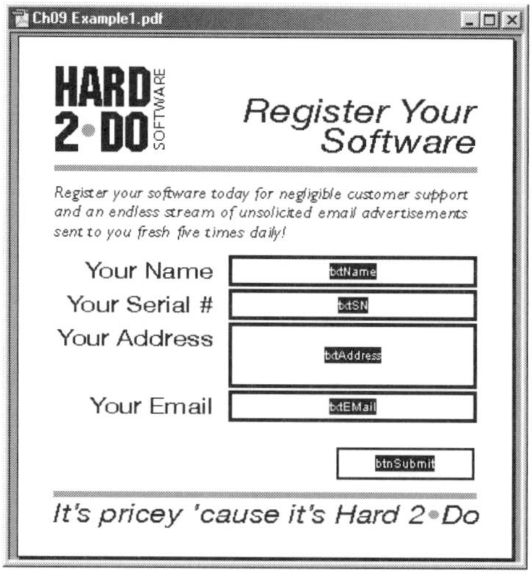

Figure 11.2 We shall check the text the user types into two of the text fields in this form to make sure it's valid.

In both cases, if the user types invalid text into the field, our form will post an alert, letting them know there's a problem, as in **Figure 11.3**.

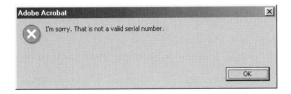

Figure 11.3   *If the user enters invalid text into one of the text fields, our form will display a warning message.*

The JavaScript

Approaching the Problem

We are going to do validation checking on these fields by writing a validation JavaScript for each field. Acrobat executes a field's validation JavaScript when the user exits the field. Our JavaScript's purpose will be to look at the text the user entered into the form field and decide whether or not the text is valid. If it's not valid, the script will tell Acrobat to reject the user's entry, causing the field to revert to its default value, which is usually blank.

Within the validation JavaScript, we shall check the correctness of the user's input by testing it against a regular expression, as we did in Chapter 10. This will give us a compact, precise way of comparing the field's text to the desired pattern.

Our example form will give us a chance to look at three regular expressions of increasing complexity, adding to the formatting codes we discussed in the previous chapter. As we saw in that chapter, regular expressions are among the most exotic, cryptic-looking parts of JavaScript, and many people never really acquire a taste for them.

That said, regular expressions are well worth learning, because they make it easy to accomplish a slew of important text-related tasks—field validation, checking for illegal characters, and so on—that are otherwise painfully difficult. If you wish, however, you can skip the chapters in this book that deal with regular expressions (Chapters 8, 9, and 10) and return to them at a later time; the rest of the book does not depend on them.

The Name Field

Let us start with our name text field, txtName. We are going to add a validation JavaScript to this field that determines whether its text is a valid name. This JavaScript is going to be very simple-minded about what constitutes a valid name. The text in txtName will be considered a valid name if it consists of the following sequence:

- a capital letter, followed by…

- one or more lowercase letters, followed by…

- a single space character, followed by…

- a capital letter, followed by…

- one or more lowercase letters, followed by…

- the end of the string.

As in the previous chapter, we need to create a regular expression that describes this sequence.

The regular expression

For txtName, we shall use a regular expression that describes our *first name-last name* sequence; we'll assign this expression to a variable, re, as we did in Chapter 10.

```
var re = /^[A-Z][a-z]+ [A-Z][a-z]+$/
```

Let's examine each metacharacter in this regular expression to see what it means. Some of this will be review from the last chapter.

```
/^[A-Z][a-z]+ [A-Z][a-z]+$/
```

Remember that a regular expression begins and ends with a slash. These slashes unambiguously indicate the extent of the regular expression in the JavaScript code.

```
/^[A-Z][a-z]+ [A-Z][a-z]+$/
```

The caret marks the beginning of our string. The sequence defined by this regular expression must be at the beginning of the string to be a match.

```
/^[A-Z][a-z]+ [A-Z][a-z]+$/
```

Brackets in a regular expression will match any one of the characters inside the brackets. You can use a hyphen to indicate a range of characters. In our case, we specified [A-Z], which would match any uppercase alphabetic character. Putting it simply, our string must start with a capital letter.

/^[A-Z][a-z]+ [A-Z][a-z]+$/

In a similar manner, [a-z] matches any single lowercase letter. The problem is that, in a name, the initial capital letter is followed by *an unknown number* of lowercase letters. That's where the plus sign comes in handy. A plus sign following a character specification ([a-z], in our case) indicates that there should be one or more of that character specification. It doesn't matter how many of those characters there are, as long as there is at least one.

So far, our regular expression indicates that the string we are testing should start with a capital letter and be followed by one or more lowercase letters: *John, Barbara, Elizabeth, Gigi,* and so on. This adequately specifies the first name.

/^[A-Z][a-z]+ [A-Z][a-z]+$/

Note the space between the plus sign (+) and [A–Z]

The space character between the first- and last-name specifications in our regular expression will match a single space character in the string we test. We are saying that the first and last names must be separated by a single space character.

(There are some alternatives we could have used here instead of the space character. Specifically, either \b or \s can be used to indicate a word break; see **Table 11.1**, at the end of the chapter, for more information on these two metacharacters.)

/^[A-Z][a-z]+ [A-Z][a-z]+$/

The specification for the last name is identical to that for the first name: a capital letter, followed by one or more lowercase letters.

/^[A-Z][a-z]+ [A-Z][a-z]+$/

Finally, the dollar sign indicates the end of the string. This means that our sequence must end at the end of the string for that string to be a match.

This regular expression is admittedly simplistic; any of us can come up with a large number of names that will not match this sequence. For now, however, let's leave it at this. Chapter 19 lists some sources of Regular Expressions on the Web; many of these sites have more all-inclusive expressions for testing names.

Table 11.1, at the end of this chapter, presents some additional regular-expression metacharacters appropriate for examining sets of characters.

The validation script

Having written our regular expression, let's write the validation script for our txtName field, teaching it to accept only valid names. You type a validation JavaScript into the Validate panel of a form field's properties.

To type in the validation JavaScript, start with the Form tool selected and do the following:

1. Double-click the txName field to get to its properties.

Acrobat will present you with the Field Properties dialog box.

2. Go to the Validate tab (**Figure 11.4**).

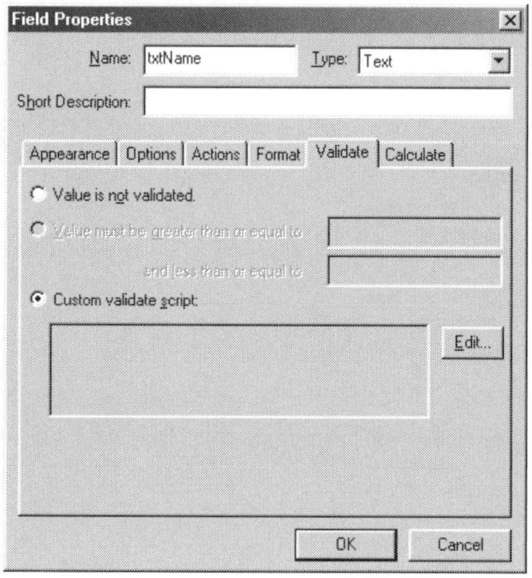

Figure 11.4 *You create a validation JavaScript by double-clicking the combo box and then going to the Validate panel in the resulting Field Properties dialog box.*

3. Select the "Custom validate script" radio button.

4. Click the Edit button.

You will now be looking at the JavaScript Edit dialog box (**Figure 11.5**).

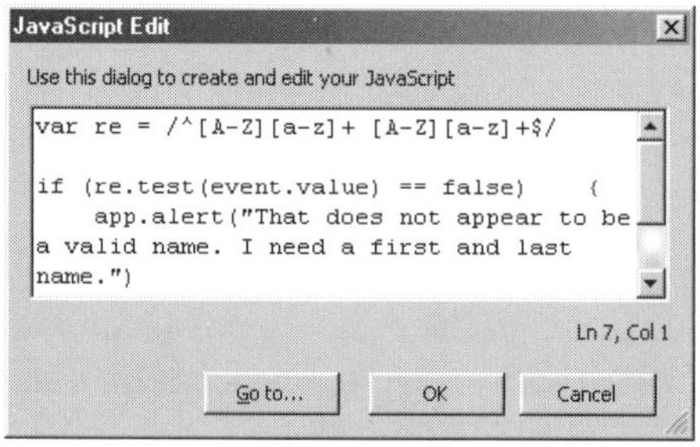

Figure 11.5 *Type your validation JavaScript into the JavaScript Edit dialog box, as usual.*

5. Type in the following script:

```
var re = /^[A-Z][a-z]+ [A-Z][a-z]+$/
```

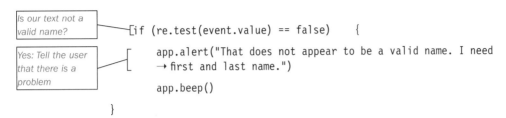

```
if (re.test(event.value) == false)    {
    app.alert("That does not appear to be a valid name. I need
    → first and last name.")
    app.beep()
}
```

6. Close all dialog boxes.

7. Try it out: Return to the Hand tool and type a name into the name field. If you type anything other than a *first name-space-last name* sequence, Acrobat will beep and complain with an alert, as in **Figure 11.3**.

The code in detail

```
var re = /^[A-Z][a-z]+ [A-Z][a-z]+$/
```

This is our definition of the RegEx object, re, as we discussed earlier. This object's regular expression will match any *first name-space-last name* string.

```
if (re.test(event.value) == false)    {

    ...

}
```

Here, we test the value of our event object (event.value is the text currently held by our text field) to see if it matches the regular expression in re. Our if operator checks to see if the test is false—that is, if the text in our name field is *not* a *first name-space-last name* sequence. If the test yields a result of false, then if will execute the statements in the braces.

```
app.alert("That does not appear to be a valid name. I need a first
→ and last name.")
```

```
app.beep()
```

In our case, if the name is not what we want, the JavaScript presents an alert warning the user and then beeps.

Serial Number Field

The Serial Number field needs to receive a seemingly random series of characters and determine whether the series matches the pattern for this company's serial numbers. An example of a valid number for this company would look something like this:

A6BF-479X-2139

That is, a valid account number will consist of the following, in this order:

- a single capital letter,…

- a numeral,…

- two capital letters,…

- a hyphen,…

- three numerals,…

- and so on.

The regular expression

The regular expression that describes our pattern looks like this:

```
var re = /^[A-Z]\d[A-Z]{2}-\d{3}[A-Z]-\d{4}$/
```

This is starting to look decidedly long and complex, but it really isn't particularly difficult; as usual, we just need to take it a bit at a time.

After the /^ that starts the regular expression and indicates the start of the string, we have the following:

```
/^[A-Z]\d[A-Z]{2}-\d{3}[A-Z]-\d{4}$/
```

As in our name field, [A-Z] indicates a single character from *A* to *Z*.

```
/^[A-Z]\d[A-Z]{2}-\d{3}[A-Z]-\d{4}$/
```

Backslash-d matches a single numerical digit, that is, a single character from 0 to 9. It's equivalent to [0-9].

```
/^[A-Z]\d[A-Z]{2}-\d{3}[A-Z]-\d{4}$/
```

Our account number now calls for two capital letters. We could do this with two [A-Z] codes in succession, but this would become unwieldy if we needed, say, ten capital letters in a row.

A numeral in braces ({2}, in our case) indicates a repetition of the preceding code that many times. Thus, [A-Z]{2} specifies a run of two capital letters.

The braces can have two numbers in them, separated by commas, indicating a minimum and maximum character count. For example, [A-Z]{2,5} indicates at least 2, but not more than 5, capital letters.

```
/^[A-Z]\d[A-Z]{2}-\d{3}[A-Z]-\d{4}$/
```

The dash, for a wonder, isn't a metacharacter; it simply specifies there should be a literal dash in the string at this point.

The remainder of the regular expression introduces no new codes; we have:

- \d{3}[A-Z]-, three numerals, a capital letter, and a dash

- \d{4}, four numerals

- $/, the end of the string and the end of the regular expression

The validation script

The validation script for the txtSN fields is remarkably like that we used for the txtName field. The script will see if the field's contents match our regular expression and, if not, will beep and complain.

To enter the txtSN field's validation script, follow the numbered steps we used for txtName, but type in the following script instead of the txtName script:

```
var re = /^[A-Z]\d[A-Z]{2}-\d{3}[A-Z]-\d{4}$/

if (re.test(event.value) == false)    {
    app.alert("I'm sorry. That is not a valid account number.")
    app.beep()
}
```

If you compare this script to the one for txtName, you'll see it's identical except for the regular expression and the text in the alert.

I won't step through this in detail, since it exactly matches the logic of our previous JavaScript.

Having typed in the validation script, try it out. Return to the hand tool and enter some account numbers. The field will accept only those that conform to our regular expression.

Enhancements

Blank Fields

One problem with our validation JavaScripts as they are is that if the user leaves a field blank, our JavaScript will report it as bad entry. Technically, this is correct, since a zero-character string is, indeed, a bad email address. However, it makes for an annoying user interface; every time the user clicks in a form field and then, changing his or her mind, clicks somewhere else, our form will bleat about invalid text in the field.

We would like our validation code to examine the field contents only if the user has typed something into the field. This is easily done with a minor modification to our present validation JavaScripts. Here is the new version of the txtName script:

```
var re = /^[A-Z][a-z]+ [A-Z][a-z]+$/
```

Is the field not blank?

Is the text not a match?

```
if (event.value != "") {
    if (re.test(event.value) == false) {
        app.alert("That does not appear to be a valid name. I need a
        → first and last name.")
        app.beep()
    }
}
```

Here we have placed a new `if` statement around the script's original `if` statement.

```
if (event.value != "") {
```

This `if` command looks to see if the text the user typed into the form field is *not* a blank. ("`!=`" means *is not equal to* in JavaScript.) Only if this is true (if the field is not blank) will `if` execute our JavaScript code that tests the field contents. If the field is blank, the JavaScript will do nothing at all. This will prevent the user from being annoyed by unnecessary alerts.

Rejecting Bad Input

The JavaScripts we use in this chapter don't actually reject bad input from the user; that is, if the user types in some incorrect text, our JavaScripts display an alert telling them about it, but it leaves their incorrect text in the form field. This is actually a good thing; it lets them fix their mistakes by editing their old text, rather than requiring them to retype the entire field.

If we *did* want Acrobat to reject bad input, however, our JavaScript would need to somehow tell Acrobat that the input is, indeed, bad. We do this by setting the rc (result code) field of the event object to false:

```
event.rc = false
```

At the end of a validation script, Acrobat looks at event.rc to determine whether your script thought the text was valid. If event.rc is false, Acrobat resets the text field to its default value (usually blank).

This line of JavaScript should be placed among the statements that are executed if the user's input fails the test against the regular expression:

```
if (re.test(event.value) == false)     {
    app.alert("That does not appear to be a valid name. I need a
    → first and last name.")
    app.beep()
    event.rc = false
}
```

Again, I think this is generally not a good idea in a form; indeed, I consider it a form of meanness, since it forces the user, in the case of an error, to reenter all of the field's text, rather than just edit it.

Regular Expressions from the Web

We have written regular expressions that match the name of the person using our form and the serial number of the software he or she bought. We still have the email field to deal with, and in a real registration form there would be telephone numbers, zip codes, and many other fields, any of which we might want to validate before the user submitted the data to our registration site.

Writing regular expressions to validate every text field in a form can be tedious. Happily, there are many sites on the World Wide Web that have regular expressions you can use for free: Just copy and paste the expression from the Web page into your form field's validation script.

See Chapter 19 for a list of regular-expression resources on the Web.

More Metacharacters

Table 11.1 presents some of the template codes that are most applicable to testing sets of characters. Refer to Chapter 10 for more codes that are appropriate to that chapter's tasks. Appendix B presents a full list of all regular-expression codes.

Table 11.1 *Single-Character Regular-Expression Codes*

CODE	MEANING
*	Must follow a character specification; indicates zero or more instances of that specification. Thus, ba+d would match *bd, bad, baaad,* and so on.
+	Matches the preceding character specification one or more times.
?	Matches the preceding character zero or one time. Thus, ba?d would match *bd* and *bad,* but not *baaad.*
{n}	Where n is a number: matches exactly *n* instances of the preceding specification. Thus, Du{3}de would match only *Duuude.*
{n,m}	Where n and m are numbers: matches at least *n* but not more than *m* instances of the preceding specification. Du{1,3}de will match *Dude, Duude,* and *Duuude.*
\b	Matches any word boundary, including the beginning of the string, a space character, a tab, or a new line.
\s	Matches any single whitespace character, including line breaks, tabs, new lines, and so on. This differs from \b in including some exotic characters, such as vertical tabs.

12

Formatting Text Fields

When I first started working with Acrobat forms, one of the features that impressed the socks off me was the autoformatting capability of its text fields. Select a predefined format in the Format pane of the Field Properties dialog box, and the form field automatically takes whatever text you typed into it and reformats it into a Zip code, a telephone number, a currency format, and so on. Very nifty.

I was young then, and have lived much since. Among the minor nuggets of wisdom I've accumulated along the way is that there is no magic in Acrobat's automatically formatted text fields. With a little JavaScript knowledge and some tolerance for regular expressions, you can easily create your own text fields that automatically format themselves.

In this chapter, we shall learn the basics of how to specify the formatting of a text field. This lesson will build on the discussion of regular expressions in the previous two chapters; you *must* read those chapters before attempting this one.

The Project

We are going to add automatic formatting to the telephone field in the form in **Figures 12.1** and **12.2**. Our script will reformat the user's input in the format of an American telephone number: 1-*area code-prefix-number*. (This is different than Acrobat's built-in telephone format, which places parentheses around the area code.)

Figure 12.1   *We are going to add a format JavaScript to this form that will change the input in the telephone field to 1-nnn-nnn-nnnn format.*

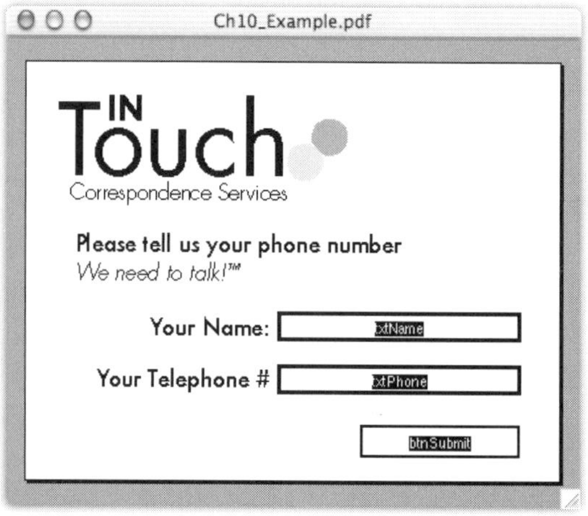

Figure 12.2   *There are two text fields in this form, txtName and txtPhone.*

The Format Panel

We specify a format for a form field by going to the Format panel in the Field Properties dialog box (**Figure 12.3**). This panel allows us to select from among a variety of predefined formats; if you need a format that isn't included in the predefined list, you can select the Custom option from the Category list, as in the figure, and then type in a JavaScript that specifies how the text should appear to the user. This JavaScript is referred to as a *format JavaScript*.

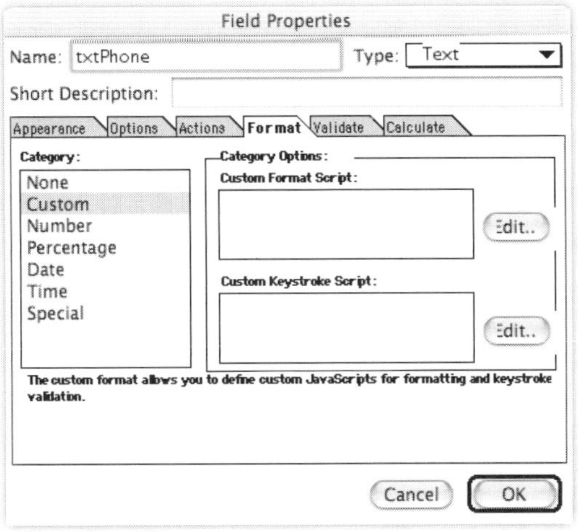

Figure 12.3 *You enter format JavaScripts into the Format panel of the Field Properties dialog box.*

A format JavaScript must set the property `event.value` to whatever text the user should see:

```
event.value = "Formatted Text"
```

This text becomes the visible representation of the field's value, but it does *not* change the actual field contents. When the user exits the field (by tabbing out or clicking on something else), Acrobat executes the format script, changing the field's appearance. When the user reenters the field, the text reverts to exactly what he or she had originally typed in (**Figure 12.4**). This is something that Acrobat always does with a formatted field; you have no control over this.

Note that the format JavaScript is executed when the user leaves the form field; in this way, it is similar to a JavaScript attached to the On Blur event. However, the format JavaScript is a completely separate mechanism; when the user leaves a text field, Acrobat executes both the format JavaScript and the On Blur JavaScript, in that order.

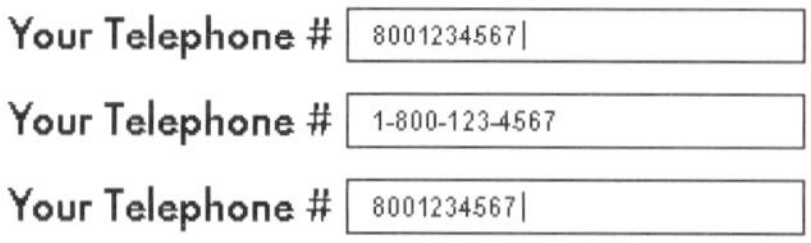

Your Telephone # | 8001234567|

Your Telephone # | 1-800-123-4567

Your Telephone # | 8001234567|

Figure 12.4 *In the top illustration, the user types numbers into a text field. In the middle, once the user clicks outside of the field, the field's format JavaScript goes to work, changing the user's input into proper format. In the bottom picture, when the user reenters the field; the field's text reverts to the user's original input.*

Parentheses in Regular Expressions

In our format JavaScript for the telephone field, we are going to use the following regular expression:

```
var re7Digits = /^(\d{3})(\d{4})$/
```

This regular expression has two parts:

- $(\d{3})$—This specifies three numeric characters in a row. (Backslash-d matches a single numeric digit; {3} says we have three of them.) Since this expression occurs at the beginning of the string, this will match the three-digit prefix of our telephone number. Note that this specification is in parentheses; we shall discuss the significance of this in a moment.

- $(\d{4})$—This will match the remaining four digits of our telephone number. This, too, is in parentheses.

The parentheses cause something special to happen when we test a string against this regular expression. In the previous chapter, we saw that parentheses in a regular expression cause the specifications they contain to be treated as a single unit. This is still true, but there's more.

Once the regular expression has been used to test a string, your JavaScript can refer to text that matched the parenthetical specification using special properties named RegExp.$1, RegExp.$2, RegExp.$3, up through RegExp.$9. RegExp.$1 will refer to the text that matched the first parenthetical expression; RegExp.$2 will refer to the second parenthetical match, and so on up to the ninth match, referred to as RegExp.$9.

This sounds more confusing than the concept really is; it will help to look at an example. Let us test a seven-digit string using our regular expression:

```
var re7Digits = /^(\d{3})(\d{4})$/
re7Digits.test("8124796")
```

After this test, `RegExp.$1` will refer to the first three digits in our number—812—and `RegExp.$2` will refer to the final four digits—4796—the second parenthetical match.

We can reformat this seven-digit number into a proper U.S. telephone number (**Figure 12.5**) by concatenating the two strings with a hyphen placed between them:

```
event.value = RegExp.$1 + "-" + RegExp.$2
```

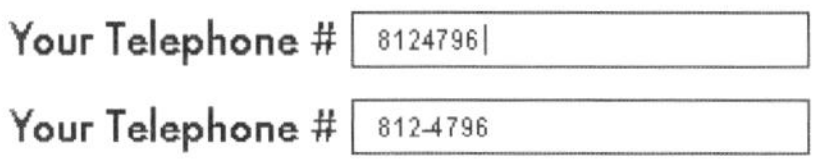

Your Telephone # `8124796`

Your Telephone # `812-4796`

Figure 12.5   *The regular expression /^(\d{3})(\d{4})$/ allows us to separate the first three and final four digits of a seven-digit number. We can then display them as a properly hyphenated telephone number, as in the bottom field.*

The JavaScript

We are going to write a format JavaScript for the txtPhone field pictured in **Figures 12.1** and **12.2**. This JavaScript should take whatever the user enters into the text field, separate it into telephone number components, and then reassemble them into a properly formatted U.S. telephone number (**Figure 12.6**).

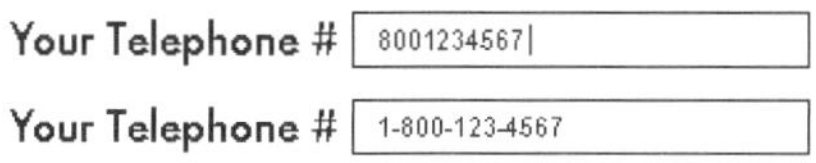

Your Telephone # `8001234567`

Your Telephone # `1-800-123-4567`

Figure 12.6   *Our telephone field's JavaScript will reformat the field's contents (top) into a properly formatted telephone number with area code (bottom).*

There are two situations we shall handle:

- The user enters seven digits (1234567); this we shall format as a local number (123-4567).

- The user enters ten digits (1234567890); we shall format this as a long-distance number (1-123-456-7890).

Our JavaScript will contain two regular expressions, one for each case, and two if statements that reformat our text field according to the situation. If the user enters anything other than a seven- or ten-digit number, we shall leave the input unchanged; Acrobat will display it exactly as the user typed it.

To type in the format JavaScript:

Start with the Form tool selected.

1. Double-click the txtPhone field to access its properties.

Acrobat will present you with the Field Properties dialog box (**Figure 12.3**).

2. Go to the Format panel.

3. Select Custom in the Category list.

4. Click on the Edit button next to the Custom Format Script text box.

The JavaScript Edit dialog box opens (**Figure 12.7**).

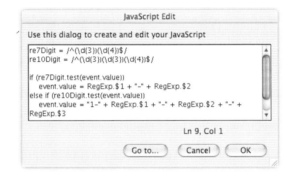

Figure 12.7 *Type your format JavaScript into the JavaScript Edit dialog box, as usual.*

5. Type in the following script:

Our two regular expressions

```
var re7Digits = /^(\d{3})(\d{4})$/
var re10Digits = /^(\d{3})(\d{3})(\d{4})$/
```

Do this for a seven-digit number

```
if (re7Digits.test(event.value))
    event.value = RegExp.$1 + "-" + RegExp.$2
else if (re10Digits.test(event.value))
```

Otherwise, do this for a ten-digit number

```
    event.value = "1-" + RegExp.$1 + "-" + RegExp.$2 + "-" +
    RegExp.$3
```

6. Close all dialog boxes.

7. Try it out: Return to the Hand tool and type a seven- or ten-digit number into the telephone field. The JavaScript will reformat your entry into a valid telephone number.

The code in detail

```
var re7Digits = /^(\d{3})(\d{4})$/
var re10Digits = /^(\d{3})(\d{3})(\d{4})$/
```

We start by defining two regular expressions. The first is the expression we examined earlier; this will match any seven-digit numeric string. The second expression matches a ten-digit long-distance number. Its three parenthetical expressions correspond to the three-digit area code, the three-digit prefix, and the four remaining digits in the telephone number. We will be able to refer to these later as RegExp.$1, RegExp.$2, and RegExp.$3.

```
if (re7Digits.test(event.value))
```

Here we test our form field contents against the seven-digit regular expression within a call to the if command. If the string matches our regular expression, if will execute the next line in our JavaScript.

```
event.value = RegExp.$1 + "-" + RegExp.$2
```

This line will be executed only if the if command's test evaluated to true, that is, if our string is a seven-digit number. This line assembles the display version of our telephone number by concatenating the prefix (RegExp.$1), a hyphen, and the remaining four-digit telephone number (RegExp.$2).

Naming Regular Expressions

In Chapters 10 and 11 we always gave the name re to the variable associated with our regular expression. It's a good, mnemonic name, and we never needed any other names, since we hadn't used more than one regular expression in our JavaScripts. This chapter's example, however, has two regular expressions, so we need to give different names to their variables: re7Digits and re10Digits. I picked these names to remind me what they are; there is nothing otherwise special about them.

You can name regular expression variables any way you want: myRegExp, re1, re2, re3, telephoneNumberPattern, or whatever. I suggest striving for simple names that are also somewhat descriptive.

```
else if (re10Digits.test(event.value))
    event.value = "1-" + RegExp.$1 + "-" + RegExp.$2 + "-" + RegExp.$3
```

The else command specifies one or more JavaScript statements that should be carried out if the corresponding if comparison failed, that is, if the user's input was not a seven-digit number.

In our script, the else is followed by another if, which tests the user's input against the ten-digit regular expression. If they match, then we assemble a long-distance number in 1-*nnn-nnn-nnnn* format. Remember that RegExp.$1, RegExp.$2, and RegExp.$3 will correspond to the area code, the prefix, and the rest of the telephone number.

Validation vs. Formatting

Notice what our format JavaScript did *not* do: It did not reject the user's input if the text field contained anything other than numbers, or the incorrect amount of numbers. If the string fails to match both of the regular expressions, we make no change to the displayed input; we simply leave it as the user entered it.

A format JavaScript's only assignment is to reformat the appearance of what the user types into the text field so that it conforms to an expected layout of characters.

Actually rejecting a form's contents because it fails to conform to some requirement is the domain of the validation script, as we discussed in Chapter 11. These are the scripts that examine the contents of the text field and then alert the user if the contents are invalid.

The validation script for a telephone number would be similar to the example script we used in Chapter 11 to validate a serial number; review that script, and you'll see that you can adapt it to fit a telephone number: Your validation script would use a regular expression to determine whether the user's input was a valid telephone number, and then the script would tell Acrobat to reject the input if it was invalid.

Note that if you do attach a validation script to your telephone field, that field will now have two scripts attached to it: the validation script and the format script. This is perfectly acceptable; you can attach as many JavaScripts as you wish to a form field.

13

Alerts and Dialog Boxes

One of the most important activities for any computer program or script is communication with the user. Most of the tools that Acrobat JavaScript provides allow the user to communicate with the script; text fields, buttons, check boxes, and all the form field types allow the user to supply information to be processed by the JavaScript. What about communication in the opposite direction? How does a JavaScript talk back to the user?

There is one method we've used since Chapter 2 to tell the user something or other: alerts. We have periodically used the `app.alert` method to display an alert to the user containing a message and an OK button, such as that in **Figure 13.1**.

In this chapter, we're going to see some of the additional capabilities of the `app.alert` method. By supplying additional arguments to the method, we can change the icon displayed in the alert and specify different buttons in place of the default OK button. We are also going to look at a useful alternative to `alert`, the `app.response` method, which asks the user a question and lets him or her type in an answer.

Displaying Alerts: app.alert

Since Chapter 2, we have used the `alert` method in its simplest form, passing it only the string to display in the alert. For example, the JavaScript in the following line presents an alert like that shown in **Figure 13.1**.

```
app.alert("That is not the password! ")
```

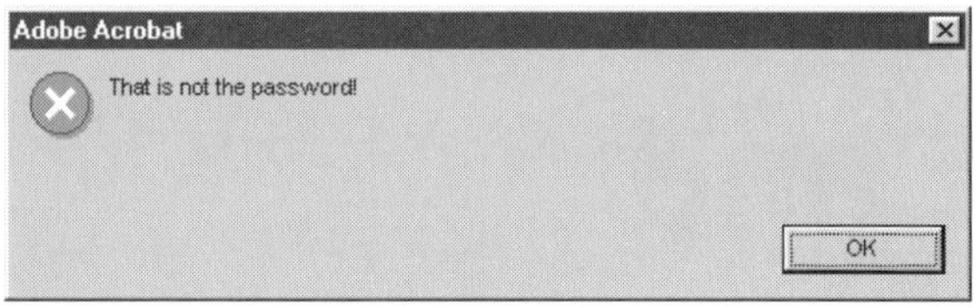

Figure 13.1 *By default,* `app.alert` *displays a message, a Halt icon, and an OK button.*

However, the `alert` method can actually take up to three arguments, a string, and two numbers:

```
app.alert("Are you sure you want to close the form?", 2, 2)
```

The three arguments are as follows:

- A string containing the text that should be displayed in the alert

- A number from 0 to 3 indicating which icon should appear in the alert

- A number from 0 to 3 indicating which buttons should appear in the alert

The second two arguments are optional. If you don't supply them, Acrobat uses the Halt icon and the OK button; this is what we've done in all our alerts to this point.

Alert Icons

The Halt icon in **Figure 13.1** indicates that something has gone so wrong that users should stop what they're doing.

However, you don't always want quite so emphatic an icon in your alerts. In that case, you may supply a second argument to `app.alert`, an icon number that indicates which icon should appear in the alert.

For example, the following line of JavaScript code produces the alert in **Figure 13.2**.

```
app.alert("Are you sure you want to close the form?", 2, 2)
```

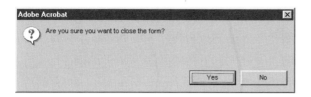

Figure 13.2 *Specifying an icon code of 2 tells* `app.alert` *to display a Question icon rather than the default Halt icon.*

The second argument, a 2, specifies that the alert should have a Question icon, rather than the default Halt icon.

The icon number in `app.alert` may have values 0 through 3, producing the results listed in **Table 13.1**. Note that the Macintosh and Windows versions of each icon are different, although they do convey roughly the same idea. Notice also that the Mac doesn't have a separate icon for Question; it uses the same icon as for Warning.

Table 13.1 *Alert Icon Codes*

ICON NAME	CODE	MAC	WINDOWS
Halt	0		
Warning	1		
Question	2		
Info	3		

Alert Buttons

The third argument to `app.alert` is also an integer from 0 to 3; each value specifies a particular set of buttons that should be presented to the user, as in **Table 13.2**.

By default, `app.alert` supplies an alert that has a single OK button. However, just as you can specify the icon that should appear in an alert, you can also specify a set of buttons that should be presented to the user. Note that the alert in **Figure 13.2** has two buttons, labeled Yes and No; this was a result of the 2 that we passed as the third argument in the corresponding call to `app.alert`:

```
app.alert("Are you sure you want to close the form?", 2, 2)
```

Table 13.2 *Alert Button Codes*

BUTTONS	CODE	ICON
OK	0	OK
OK, Cancel	1	OK Cancel
Yes, No	2	Yes No
Cancel, Yes, No	3	Cancel Yes No

How can your JavaScript determine which button the user has clicked? The app.alert method returns a number that indicates which button was selected by the user. The way you would use app.alert with button codes 1, 2, or 3 would be like this:

```
var btnCode = app.alert("Are you sure you want to close the form?",
→ 2, 2)
```

In this line of JavaScript, the variable btnCode will be assigned a number (3 or 4, in this case) that indicates whether the user clicked the Yes or the No button. (As always, there is nothing particularly special about the name btnCode; I picked it to remind me what the variable refers to.)

The value returned by app.alert will be a number from 1 to 4, as listed in **Table 13.3**.

Table 13.3 *app.alert Return Values*

VALUE	MEANING
1	OK
2	Cancel
3	No
4	Yes

Asking a Question: app.response

Acrobat provides an easy way for your JavaScript program to ask the user a simple question. The app.response method presents a dialog box to the user that displays a question and lets the user type in a response.

A typical call to app.response, producing the query in **Figure 13.3** is as follows:

```
var pwd = app.response("What is the password?","Security
→ Check","",true)
```

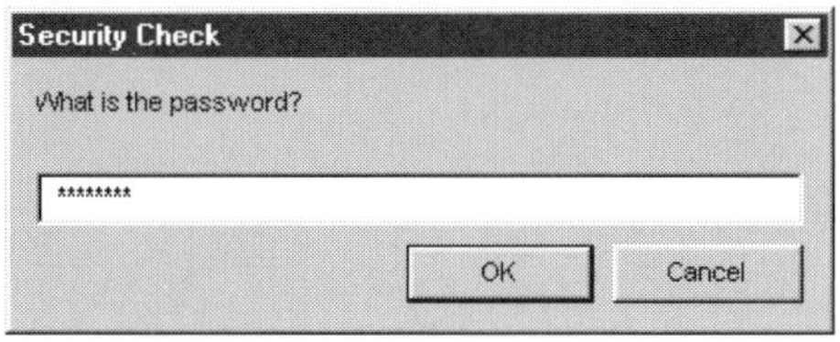

Figure 13.3 *The* app.response *method displays a dialog box that presents a question and lets the user type a response. If you wish, the dialog box will display the user's input as bullets instead of alphanumeric characters.*

The app.response command takes four arguments, of which only the first is required; the others are optional:

- A string holding the question to be presented to the user.

- A string that will be used as the title of the dialog box. Though it's technically optional, you really should supply a title string; the default title provided by app.response will be cryptic at best and may panic some of your more sensitive users. (For example, on my computer, the default title was "ECMAScript.")

- A string that indicates the default user response. This text will be already entered into the text field when the dialog box is presented to the user; all the user has to do is click OK to provide this response.

  For example, in a form intended for the U.S. market, a response dialog box that asks for nationality might provide *United States* as the default response. Note that in my example above, I passed an empty string (""), indicating that I didn't want a default response.

- A Boolean that, if true, tells app.response that this field is a password field; characters typed into the text field will be displayed as bullets for added security, as in **Figure 13.3**. If you omit this Boolean, app.response will display typed characters normally.

If the user clicks the OK button, the app.response command returns a string that contains the text the user typed into the text field. On the other hand, if the user clicks the Cancel button, then app.response returns a **null object**. This is a special kind of JavaScript object that is often used to represent "no response." The JavaScript that calls app.response will need to test the return value to see if it's a null object; if so, then we know the user clicked Cancel. We'll see how to do this in our example below.

The Project

(Files: Ch13_Example1.pdf, Ch13_Example1_raw.pdf)

We are going to add several alerts to the form in **Figure 13.4**. This form has two buttons, labeled Submit Order and Close Form; we shall attach our JavaScripts to these fields' Mouse Up events. **Figure 13.5** shows the two form fields in this Acrobat form that are of interest to us in this chapter: btnSubmit and btnClose.

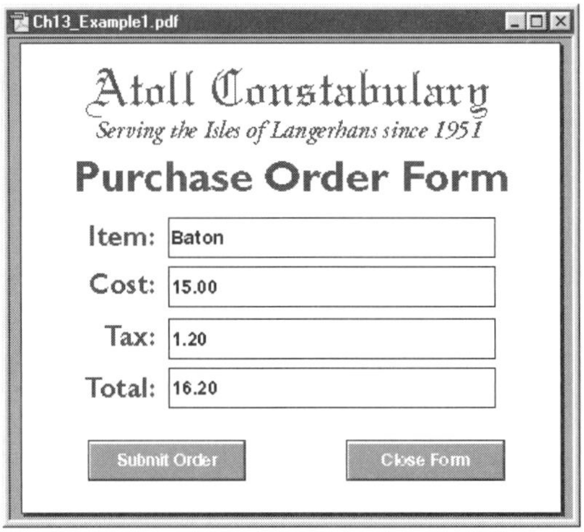

Figure 13.4 *We are going to attach JavaScripts to the two buttons in this form.*

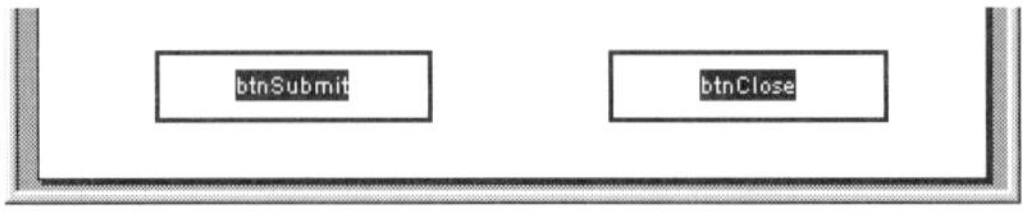

Figure 13.5 *The two form fields we're focusing on in this chapter are the two buttons: btnSubmit and btnClose.*

The JavaScripts we add to our form will do the following:

- The JavaScript attached to the Close Form button (btnClose) will display an alert asking the user whether or not the form should really close; this dialog box will have two buttons, labeled Yes and No. If the user clicks the Yes button, the form will close.

■ The script for the Submit Order button (btnSubmit) will put up a dialog box asking for a password; this dialog box will have a text field into which the user can type a word or phrase. If the password is correct, the JavaScript will submit the form to a remote site; otherwise, the JavaScript will scold the user and will not submit the form.

The Close Form Script

We shall attach a Mouse Up script to btnClose that, when the button is clicked, presents the dialog box in **Figure 13.2** on page 137. If the user clicks Yes, the script will close the Acrobat document.

To attach our Mouse Up script to btnClose:

Start with the Field Properties dialog box displaying the button's Actions panel, as in **Figure 13.6**. (See Chapter 1 for a reminder of how to get to this panel.)

1. Select the Mouse Up event and click the Add button.

You will now be looking at the Add an Action dialog box.

2. In the Add an Action dialog box, select JavaScript in the pop-up menu and click the Edit button.

Acrobat will present you with the JavaScript Edit dialog box.

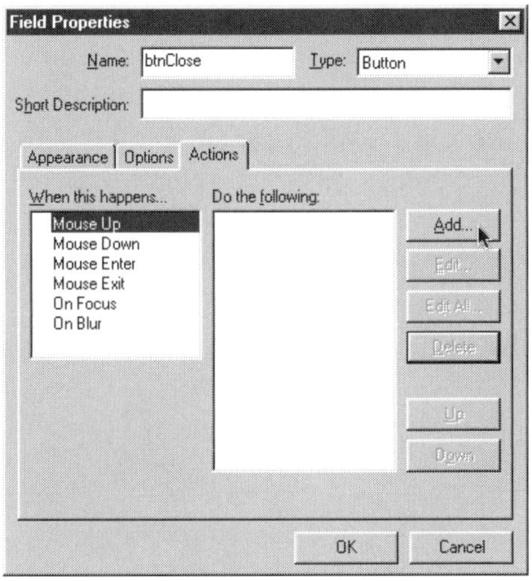

Figure 13.6 *We shall attach JavaScripts to the Mouse Up event in our two buttons.*

3. Type the following script into the JavaScript Edit dialog box:

Ask the user a question

```
var btnCode = app.alert("Are you sure you want to close the
→ form?",2,2)
```

If the user clicked "Yes"...

```
if (btnCode == 4)
```

...close the document

```
this.closeDoc(true)
```

4. Exit from all the dialog boxes until you are once again looking at your Acrobat page.

5. Try it out: Save the form to preserve the code that you entered. Then, using the Hand tool, click the Close Form button. You'll be asked if you're sure you want to close the form. Click the Yes button, and the form will close. (You did save it first, didn't you?)

The code in detail

```
var btnCode = app.alert("Are you sure you want to close the
→ form?",2,2)
```

This is the same call to `app.alert` we described earlier. This gives us the "Are you sure?" alert in **Figure 13.2**. The alert has a Question icon (the first 2 among the `app.alert` arguments), a Yes button, and a No button (the second 2).

```
if (btnCode == 4)
```

We execute a call to the `if` command that looks at the value returned by our alert (now stored in the variable, `btnCode`). When the user clicks either of the two buttons, the alert will close and a numeric code will be assigned to the variable `btnCode`. Looking at **Table 13.3**, we can see that the value of `btnCode` will be either 3 (for No) or 4 (for Yes). If `btnCode` is equal to 4, indicating the user clicked the Yes button, then `if` will execute the JavaScript line following the parenthetical comparison. (Notice that, since we have only one line after the `if` command, we can dispense with the usual braces.)

```
this.closeDoc(true)
```

Finally, if `btnCode` is equal to 4, that is, if the user clicked Yes in the alert, then `if` will execute `this.closeDoc()`, a method that closes the current document. The Boolean `true` that we are supplying as an argument tells Acrobat *not* to give the user a chance to save the document before closing. If we had supplied a `false` or omitted the Boolean altogether, Acrobat would have displayed a dialog box asking if the document should be saved.

The Submit Order Script

We are going to attach a JavaScript to the Mouse Up event for btnSubmit. When the user clicks this button, the JavaScript will present the dialog box in **Figure 13.3**, which asks for a password. The user types in a password and clicks OK (or, perhaps, chickens out and clicks Cancel).

If the user typed the correct password, then our JavaScript will submit the form to a remote server for processing, beep, and tell the user the form has been sent. Otherwise, the script presents an alert saying the password is incorrect (**Figure 13.7**) and does *not* submit the data for processing.

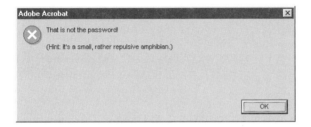

Figure 13.7 *If the user enters the wrong password, our JavaScript will inform them of this fact. Note that the message in this alert consists of two lines of text, double-spaced.*

The JavaScript

To attach our Mouse Up script to the btnSubmit button:

Start with the Field Properties dialog box displaying the Actions panel, similar to **Figure 13.6**. (Again, see Chapter 1 for a reminder of how to get to this panel.)

1. Select the Mouse Up event and click the Add button.

   You will now be looking at the Add an Action dialog box.

2. In the Add an Action dialog box, select JavaScript in the pop-up menu and click the Edit button.

   Acrobat will present you with the JavaScript Edit dialog box.

3. Type the following script into the JavaScript Edit dialog box:

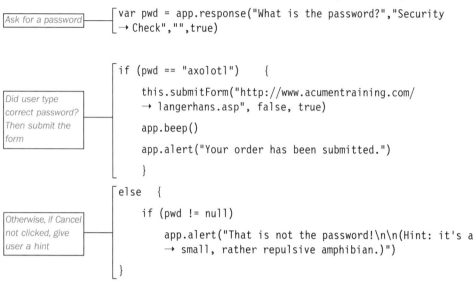

Ask for a password

```
var pwd = app.response("What is the password?","Security
→ Check","",true)
```

Did user type
correct password?
Then submit the
form

```
if (pwd == "axolotl")     {
    this.submitForm("http://www.acumentraining.com/
    → langerhans.asp", false, true)
    app.beep()
    app.alert("Your order has been submitted.")
}
```

Otherwise, if Cancel
not clicked, give
user a hint

```
else    {
    if (pwd != null)
        app.alert("That is not the password!\n\n(Hint: it's a
        → small, rather repulsive amphibian.)")
}
```

4. Exit from all the dialog boxes until you are once again looking at your Acrobat page.

5. Try it out. Return to the Hand tool and save the form; then click on the Submit Order button. When you are asked for a password, type in some text. If you type anything other than the password, you will get the "incorrect password" alert. If you click Cancel, the dialog box will quietly close.

Did I mention that the password is *axolotl*?

The code in detail

```
var pwd = app.response("What is the password?","Security
→ Check","",true)
```

Here we call the app.response method, as described earlier. The four arguments specify the question that should appear in the alert ("What is the password?"), the title of the alert ("Security Check"), the default entry in the text field (an empty string), and a Boolean true that specifies that the user's entry should be displayed as a series of bullets, as in **Figure 13.3**.

The app.response method will return one of two things: a string containing the text entered by the user, or, if the user clicked Cancel, a null object. Whichever it is, that return value will be assigned to the variable pwd.

```
if (pwd == "axolotl")     {
```

This `if` statement examines the user's input, stored in the variable, `pwd`, looking to see if it is equal to "axolotl." If so, we want to submit the data for processing.

```
this.submitForm("http://www.acumentraining.com/langerhans.asp",
→ false, true)
```

This is the first of the three lines of code that `if` executes if the user types the correct password. This line executes `this.submit`, which submits the form to a processing application. The three arguments to this method are as follows:

- A string containing the URL of the processing application. In this case, it's the Web address of a processing program that simply sends back an acknowledgement. A real processing application would do something like take the form data and place it in a database.

- A Boolean that indicates the format in which the data should be sent: FDF (`true`) or HTML (`false`). FDF is an Acrobat-specific format for sending form data to a processing application. We are specifying HTML for broadest compatibility with processing applications.

- A Boolean that indicates whether empty fields should be included in the data sent to the processing application. We use `true` so that the processing application will receive information about all the fields in our form, even if they are blank. (When in doubt, I consider this to be a good idea.)

This is pretty much all you need to know about submitting a form from within JavaScript. The hard part all takes place at the server, where you will need to have a processing program, at the specified URL, that is designed to expect such data. How to do this is far beyond the boundaries of this book. However, if you send the data in HTML format, as we did above, then you can use a variety of free or cheap server-based programs designed for Web forms; they will work perfectly well with your Acrobat form data. See Chapter 19 for sources of such programs.

```
app.beep()
```

```
app.alert("Your order has been submitted.", 3)
```

These are the other two lines that are executed if the `if` command's comparison is true. These two lines tell Acrobat (represented by the app object) to beep and then put up an alert, reassuring the user that all is well. Note that the call to `app.alert` specifies icon code 3, the Info icon.

```
else {
```

If an `if` comparison fails (in our case, if the user did not enter *axolotl* as the password), then the `else` command will execute the lines that follow it, enclosed in braces, in our JavaScript program.

There are actually two reasons that the user's input, the variable `pwd`, would not be equal to `axolotl`: If the user typed in the wrong text, that would cause the `if` comparison to fail; however, if the user clicked the Cancel button, then `pwd` would be a null object and this, too, would fail the test (`pwd == "axolotl"`).

```
if (pwd != null)
```

This second `if` statement, executed by the `else` command if `pwd` is not `axolotl`, further compares `pwd` with `null`. If the `pwd` variable is not null (`!=` means *is not equal to*), then we know the user did not click the Cancel button (which would have forced the `response` method to return a null object); therefore, the user entered an incorrect password into the dialog box.

```
app.alert("That is not the password!\n\n(Hint: it's a small, rather
→ repulsive amphibian.)")
```

This call to `app.alert` alert is executed by the second `if` command. The alert will be displayed to the user if the user types in an incorrect password.

Note the curious-looking \n\n in the alert's string. Backslash-n is a *metacharacter* inside a JavaScript string—that is, \n is a character sequence that actually represents some other character within the string. Specifically, \n represents a new line—a line break. If you place a \n into an alert's message string, the display text will have a line break at that point. In our JavaScript, we placed two consecutive \n sequences into our string, so our alert text displayed two lines of text, double-spaced (**Figure 13.7**).

This is your only real formatting ability within an alert box.

We discuss metacharacters in greater length, in the context of regular expressions, in Chapters 10 through 12.

14

JavaScript Functions

It happens frequently in programming that two or more scripts must carry out nearly identical activities. For example, you could have a button that submits form data for processing and another that submits data for processing and then immediately closes the form. Those two scripts would be largely identical, differing only in that one of them closes the form as its last activity. There's nothing wrong with having nearly identical JavaScripts, but it seems a pity to have to type identical code into two or more separate scripts.

In JavaScript, you can place commonly used code into a named **function**. A *function* is a JavaScript mechanism that lets you associate a series of commands with a name; you can then execute those commands by placing the name in your script exactly as you would a built-in JavaScript command or object method, such as `alert`.

In the previous chapter, we added alerts to the Submit Order button and Close Form button on our purchase order. Here, we are going to extend that form by using a function to make the form's behavior a little more intelligent. In our new version of the form, the Close Form button will detect whether we have submitted the order yet and, if we haven't, will give us the opportunity to do so, carrying out exactly the same set of steps as the Submit Order button. This will take very little effort once we understand how functions work.

This is an important chapter to read; future chapters will build on our knowledge of functions.

JavaScript Functions

As I said earlier, a JavaScript function is a means of storing a set of JavaScript commands and associating them with a name. Later, a JavaScript can execute the function's contents by using the function's name in code.

Creating a Function

Consider the following JavaScript, which defines and then uses a function named BeepAlert:

```
function BeepAlert()    {
    app.beep()
    app.alert("Stop what you are doing!!")
}
```

```
BeepAlert()
```

A function definition, like the one above, consists of the following:

- The word function, which declares that what follows is a function definition

- The name of the new function—in our case, BeepAlert

  The JavaScript function name can contain, and is restricted to, any combination of alphanumeric characters, underscores, and dollar signs. Valid function names could include, for example: Beep_Alert, InspectBunnyToes9, and $FormatAsSloth. There is no significance attached to any of the "special" characters; use them as esthetics and readability dictate. As always, brief but descriptive is your goal in a name.

- A set of parentheses containing whatever arguments the new function will need

  Our parentheses are empty, indicating that this function doesn't take any arguments. We shall look at this in more detail below.

- A pair of braces enclosing the JavaScript statements that should be executed when the function is used

  The JavaScript code in the braces is referred to as the **body** of the function. This body can contain as much or as little JavaScript code as you need. In our case, our function's body consists of only two JavaScript lines: a call to app.beep and a call to app.alert.

Once BeepAlert is defined, we can use the function within that script exactly as though it were a built-in JavaScript command. Our sample script ends with a call to the function BeepAlert(); this causes Acrobat to execute the code in the function's body, beeping and then displaying the alert shown in **Figure 14.1.**

Figure 14.1 *Our* BeepAlert *function beeps and displays this alert.*

Why is this useful? In the case of our BeepAlert function, the value is arguably minimal, because the function doesn't do very much; the body contains only two statements. However, the JavaScript code in the body of a function can be as complex as you wish. That code can then be invoked when needed with a single call to the function's name. This reduces typing (and the potential of introducing errors) and clutter in your JavaScript code—worthwhile goals.

Function arguments

One characteristic of our BeepAlert function is that the alert it displays always has the same text in it: It always says, "Stop what you are doing!!" Let's change our function definition so that the function will expect to be told which text and which icon to display in the alert it presents:

```
function BeepAlert(txt, icn)     {
    app.beep()
    app.alert(txt,icn)
}


BeepAlert("But why can't I have a dinosaur? Just a little one?", 2)
BeepAlert("Please?", 2)
BeepAlert("Pretty please?", 2)
BeepAlert("I'll cry!", 0)
```

Here we have an alternative definition of BeepAlert. This version has two comma-separated names in its initial parentheses, indicating that the function will now take two arguments, named txt and icn. When we execute BeepAlert, we must pass two values within the parentheses, as we did in our sample code above:

```
BeepAlert("Please?", 2)
```

JavaScript will automatically create two variables named txt and icn and assign the first argument (the string ("Please?") to the txt variable and the second argument (the number 2) to icn. There is nothing special about the names txt and icn. I picked them to remind me of how I intend to use these arguments in the function body: txt will be a string containing the text for the alert box; icn will be the icon code for the alert box.

Within our function body, we use the variables txt and icn in our call to app.alert:

```
app.alert(txt, icn)
```

The app.alert method will receive the values of txt and icn (for example, "Please?" and 2) as its arguments, displaying the alert in **Figure 14.2**.

Figure 14.2 BeepAlert *passes the* txt *and* icn *variables to* app.alert, *which uses them as the text and icon code for the resulting alert.*

Project 1: Functions in Document JavaScripts

(Files: Ch14_Example1.pdf, Ch14_Example1_Raw.pdf)

JavaScript functions become most useful when you define them in a Document JavaScript. (You should skim Chapter 2 for a review of how Document JavaScripts work.) Functions defined in a Document JavaScript are accessible from within any JavaScript throughout the Acrobat document. This can make your Form Field scripts neat and compact, since much

Naming Argument Variables

Our definition of `BeepAlert` starts as follows:

```
function BeepAlert(txt, icn)
```

This declares that `BeepAlert` is a function, that it takes two arguments, and that these two arguments will be assigned variable names `txt` and `icn`. It does *not* indicate what kind of data `BeepAlert` wants `txt` and `icn` to be. Are they both numbers? Both strings? A number and a Boolean?

What actually determines which kind of data `BeepAlert` expects is how it eventually uses these arguments. `BeepAlert` uses its arguments in a call to the `app.alert` method:

```
app.alert(txt, icn)
```

This method, we know from experience, takes a string and a number. So that is what `txt` and `icn` must be: a string and a number. (The *Acrobat JavaScript Object Specification* lists the arguments required by every method in every object in Acrobat JavaScript; you can get to this document in Acrobat by selecting Help > Acrobat JavaScript Guide.)

It's important to pick variable names for your functions' arguments that remind you what kind of data they are supposed to contain. If I had named `BeepAlert`'s arguments `arg1` and `arg2`, I would have had no way of knowing what these arguments were supposed to be except by examining the definition of `BeepAlert`; that can be tedious if the function in question is complex.

You should pick argument names that remind you of their purpose and, therefore, of what kind of data they need to be. Some people give each argument name a prefix that indicates what kind of data it should be:

```
function BeepAlert(strAlertText, numIcon)
```

Looking at the above line, I know that `BeepAlert` takes a string and a number as its arguments. Typical prefixes are `str`, `num`, `bool`, and `ary` (arrays). There's no standardization here, so feel free to make up your own prefixes.

of the code can be moved out of the Form Field script and into a function in a Document JavaScript.

In this example, we shall take the JavaScript we looked at above, which defines and uses the `BeepAlert` function, and attach it to the form pictured in **Figure 14.3**. This is an utterly frivolous form with no useful purpose except to demonstrate function definitions; we'll move on to a more useful example later.

Figure 14.3 *We are going to attach our* BeepAlert *definition to this form as a Document JavaScript and attach the calls to* BeepAlert *to the button as a Mouse Up JavaScript.*

We are going to split our original JavaScript code into two parts:

- The BeepAlert function definition, which we shall place into a Document JavaScript.

- The four calls to BeepAlert, which we shall attach to the form's single button as a Mouse Up event. These alerts beg for a dinosaur in increasingly whiny tones (**Figure 14.4**).

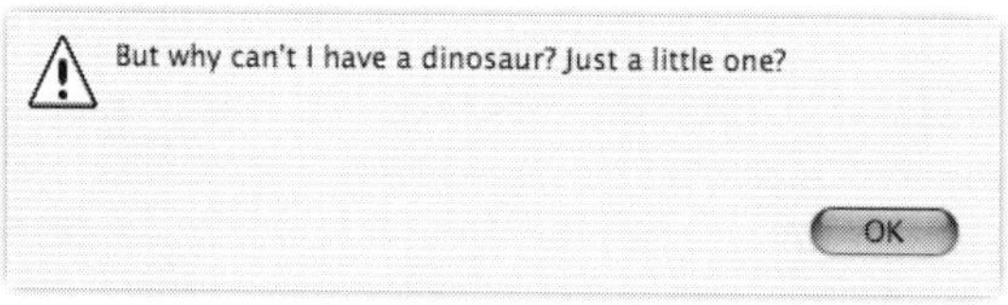

Figure 14.4 *Our* BeepAlert *function displays an alert and beeps.*

The Document JavaScript

To attach the function definition to the Acrobat file as a Document script:

Start with the file open in Acrobat.

1. Select Tools > JavaScript > Document JavaScripts.

   Acrobat will present you with the JavaScript Functions dialog box (**Figure 14.5**).

2. Type BeepAlert into the Script Name field and click the Add button.

   Acrobat will present you with the usual JavaScript Edit dialog box.

3. Type the definition of Beep Alert into the dialog box:

```
function BeepAlert(txt, icn)    {
    app.beep()
    app.alert(txt,icn)
}
```

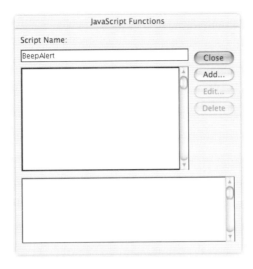

Figure 14.5 *Type a descriptive name into the JavaScript Functions dialog box and click the Add button. The name doesn't have to match the name of the function we are defining, but that will help you remember what that Document JavaScript does.*

4. Close all dialog boxes until you are back at the Acrobat page.

Now we've typed in the definition of our function as a Document JavaScript. This function will be available to all the form fields in our document. This is only half the task, however; now we must type in a JavaScript that uses our function.

Form Field JavaScript

Let's now attach a JavaScript containing our four calls to the BeepAlert function to the Mouse Up event in the form's single button, whose name is btnIWanit

To attach the Mouse Up script to btnIWanit:

Start with the button's Field Properties dialog box displaying the Actions panel, as in **Figure 14.6**. (See Chapter 1 for a reminder of how to do this.)

1. Select the Mouse Up event and click the Add button.

You will now be looking at the Add an Action dialog box.

2. In the Add an Action dialog box, select JavaScript in the pop-up menu and click the Edit button.

Acrobat will present you with the JavaScript Edit dialog box.

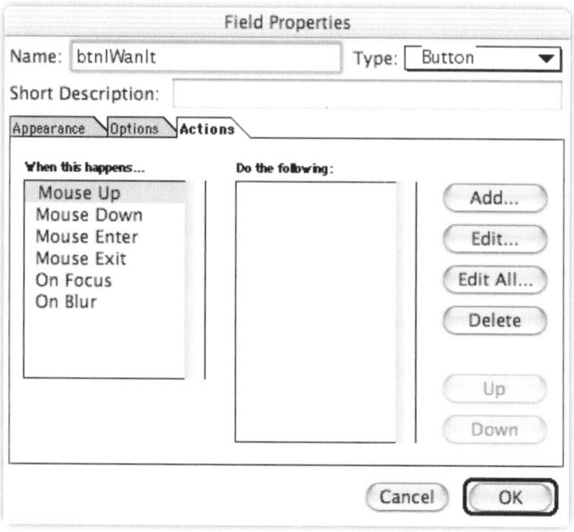

Figure 14.6 *We shall attach a JavaScript that calls* BeepAlert *to the Mouse Up event of the btnIWanit button.*

3. Type the following script into the JavaScript Edit dialog box:

> *This script simply calls BeepAlert four times*

```
BeepAlert("But why can't I have a dinosaur?
→ Just a little one?", 2)

BeepAlert("Please?", 2)

BeepAlert("Pretty please?", 2)

BeepAlert("I'll cry!", 0)
```

4. Exit from all the dialog boxes until you are once again looking at your Acrobat page.

5. Try it out. Return to the Hand tool and click on the "I Wan' It!" button. Acrobat will display the four alerts in turn, each a call to BeepAlert.

The significance of this example is that our button's JavaScript could use the function BeepAlert without having to define it; once the function is defined in a Document JavaScript, that function can be used in any JavaScript in the Acrobat file.

Project 2: Two Buttons Sharing Code

Now, let's use our new knowledge of functions to improve our example from the previous chapter. In Chapter 13, we added two JavaScripts to the form in **Figure 14.7**. The two JavaScripts, attached to btnSubmit and btnClose (**Figure 14.8**), did the following:

■   The Submit Order button's script asked for a password and, if the password was correctly supplied, submitted the form data to an external server for processing.

■   The Close Form button's script asked if you were sure you want to close the form, letting you cancel the closure. If you clicked the Yes button, the script then closed the form.

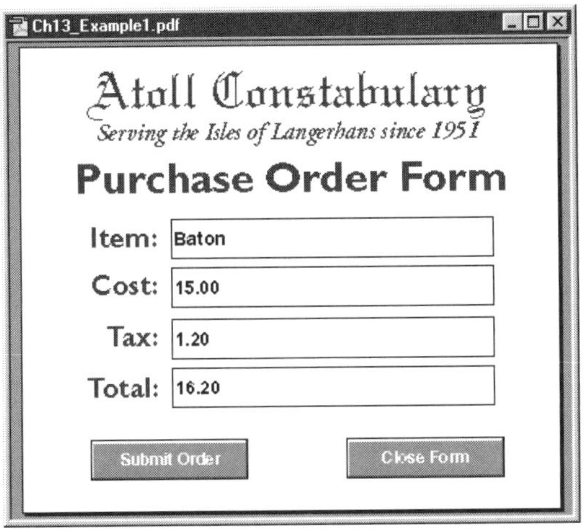

Figure 14.7   *We are going to modify the JavaScripts we attached to this form in Chapter 13.*

Figure 14.8   *The two buttons in this form are btnSubmit and btnClose.*

I would like to improve the Close Form button's behavior. I want the JavaScript attached to btnClose to check to see if the form has yet been submitted to a remote site for processing. If so, then the script will simply close the document. If the form has *not* been submitted, then I want the JavaScript to ask the user if he or she wants to submit the form before closing (**Figure 14.9**). If the user clicks No, then the script will close the document; if the user clicks Yes, then the Close Form button's script should do *exactly* what the Submit Order button normally does: ask for a password and submit the data for processing if the user supplies the correct password.

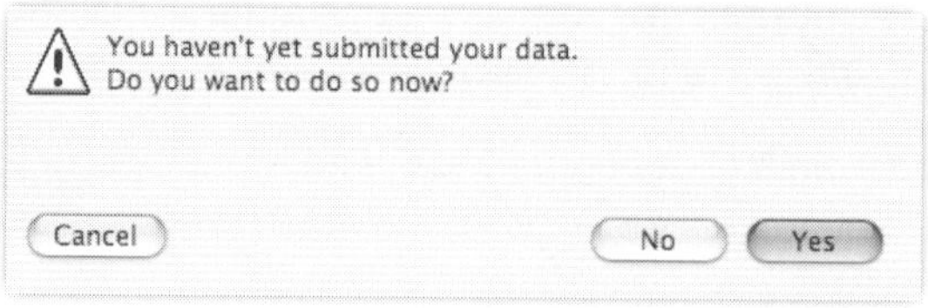

Figure 14.9 *The JavaScript attached to the Close Form button will check to see whether the form has been submitted for processing. If it hasn't, the script will ask the user if the form should be submitted now.*

Before going any further, you should read Chapter 13, if you haven't done so recently. In the discussion of this project's JavaScript, I shall be describing the changes we make to the Chapter 13 scripts, but I won't be stepping through the original code in great detail.

Approaching the Problem

We are going to make four changes to the JavaScripts from the previous chapter:

- We shall create a Document JavaScript that defines a Boolean variable named gBeenSubmitted, which we shall set initially to false.

  We shall use this variable as an indicator of whether the form has been submitted. Its initial value is false, but we shall set it to true whenever we submit the data for processing. Thus, any JavaScript can look at the value of gBeenSubmitted to determine if the data has been submitted yet.

  A variable like gBeenSubmitted, which is being used to indicate whether a certain action has taken place, is referred to in programming as a **flag**. You would describe gBeenSubmitted as a flag that indicates whether the document has been submitted.

- We shall define a function named SubmitData in a Document JavaScript.

  This function's body will be nearly identical to the JavaScript attached to the last chapter's btnSubmit button. The only difference is that this JavaScript will set gBeenSubmitted to true.

  For convenience, we shall define the SubmitData function and the gBeenSubmitted flag in the same Document JavaScript.

- The Mouse Up JavaScript attached to the Submit Order button now just makes a call to the SubmitData function, rather than containing all of the original JavaScript code in the previous chapter. (We have moved that code into the function.)

- The Mouse Up JavaScript attached to the Close Form button does the following: It checks gBeenSubmitted to see if the form has been submitted; if so, it closes the document; if not, it asks the user if the form *should* be submitted; if so, it executes SubmitForm and then closes the document.

The JavaScripts

The Document JavaScript

To add the Document JavaScript to our form, follow the numbered steps for the Document JavaScript from the "Want-a-Dinosaur" BeepAlert example, but pick a different name for the script (**Figure 14.10**).

In the JavaScript Functions dialog box, type the following JavaScript code for this script:

```
var gBeenSubmitted = false
```
The "form was submitted" flag

```
function SubmitForm()
{
    var pwd = app.response("What is the password?","Security
    → Check","",true)
```
Ask for a password

```
    if (pwd == "axolotl")     {
        this.submitForm("http://www.Langerhans.gov/orders.asp")
        app.beep()
        app.alert("Your order has been submitted.")
```
Correct password: submit the form

```
        gBeenSubmitted = true
```
Set our flag to true

```
    }
    else    {
        if (pwd != null)
            app.alert("That is not the password!\n\n(Hint: it's a
            → small, rather repulsive amphibian.)")
```
Wrong password: alert the user

```
    }
}
```

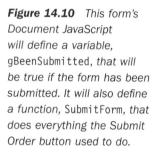

Figure 14.10 *This form's Document JavaScript will define a variable, gBeenSubmitted, that will be true if the form has been submitted. It will also define a function, SubmitForm, that does everything the Submit Order button used to do.*

This script does two things, both of which we described above: It defines a variable named gBeenSubmitted, setting it to false, and it creates a function named SubmitForm.

SubmitForm's body is identical to the Mouse Up script we attached to the Submit Order button in Chapter 13. You should reread the description of that script for a detailed look at its activities. In overview, however, this function, when executed, does the following:

- It asks the user for a password with app.response.

- If the user types in *axolotl,* which is the password, the function submits the form for processing, beeps, and puts up an alert telling the user all is well. The function then sets gBeenSubmitted to true, which the original script did not do.

- If the user did not type in *axolotl,* the function looks to see if the object returned by app.response was not a null object; if it was not (meaning the user didn't click Cancel*),* the function tells the user that the password was incorrect (**Figure 14.11**).

Once we've defined this function, any JavaScript in this Acrobat document can now carry the set of activities that the old Submit Order button did by simply executing SubmitForm.

Figure 14.11 *As in the previous chapter's script, if the user types in the wrong password, the form will let them know. The difference is that this can now happen in either the Submit Order button's or the Close Form button's JavaScript.*

The Submit button script

The new Mouse Up script for btnSubmit becomes very short: a single call to the SubmitForm function.

To attach the new script to btnSubmit, follow the numbered steps that we used for btnIWannit, above, except use the following for your JavaScript (**Figure 14.12**):

```
SubmitForm()
```

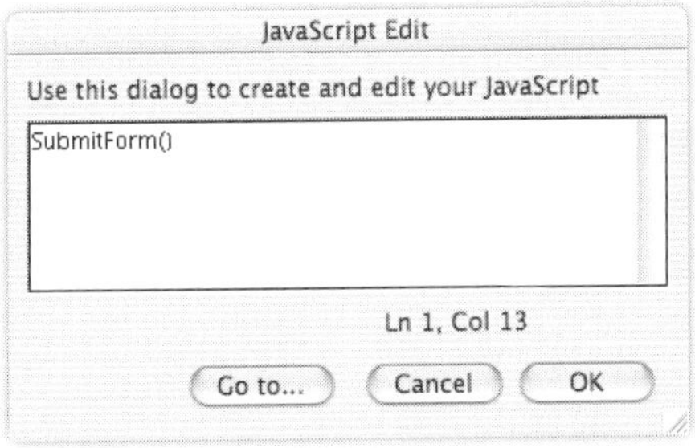

Figure 14.12 *The use of the* SubmitForm *function makes for an exceptionally tidy JavaScript.*

Pretty simple, eh? Since our new SubmitForm function does everything the old btnSubmit script did, our new script needs only to call that function.

The Close button script

We want the JavaScript for btnClose to do the following:

- If the form has already been submitted, it should simply close the document.

- If the form has not been submitted, the JavaScript should ask the user if he or she would like to submit the form.

- If the answer is no, the JavaScript should simply close the document.

- If the answer is yes, the JavaScript should call SubmitForm, submitting the document for processing.

Let's see how we do this.

To attach the new Mouse Up script to btnClose, follow the numbered steps that we used for btnIWannit, above, except use the following for your JavaScript:

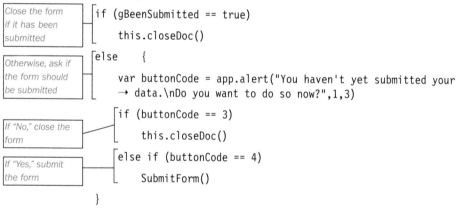

```
                    if (gBeenSubmitted == true)
                        this.closeDoc()

                    else    {
                        var buttonCode = app.alert("You haven't yet submitted your
                        → data.\nDo you want to do so now?",1,3)

                        if (buttonCode == 3)
                            this.closeDoc()

                        else if (buttonCode == 4)
                            SubmitForm()
                    }
```

Close the form if it has been submitted

Otherwise, ask if the form should be submitted

If "No," close the form

If "Yes," submit the form

Let's look at this step by step.

```
if (gBeenSubmitted == true)
    this.closeDoc()
```

Here we have an if command that examines the gBeenSubmitted variable to see if it is true, indicating that the form has been submitted. If so, if closes the Acrobat document.

```
else    {
```

If our `if` comparison failed, meaning the form has not been submitted, then we shall execute a series of JavaScript lines, enclosed in braces, that follow the `else` command. The `else` command's braces, in our case, enclose another complete `if-else` pair. (This is referred to as a "nested if-else.")

```
var buttonCode = app.alert("You haven't yet...now?",1,3)
```

The first thing our script does if the form data hasn't been submitted for processing is to ask the user if it *should* be submitted (see **Figure 14.9**). Note that we are passing *3* as the button code; this gives us an alert with three buttons: Yes, No, and Cancel. Also, we passed *1* as the icon code, giving our alert a "Warning" icon. (See Chapter 13 for a reminder of button and icon code values.)

The `app.alert` method will return a value that is assigned to the `buttonCode` variable; this will be one of three values, depending on which button the user clicks: 3 (No), 4 (Yes), or null (Cancel).

```
if (buttonCode == 3)
    this.closeDoc()
```

If the `buttonCode` variable has a value of 3, indicating that the user clicked the alert's No button, then we shall exit from the Acrobat document.

```
else if (buttonCode == 4)
    SubmitForm()
```

Otherwise, we check to see if the user clicked the Yes button; if so, we execute the `SubmitForm` function. In this case, everything that normally happens when the user clicks the Submit Order button will happen here: ask for a password, then submit the form or not, depending on the validity of the password.

Functions give you a convenient way to package recurring code in your JavaScripts. They are an extremely common feature of programs written in any programming language; we shall be defining functions in scripts periodically throughout the rest of this book.

Creating Pop-Up Menus

One seldom-used but quite useful feature of Acrobat's JavaScript is the capability to present a pop-up menu when the user clicks on a form field. There are a variety of situations, including this chapter's project, where a pop-up menu is the best solution for letting the user select among a set of options that apply to the object they clicked.

In this chapter, we shall see how to create these menus. It's very easy, entailing the call to one, straightforward method of the app object, named popUpMenu.

app.popUpMenu

The app.popUpMenu method makes a pop-up menu appear at the mouse pointer's position on the screen. You would typically call this method in a JavaScript attached to a form field's Mouse Down event.

A call to app.popUpMenu looks something like this:

```
var result = app.popUpMenu(item1, item2, item3,…)
```

Each item in the arguments you pass to the method can be one of two things:

- A string, which will become an entry in the pop-up menu

- An array of strings, which will become a submenu. The first string in the array will be the name of the submenu; the remaining strings in the array become items within the submenu. (See Chapter 6 for an introduction to arrays.)

Thus, the following line of JavaScript would create the pop-up menu in **Figure 15.1**:

```
var result = app.popUpMenu("A", ["B", "C", "D"], "E")
```

Figure 15.1 *The* app.popUpMenu *method creates a pop-up menu at the mouse pointer's position. The pop-up menu may have its own submenus, if you wish.*

The popUpMenu method returns a string that contains the text of the item the user selected. For example, the selection pictured in **Figure 15.1** would result in the variable, result, receiving the string value "C". If the user exits the menu without selecting an item (usually by clicking outside the pop-up menu), then popUpMenu returns a null object. (Remember that a *null object* is a JavaScript object that has no value, usually used to indicate Cancel in a JavaScript.)

The *switch* Command

Consider the call above to app.popUpMenu. The variable, result, will receive one of four possible strings as its value: "A", "C", "D", or "E", reflecting the user's choice from the pop-up menu. Note that "B" is the title of the submenu and so is not selectable by the user.

Our JavaScript will want to carry out some action based on the user's selection. We could do this with a set of if-else statements:

```
if (result == "A")    {
    ... do the A stuff ...
}
else if (result == "C")    {
    ... do the C stuff ...
}
else if (result == "D")    {
    ... do the D stuff ...
}
else if (result == "E")    {
    ... do the E stuff ...
}
else    {
    ... do this if result isn't A, C, D, or E ...
}
```

These cascaded if-else commands will work, and there is nothing wrong with solving the problem this way. However, this kind of activity—carrying out one of several possible actions depending on the value of a particular variable—is so common that JavaScript provides a command specifically for doing this: the switch command:

```
switch (result)  {
    case "A":
        ... do the A stuff ...
        ... could be several lines ...
        break
    case "C":
        ... do the C stuff ...
        break
    case "D":
        ... do the D stuff ...
        break
    case "E":
        ... do the E stuff ...
```

```
        break
    default:
        ... do this if nothing else matches ...
        break
}
```

The switch command is followed by a variable name in parentheses, which is, in turn, followed by a pair of braces that enclose a series of case statements. Each case statement specifies what should happen if the variable being tested has a particular value.

Each case statement is followed by the value that it tests for; case "A": precedes a set of statements that should be executed if result has a value of "A". Note the colon that follows the "A"; this separates the value to which that particular case applies from the JavaScript statements that should be executed if that case is valid.

If result does not match any of the case statements, then switch will do nothing unless you have included a default entry. If you include default, then switch will execute the statements following the colon if the variable didn't match any of the case statements.

The *break* Command

The break statement marks the end of a set of JavaScript statements associated with a particular case. If the break statement is missing, you get somewhat unexpected results: switch will execute *all* of the remaining JavaScript statements in the switch braces until it finally encounters a break. For example, presume that result were "C" in the following switch:

```
switch (result) {
    case "C":
        ... do the C stuff ...
    case "D":
        ... do the D stuff ...
        break
}
```

In this case, switch would execute the C stuff and, since the C stuff isn't ended with a break, it would continue on and execute the D stuff, as well.

Omitting the break statement can be useful occasionally, but usually you will end each case block with a break.

The Project

(Files: Ch15_Example1.pdf, Ch15_Example1_raw.pdf)

In this chapter, we are going to add three pop-up menus to the catalog pictured in **Figure 15.2**. Each of the three thumbnails on the catalog's first page has a small, downward-pointing arrowhead. When the user clicks on that arrowhead, the document presents a pop-up menu that lets the user choose to see a close-up of the picture, read a short profile of the photographer, or order a full-resolution version of the photograph (**Figure 15.3**).

Figure 15.2 We are going to add pop-up menus that will appear when the user clicks on the arrowheads in the lower-right corner of each thumbnail.

Figure 15.3 Each thumbnail's pop-up menu will contain three items and a horizontal dividing line.

The catalog pages

This catalog is an eight-page document:

■ Page 1 is the initial page the user sees; this contains the thumbnails and a Close button.

■ Pages 2, 3, and 4 display the photographs' close-ups (**Figure 15.4**); showing the user a close-up means simply moving to that page in the Acrobat file.

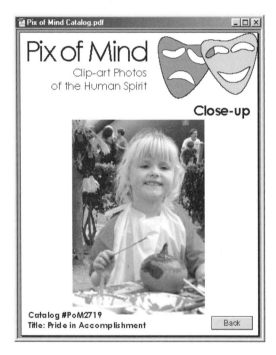

Figure 15.4 *Each thumbnail has a corresponding page in the Acrobat file that presents a larger version of the image.*

■ Page 5 is a fairly unremarkable order form, allowing the user to order full-resolution versions of the photographs (see **Figure 15.9**).

■ Pages 6, 7, and 8 present the artists' profiles to the user (**Figure 15.5**). Each page has the profile of a particular photographer.

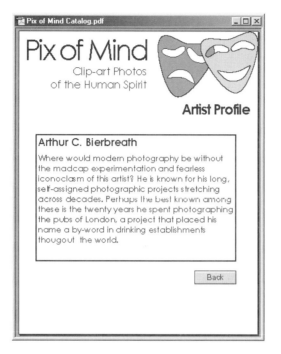

Figure 15.5 *Pages 6 through 8 in our Acrobat file present profiles of the photographers.*

We shall be looking in detail only at page 1 of this file, since this is where we are creating our pop-up menus. You may want to take a look at the controls on the other pages; there's nothing there that we haven't discussed.

The pop-up menus

The arrowhead in the lower-right corner of each thumbnail is actually part of the thumbnail itself. We are going to attach our pop-up menus to three "invisible" buttons that I have placed over each of these arrowheads (**Figure 15.6**).

Figure 15.6 *Each thumbnail has a small button in the lower-right corner. This is the button to which that thumbnail's pop-up menu script will be attached.*

These buttons are not really hidden; they are invisible because I created them with no border, background, or label (**Figure 15.7**). The visual elements I needed for the form (specifically, the arrowhead) were already on the Acrobat page; all I needed was a button to which I could attach a pop-up menu.

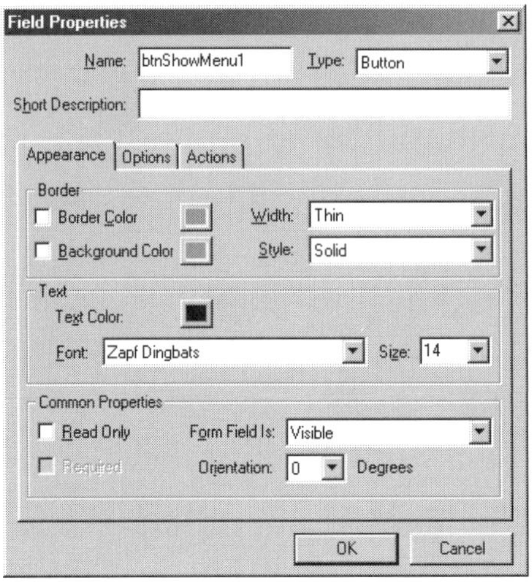

Figure 15.7 The button overlaying each thumbnail appears to be invisible because it has no border, background, or label. But note that the button is set to Visible.

These "invisible" buttons are named, from left to right, btnShowMenu1, btnShowMenu2, and btnShowMenu3. To each of these we shall attach a JavaScript associated with the Mouse Down event; this JavaScript will display a pop-up menu and then do something appropriate to what the user has selected.

Our pop-up menus will each offer the following selections to the user (see **Figure 15.3**):

■ *See close-up*—The user will be taken to the page that contains the close-up of that particular image; this will be page 2, 3, or 4, depending upon which thumbnail's button the user clicks.

■ *About the artist*—The user will be taken to page 6, 7, or 8 of the document, depending on which artist profile the user selected.

■ *Order form*—The user will be taken to page 5, the order form page.

The JavaScript

Unusually, we are going to attach our JavaScripts to the buttons' Mouse Down event; this is because proper behavior for a pop-up menu calls for the menu to appear immediately upon the user clicking the control, not clicking and releasing, as is true of most actions in a form field.

We are going to look in detail at how to attach the Mouse Down script to btnShowMenu1, which overlays the leftmost image, and then we will step through its code. We shall examine the other buttons' scripts only cursorily, because they are nearly identical to the first.

To attach the JavaScript to the Mouse Down event:

Start with the Field Properties dialog box displaying the Actions panel, as in **Figure 15.8**. (See Chapter 1 for a reminder of how to get to this panel.)

1. Select the Mouse Down event and click the Add button.

    You will now be looking at the Add an Action dialog box.

2. In the Add an Action dialog box, select JavaScript in the pop-up menu and click the Edit button.

    Acrobat will present you with the usual JavaScript Edit dialog box.

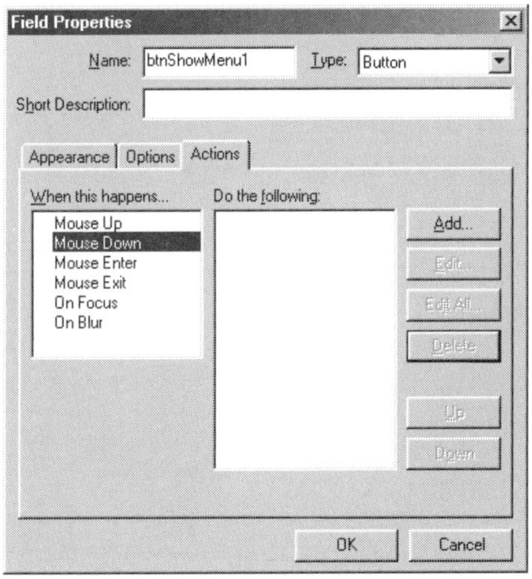

Figure 15.8 *A JavaScript that creates a pop-up menu should be attached to a form field's Mouse Down event.*

3. Type the following script into the JavaScript Edit dialog box:

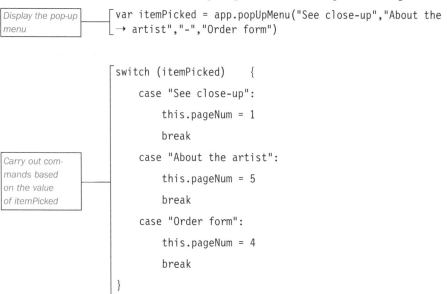

Display the pop-up menu

```
var itemPicked = app.popUpMenu("See close-up","About the
→ artist","-","Order form")
```

Carry out commands based on the value of itemPicked

```
switch (itemPicked)    {
    case "See close-up":
        this.pageNum = 1
        break
    case "About the artist":
        this.pageNum = 5
        break
    case "Order form":
        this.pageNum = 4
        break
}
```

4. Exit from all the dialog boxes until you are once again looking at your Acrobat page.

5. Try it out: Return to the Hand tool and click on the arrow in the leftmost thumbnail. A pop-up menu will appear, allowing you to choose among three items. Select each menu item in turn, seeing how the form behaves.

The code in detail

```
var itemPicked = app.popUpMenu("See close-up","About the artist",
→ "-","Order form")
```

This script starts by presenting the pop-up menu. Looking at the arguments we pass to popUpMenu, we can see our pop-up menu will have four items in it:

- See close-up

- About the artist

- - (a hyphen)

   A single hyphen has a special meaning to popUpMenu; it specifies that a break in the menu, usually a horizontal line, should appear at that point.

- Order form

When the user selects an item or clicks elsewhere in the form, app.popUpMenu will return either the text of the selected item or a null object if the user closed the pop-up menu without selecting anything.

In our code, the string or null object returned by app.popUpMenu is assigned to the variable itemPicked. As usual, there is nothing special about this name; I chose it to be short and mnemonic.

```
switch (itemPicked)     {
```

We now are going to execute a switch on the variable itemPicked. The braces will enclose case statements that together examine itemPicked and execute JavaScript commands appropriate to each possible value.

```
case "See close-up":
    this.pageNum = 1
    break
```

This case statement handles the instance where itemPicked is "See close-up", setting this.pageNum to 1. (You may remember from Chapter 1 that the this.pageNum property contains the page currently viewed by the user; setting this to 1 changes the current page to page 1.) In a JavaScript, page 1 is the second page in the Acrobat file (remember that JavaScript counts pages from zero); this page is the close-up page for the first thumbnail (see **Figure 15.4**).

```
case "About the artist":
    this.pageNum = 5
    break
```

Here we handle the case where itemPicked is "About the artist", moving to page 5 in the Acrobat document.

```
case "Order form":
    this.pageNum = 4
    break
```

Finally, we handle the "Order form" case by moving to page 4, which is the order form page (**Figure 15.9**).

No default

Note that our switch statement didn't include a default block. This is because I didn't want to do anything if itemPicked was something other than what I am looking for. If I had wished, I could have had a final, default block in my switch statement:

```
default:
    app.alert("I do not understand what you mean. ")
    break
```

Figure 15.9 *Selecting "Order form" from our pop-up menu takes the user, not unreasonably, to the order form page.*

The Other Buttons

The Mouse Down JavaScripts for btnShowMenu2 and btnShowMenu3 are nearly identical to those for btnShowMenu1, above. They differ from the btnShowMenu1 script only in that the page numbers to which we send the user for the close-up and the artist profile are different for each thumbnail.

For each of the other two buttons, follow the numbered steps above, but with the following JavaScripts:

For btnShowMenu2:

```
var itemPicked = app.popUpMenu("See close-up","About the artist",
→ "-","Order form")

switch (itemPicked)    {
    case "See close-up":
        this.pageNum = 2
        break
```

```
    case "About the artist":
        this.pageNum = 6
        break
    case "Order form":
    this.pageNum = 4
    break
}
```

For btnShowMenu3:

```
var itemPicked = app.popUpMenu("See close-up","About the artist",
→ "-","Order form")
```

```
switch (itemPicked)    {
    case "See close-up":
        this.pageNum = 3
        break
    case "About the artist":
        this.pageNum = 7
        break
    case "Order form":
    this.pageNum = 4
    break
}
```

Customization Notes

Functions in `case` **Code**

In our example, each case statement does only one thing: It moves the viewer to a particular page by setting the value of this.pageNum. However, the JavaScript in a case block can contain any collection of JavaScript statements you wish. For example, we could have added a Close Form item to our pop-up menu with a corresponding case entry that looks like this:

```
case "Close Form":
    var btn = app.alert("Are you sure you want to quit?",2,2)
    if (btn ==  2)
        this.closeDoc()
    break
```

The above case block asks if the user really wants to quit (**Figure 15.10**); if he or she clicks the Yes button, then the case block closes the document with a call to this.closeDoc. (See Chapter 13 for the details of the app.alert function.)

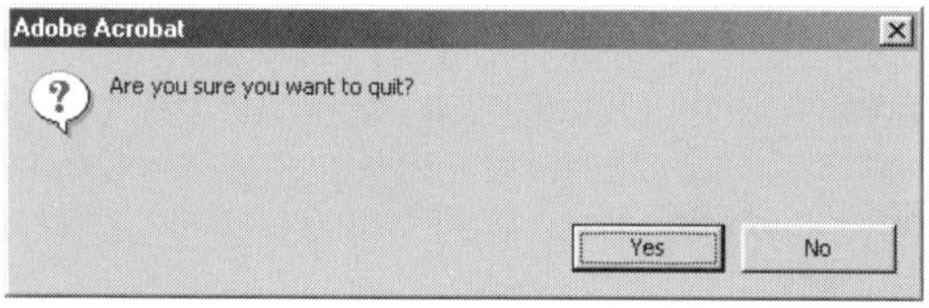

Figure 15.10 *Our sample case statement confirms that the user wants to quit the form and, if so, closes the document.*

There is no limit to the amount of JavaScript a case block can contain. However, if there are going to be more than a few lines, I prefer to define a function that does that activity and have the case statement simply execute the function; this makes the case block tidier and easier to read.

For example, we could create a Document JavaScript in our Acrobat file (see Chapter 2 for a reminder of how Document JavaScripts work) that defines a function named CloseIfSure, as follows:

```
function CloseIfSure()    {
    var btn = app.alert("Are you sure you want to quit?",2,2)
    if (btn ==  2)
        this.closeDoc()
}
```

This function does exactly what our previous case block did: It asks the user if he or she really wants to quit and, if so, closes the document. Having defined our CloseIfSure function, our case statement can now simply call the function:

```
case "Close Form":
    CloseIfSure()
    break
```

This is more readable than the original case block. The more complex the case block, the more helpful it is to move that code into a function and let the case simply execute the function.

Pop-Up Menu User Interface

It's important that you give the user an indication that clicking at a certain point on the page will yield a pop-up menu. In our examples, I used a downward-pointing arrowhead (**Figure 15.11**), which is a fairly common icon meaning "click here for more choices." I added this downward arrowhead to the original thumbnail images in Adobe Photoshop because our buttons are defined as having no background, border, or label.

As an alternative, I could have left the thumbnails unmodified and used a button whose label is *t* and whose label font is Zapf Dingbats; this would produce the following symbol: ▼. Although this method works perfectly well, I think Photoshop gives better control over the exact appearance of the arrowhead; for instance, you can apply effects like anti-aliasing, which smoothes any jagged lines.

Figure 15.11 *In our thumbnails, the downward-pointing arrowhead was added to the thumbnail image in an image editor.*

Interacting with Databases

An Acrobat form is a data collection device; its fields allow a user to supply information needed to carry out some task: order a book, register for a class, or supply an item for the International Elvis Sighting Registry. Having collected the data, an Acrobat form must do something with it. In a corporate environment, the most common thing to do is to submit the data, sending it to a server-based application that puts the data into a database on the company's server. In this case, Acrobat does not directly interact with the database; the form sends the data to a program written in Java, PHP, ASP or some other scripting language; it is this other program, running on a server, that actually manipulates the database.

However, as an alternative, Acrobat JavaScript gives a form the ability to directly "talk" to a database. Using a set of JavaScript objects that together implement something called **ADBC** (Adobe Database Connectivity), an Acrobat document can actually become the user interface for a database. The fields in the document can "automatically" (from the standpoint of the user) populate themselves with data from the database, and the user can enter new data and have it added to the database. In fact, anything you can do with the database can be done from within an Acrobat file, subject to three limitations:

- The database must use a language called SQL to communicate with the outside world.

- The database must connect to client computers using a Microsoft technology called ODBC (Open Database Connectivity).

- The form must be viewed from a Windows computer. Unfortunately, there is no support for ADBC in the Macintosh version of Acrobat.

This chapter and the next present the basics of communicating with a database from within your JavaScripts. There is so much to discuss in even this light introduction to the topic that I have divided it into two chapters, mostly to make the topic a little less panic-inducing.

This chapter presents an overview of SQL and ODBC and then looks at the JavaScript objects Acrobat provides for accessing information within a database.

In Chapter 17, we shall apply what we have learned to a sample form that reads and displays data from a database.

These chapters will get you started in carrying out basic activities with databases from within Acrobat. They do, however, present only a light introduction to the database language, SQL; there are entire books written on the subject. If you need to do more than what these chapters describe, you will want to read a separate book on SQL. (My favorite introduction to SQL is Peachpit Press's *SQL: Visual Quickstart Guide,* by Chris Fehily, but there are many books on the subject at your local bookstore.)

Database Basics

A database is a collection of tabular information residing on a computer. In the modern world, databases keep track of virtually everything about everyone; banks, credit cards companies, advertising agencies, telemarketing firms, insurance companies, veterinary clinics, and struggling authors of technical books all keep their information about customers and vendors on computer-resident databases. Microsoft Access and FileMaker Pro are examples of software that lets you manipulate the data in a database: You can add, remove, and modify data, generate reports from the data, and so on.

In a corporate setting, database software usually resides on a server and the data is accessed across a network; when you browse Amazon.com's products, you are looking at information taken from Amazon.com's database of products, using a Web server as the "front end." For a database to be used across a network, there needs to be a standard language that is used to request information from a database ("Give me all the CDs by the band Pink Swollen Toes.") and a standard way to get those requests to the database application.

This sort of setup is what we shall briefly examine here. We shall look at SQL, a query language that is understood by many databases, and ODBC, a common method for connecting with a database across a network. SQL is the language you use to ask a question of a database; ODBC is how that question gets to the database software.

SQL

SQL (pronounced "S-Q-L") is a language that is used to issue commands to a wide range of database software. In addition to commercial database software that understands SQL, such as Microsoft Access, there is also some very powerful free SQL software available; I'm particularly fond of MySQL, for example.

SQL is a well-defined, published, standard language; however, various database management software packages often differ slightly in their implementation of that standard. Access, MySQL, PostgreSQL, and most other database management software each provide a slightly different variant of the standard SQL. (This is analogous to all of the variants of English: American, British, Australian, and so on.) Everything we discuss in this book, however, is sufficiently basic that it will work with any SQL database software.

Whence *SQL?*

The name *SQL* originally stood for Structured Query Language. However, because that phrase does not really describe the language, ANSI (the American National Standards Institute) has declared that the initials no longer stand for anything; the language's name is *SQL,* pure and simple.

Proper pronunciation is "S-Q-L." You will often hear people say "Sequel," but that's not correct. Among other things, there is a commercial SQL database product named Sequel and that company is understandably touchy about the name becoming generic.

I sometimes pronounce it "Squeal," but that's mostly a reflection of many people's initial reaction to learning the language.

SQL databases and tables

An SQL database is a collection of two-dimensional tables. Consider **Figure 16.1**. This diagram depicts part of an SQL database for a corporate customer list. In the fragment we see in the figure, the database named Customers has three tables: ClientData, Companies, and Spouses. Each of these tables is conceptually similar to a spreadsheet, containing data organized into rows and columns. Each column must have a unique title that identifies it within that table.

Database: Customers

Table: ClientData

FirstName	LastName	Address
Charles	Gilligan	3rd Palm Dr.
Skipper	Aangstrom	213 Minnow
Thurston	Howell	1 Beach Dr.
Mary Ann	Baker	Next Tree

Table: Companies

Name	President	Product
Red-A, Inc.	H. Prynn	Bath Oils
White Fence	T. Sawyer	House Paint
Eye C. U.	P. Marlowe	Investigations
Curly Hair	H. Poirot	Grooming

Table: Spouses

Name	Spouse	Happy
Lovey	Thurston	Delirious

Figure 16.1 *An SQL database contains one or more tables made up of data arranged in rows and columns.*

Thus, in the figure, the table ClientData contains columns named FirstName, LastName, Address, and so on; this is the information the database stores for each person—on each row—in that table.

To get to data within an SQL database, you must specify:

- The table from which you want to draw data (for example, ClientData)

- The columns you want to look at (LastName, Address)

- The rows that contain the information you want (the row whose LastName column contains *Smith*)

SQL is the language you use to frame such a request.

In this chapter and the next, we shall look at a couple of samples of SQL requests. This will give us a feel for what the language looks like and will provide some specific examples we can use later in our JavaScript programs.

Eventually, we will use Acrobat JavaScript commands to send these commands to a database; for the moment, we'll just concentrate on the SQL commands, themselves.

Selecting columns

The first step in using an SQL database is to tell it exactly which tables and which columns within each table you want to work with. You do this with a command like the following:

```
SELECT LastName,Address FROM ClientData
```

Here we are using the SQL SELECT command, which specifies that we want to work with data from one or more columns (LastName and Address, in our case) in one of the tables (ClientData) in the database (**Figure 16.2**). Sending this command to an SQL database tells it to "select" the data in the specified columns, a task analogous to selecting the columns in a spreadsheet.

FirstName	LastName	Address	City
Charles	Gilligan	3rd Palm...	Isleton
Skipper	Aangstrom	213 Minnow	Schooner...
David P.	Smith	32 Maple...	New York
Thurston	Howell	1 Beach Dr.	The Sands
Mary Ann	Baker	Next Tree	Over
Ginger	Smith	8 Sway Ln.	Oolala

Figure 16.2 *Here we've used the SQL* SELECT *command to select two columns of data: LastName and Address.*

The word SELECT is followed by one or more column names separated by commas. FROM is followed by the name of the table from which you want to draw data.

Nothing immediately appears to happen when we send this command to a database from within Acrobat JavaScript. The database selects the specified data but does nothing immediately visible. Our JavaScript can then request the selected data one row at a time, using each row of data to fill in form fields, perform calculations, and so on. (**Figure 16.10**, on page 189, shows a form we'll use to display data from the ClientData table.)

We shall discuss later how to obtain the column and table names. (The short answer: Ask the database designer.)

Here's a second example of the SQL SELECT command:

SELECT * FROM ClientData

An asterisk is a shorthand character meaning *every column*. This call to SELECT selects all of the columns in the table (**Figure 16.3**).

FirstName	LastName	Address	City
Charles	Gilligan	3rd Palm...	Isleton
Skipper	Aangstrom	213 Minnow	Schooner...
David P.	Smith	32 Maple...	New York
Thurston	Howell	1 Beach Dr.	The Sands
Mary Ann	Baker	Next Tree	Over
Ginger	Smith	8 Sway Ln.	Oolala

Figure 16.3 *Here our SQL SELECT command has selected all the columns in our table.*

Searching

A call to SELECT can specify, in addition to the table and column names, search criteria so that only certain rows are selected; this is done using a WHERE clause:

SELECT * FROM ClientData WHERE LastName = 'Smith'

The above example will select all the columns in the table, but only in those rows in which the value of the LastName column is 'Smith' (**Figure 16.4**). Note that SQL uses a single equals sign to mean *is equal to,* unlike JavaScript, which uses a double equals sign. Also note that SQL encloses searched-for text in a pair of single quotes, rather than the more common double quotes.

FirstName	LastName	Address	City
Charles	Gilligan	3rd Palm...	Isleton
Skipper	Aangstrom	213 Minnow	Schooner...
David P.	Smith	32 Maple...	New York
Thurston	Howell	1 Beach Dr.	The Sands
Mary Ann	Baker	Next Tree	Over
Ginger	Smith	8 Sway Ln.	Oolala

Figure 16.4 *An SQL SELECT command can tell the database to select only those rows whose LastName column contains 'Smith'.*

SQL provides a complete set of comparisons you can use to select rows. **Table 16.1** lists the comparisons you can perform in a WHERE clause.

Table 16.1 *SQL Comparison Operations*

COMPARISON	DESCRIPTION
=	Equal to
>	Greater than
>=	Greater than or equal to
<	Less than
<=	Less than or equal to
<>	Not equal to

Thus,

```
SELECT * FROM ClientData WHERE LastName > 'C'
```

would select all the rows whose LastName column has a value later in the alphabet than *C*.

SQL is a rich language for manipulating databases. In these chapters, we discuss only some very basic commands; look at any good book on SQL, and you'll find a large, varied vocabulary for performing all manner of actions on a database. That said, the simple commands we examine in this chapter and the next will actually suffice for the activities most people will likely want to perform from within an Acrobat form.

ODBC

Open Database Connectivity is a standard method by which computers can talk to databases. In human terms, if SQL is the equivalent of English, then ODBC is analogous to a telephone; it is the means by which a computer system can send messages—SQL statements—to a database.

The database to which a computer is connected is typically full-blown database software, often running on a server. Microsoft Windows, however, can treat Access database *files* as **ODBC data sources.** An ODBC data source is something that the Windows ODBC mechanism can manipulate using SQL; it can be database management software or simply a database file in a format known to ODBC, such as an Access database file. ODBC-savvy software, including Acrobat JavaScript, can read data from any ODBC data source, including Access database files.

Adding a data source to Microsoft Windows

In Windows, before you can use data from an ODBC source, you need to open that source on your computer. You do this with the ODBC Data Sources control panel.

In this chapter, we are going to use as our ODBC data source an Access file named ADBCDemo.mdb. You will find this file in the Extras folder on your Acrobat CD-ROM; you will also find it among the example files for this chapter. (Go to www.acumentraining.com/acrobatjs.html for the sample files for this book.)

If you want to follow along with the JavaScript examples for this topic, you must copy this file to your hard disk (exactly where doesn't matter) and follow the steps below. Keep in mind that we are in Windows, here, not Acrobat.

(Other environments, including Macintosh OS X, can connect to ODBC data sources, but you will need to follow those environments' documentation to see how to do so. Unfortunately, those other environments are somewhat irrelevant to us here, since only the Windows version of Acrobat supports ODBC.)

To add the as file to Windows as an ODBC data source:

Start in Windows with your Windows control panels displayed.

1. Double-click the ODBC Data Sources icon 🗿 ODBC Data Sources (32bit) .

   You will be looking at the ODBC Data Source Administrator dialog box (**Figure 16.5**). This dialog box lists all of the data sources currently available on your system. We are going to add a new data source, the Adobe demo file.

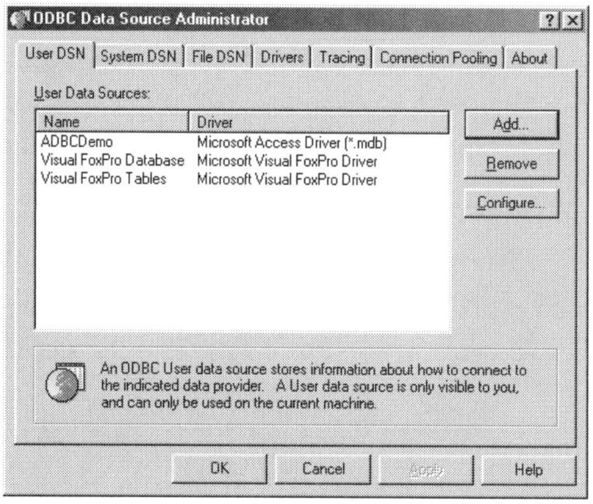

Figure 16.5 *The Data Source Administrator dialog box is where you add a new data source to those already available on your Windows machine.*

2. Click the Add button.

You will be looking at the Create New Data Source dialog box (**Figure 16.6**).

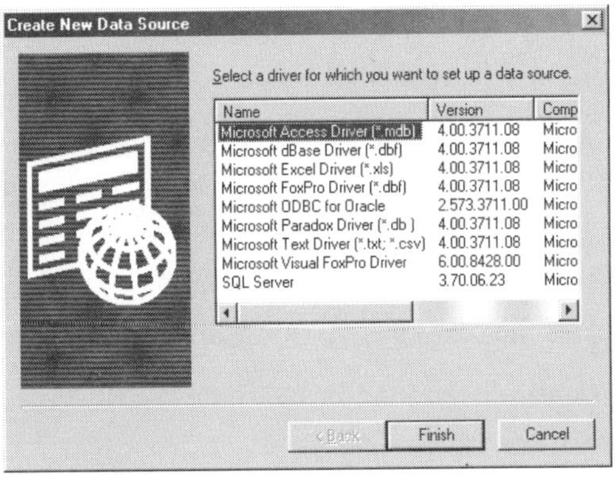

Figure 16.6 *We are going to use an Access database file (with the suffix ".mdb") as our data source.*

3. Select Microsoft Access Driver and click the Finish button.

Windows will present you with the ODBC Microsoft Access Setup dialog box (**Figure 16.7**).

4. In the Data Source Name field, type "ADBCDemo." This is the name by which the new data source will be known in our Acrobat JavaScripts.

5. Type a short description into the Description field. This can be anything you like.

6. Click the Select button and navigate in the resulting Open dialog box to the ADBCDemo.mdb file.

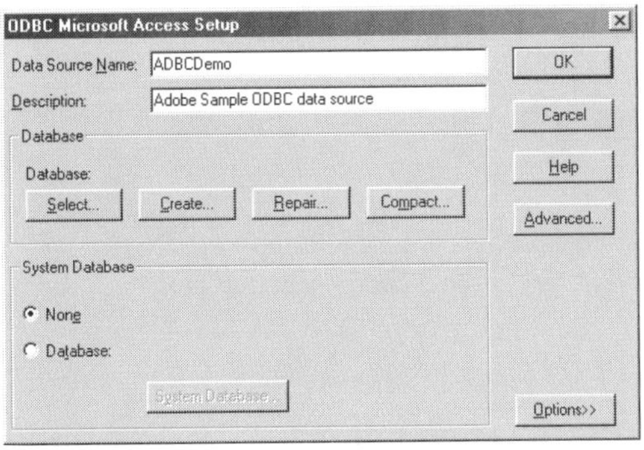

Figure 16.7 *As a final step in opening our database file as a data source, we need to click the Select button and select the actual file.*

7. Close all dialog boxes until you are back at the Windows desktop.

You will see no visible difference, but the Adobe demo file will now seen by all Windows ODBC software on this computer as a valid data source.

Turning off "read-only"

If you copied your ADBCDemo file from the Acrobat CD-ROM, you will find that it is annoyingly marked as read-only. Copying any file from a CD-ROM to your hard disk in Windows marks them as read-only; this is a continual nuisance when working with these files. Let's turn that attribute off.

To turn off the read-only attribute of your ADBCDemo.mdb file:

Start by opening the window in Windows that contains the demo file.

1. Right-click the file and select Properties in the resulting pop-up menu (**Figure 16.8**).

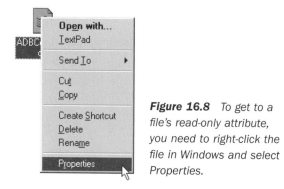

Figure 16.8 *To get to a file's read-only attribute, you need to right-click the file in Windows and select Properties.*

Windows will present you with the file's Properties dialog box.

2. Deselect the check box marked Read-only at the bottom of the dialog box (**Figure 16.9**).

Figure 16.9 *In the file's Properties dialog box, deselect the Read-only check box.*

3. Click the OK button.

Now, at last, we are ready to discuss accessing databases from Acrobat JavaScript.

ADBC

ADBC, Adobe Database Connectivity, is Adobe Acrobat's version of ODBC; using this, Acrobat JavaScripts can open a connection to an ODBC database and pass SQL commands to it. You can then select rows within the database, access the data within the selected rows, and display that data in your form.

Actually, since ADBC is simply a conduit through which you pass SQL commands to a database, you can do pretty much anything to a database from within your Acrobat JavaScripts by passing the appropriate SQL commands: You can look at data in the database, change data, add new data, delete data, and so on.

We are going to see how to pass SQL commands from an Acrobat JavaScript to an ODBC database. In the next chapter, we are going to use ADBC to create the form pictured in **Figure 16.10**. This form lets the user browse through a customer database; it connects to the ADBCDemo file we discussed in the previous section and lets the user step through each person in the database, displaying each customer's information in turn. The form also lets the user search for a specific customer by last name.

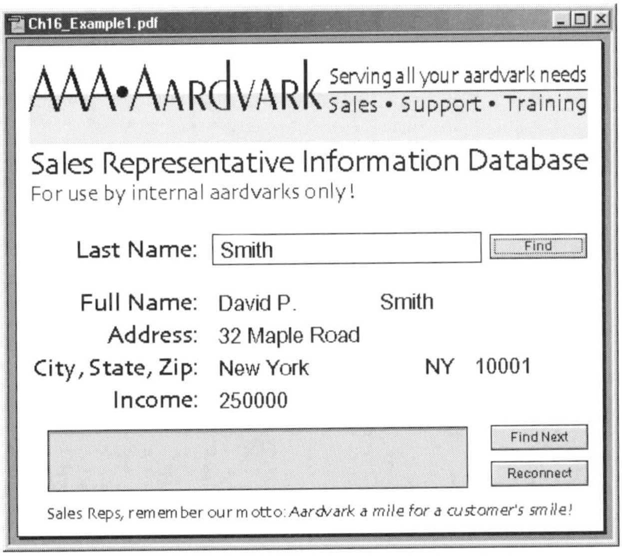

Figure 16.10 *In the next chapter, we shall use this form as a user interface for browsing and searching the ADBCDemo file.*

Database Objects

ADBC communication with a database is carried out in Acrobat JavaScript using three types of JavaScript objects:

- *ADBC object* is an object through which you connect to an ODBC database.

- *Connection object* represents a database to which your JavaScript is connected.

- *Statement object* is an object through which you send SQL statements to a connected database.

  The Statement object also provides methods by which you may use data retrieved from the database. For example, the nextRow method lets you step through the selected records in the database one row at a time. We shall look at some of these in a moment.

To use an ODBC database, an Acrobat form must do the following:

1. Use the ADBC object to open a connection to the desired database. This action yields a Connection object that will represent that connected database in our JavaScript.

   If the form's only purpose is to act as a front end to this database, then the form may open the connection in a Document JavaScript or a Page Open JavaScript. (See Chapter 2 for a reminder of how Page Open JavaScripts work.) This way, the database will be available as soon as the user opens the form.

2. Use the Connection object obtained in step 1 to get a Statement object through which you can send SQL statements to the database. This may be done in the same script that opened the database connection.

3. Repeatedly use the Statement object created in step 2 to send SQL statements to the database. This is when you actually access the contents of the database.

4. If necessary, use the Statement object's methods to manipulate the data retrieved from the database.

Let's look at the three database objects in a little more detail.

ADBC object

The ADBC object is a globally accessible object (that is, you may use it from within any JavaScript in your Acrobat file) that lets you connect to an ODBC data source available to your Windows computer. It has only one method that we care about here—newConnection, which is used with code similar to the following line:

```
var cxn = ADBC.newConnection("nameOfDataSource")
```

The newConnection method opens a connection to the data source whose name is passed to it as an argument. It returns a Connection object representing the now-open data source; in our case, we assigned that Connection object to the variable, cxn. (As usual, the name is just something I picked; it has no particular significance to JavaScript.)

If newConnection fails to open the data source (perhaps because there is no data source with that name available on that machine), then the method returns a null object. (Remember that you must install your data source in Windows, as we described above, before attempting to open a connection to it.)

Connection object

The Connection object represents an open data source within your JavaScript program; you usually get a Connection object from a call to ADBC.newConnection, as we did above.

The Connection object method that you will use most often in a form is newStatement:

```
var myStatement = cxn.newStatement()
```

This line of JavaScript uses the Connection object from our previous line of code to create a Statement object through which we can communicate with the database. As we shall see, it is through a Statement object that you send SQL commands to a database.

Statement object

The Statement object is your conduit to an open data source. The Statement object's methods allow you to send SQL statements to the data source with which it is associated and retrieve information from that data source. There are three methods of particular interest to us here: execute, nextRow, and getRow.

The execute method sends an SQL statement to the data source:

```
myStatement.execute("an SQL command")
```

The string argument must contain a valid SQL command. This may be *any* SQL command; using execute, you may read data from the data source, add new data, delete data, anything. For example, the following line of JavaScript code will select all the columns of data in the database named ClientData:

```
myStatement.execute("SELECT * FROM ClientData")
```

Note that this call to execute does not immediately hand the data over to your JavaScript. Having told the database to select all the columns of data, we need to tell it to transmit that data to our JavaScript program. This is a two-step process; first we must make a call to the nextRow method:

```
myStatement.nextRow()
```

The nextRow method tells the database to prepare to send the next row of data from the rows selected by the most recent SQL command. This data isn't immediately sent to our JavaScript program; it just tells the data source which row we will want to read. We actually fetch the data with getRow:

```
var theRow = myStatement.getRow()
```

The getRow method actually gets a row of data from the data source and returns a **Row object** that represents that data. A Row object contains a property corresponding to each column in that row; the value of that property is the database's value of that column in the current row. For example, theRow.FirstName refers to the value of the FirstName column in the current row.

Let's return to nextRow for a moment. The nextRow method tells the database to prepare to read the next row of data. What if you are already at the last row of data and there are no more rows left? If nextRow fails to move to a new row of data (usually because you have reached the end of the database), then it **throws an exception** that your JavaScript must handle somehow. To understand what this odd phrase means, we need to digress a bit, to discuss a new pair of JavaScript commands: **try** and **catch.**

The *try* and *catch* Commands

The JavaScript try and catch commands are important when you're using SQL within Acrobat. They are actually part of JavaScript's error-handling mechanism, allowing a JavaScript program to recover gracefully from errors. These two commands are intended to handle errors that occur at

run time, that is, at the time a program is executing (as opposed to when you first type in a program's code). They are important to us in this chapter because Acrobat's database-related objects use try and catch to handle out-of-data situations.

A *try* and *catch* example

Consider the following very simple (and very bad) single-line JavaScript:

```
NoSuchThing
```

This JavaScript has the serious disadvantage that there is no such function or JavaScript command as NoSuchThing. (I realize this isn't very realistic, but bear with me for a moment.) If you were to execute this script, perhaps as a button's Mouse Up action, then Acrobat would display the JavaScript Console with an error message in it (**Figure 16.11**).

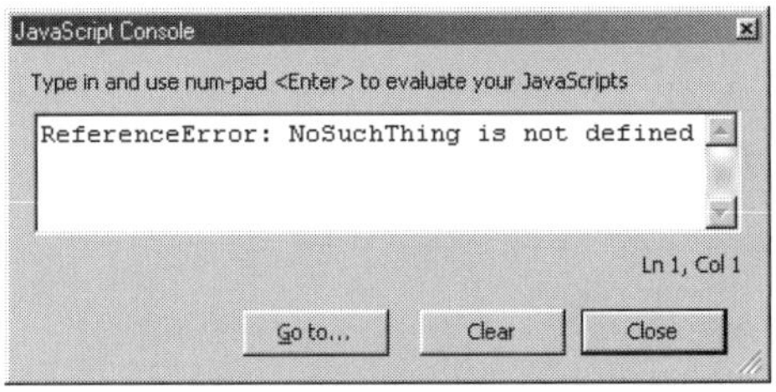

Figure 16.11 *Usually, Java-Script errors at run time are reported as an error message in the JavaScript Console window. This may cause angst in sensitive users.*

This may be alarming to a user.

You can intercept JavaScript's handling of unusual situations, including JavaScript errors, with the try and catch commands:

```
try {
    NoSuchThing
}
catch(e) {
    app.alert("Error! Nothing very much. Don't worry.\n" + e)
}
```

The try command executes the JavaScript code in the braces that follow it. If that code executes without any problem, then JavaScript ignores catch and its braces.

On the other hand, if an error occurs while executing the try block, then execution immediately drops out of the try and catch is executed. Errors within a try block generate what is called an **exception;** an exception is something that causes JavaScript execution to drop out of a `try` block. The most common example of an exception is a JavaScript error.

The `catch` command is followed by parentheses containing a variable name; the parentheses are followed by a block of JavaScript code in braces. An exception (again, usually a JavaScript error) causes JavaScript to immediately leave a `try` clause and then execute the `catch` command's JavaScript code.

Within a `catch` block, the variable we handed to `catch` (e, in our case) will refer to an **Exception object** that contains information about the current exception. In our example, we handed that Exception object to the `app.alert` method as part of the message it should print. (Displaying an Exception object in an alert prints a description of the exception—in our case, an error message, as in **Figure 16.12**.)

The term used for causing an exception in a JavaScript program is to *throw* the exception; we say that a JavaScript error *throws an exception*, which is *caught* by the `catch` command.

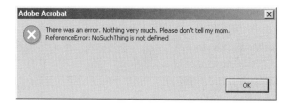

Figure 16.12 *Using* try *and* catch, *you can report errors and other exceptions yourself, presenting a more reassuring message to the user.*

NextRow and Exceptions

The reason `try` and `catch` are of interest to us is that the Statement object's `nextRow` method throws an exception if there is no more data left to read. Left to itself, JavaScript would treat this like any other error occurring at the time the script is run: It would open the JavaScript Console window and display an error message. We would like to treat the situation a little more gently.

Specifically, you should always call the `nextRow` method in a `try-catch` pair:

```
Try    {
    myStatement.nextRow()
}
catch(e)    {
    app.alert("There's no more data. Bummer.")
}
```

The `try` command executes our call to `nextRow`. If this succeeds, then execution skips over the `catch` clause and continues on. However, if `nextRow` fails, then execution drops into the `catch` clause, which tells the user that we're at the end of the data.

This technique allows you to control how to report that end-of-data message to the user.

In the next chapter, we shall use `try` and `catch` every time we advance to the next row of data when reading a database.

SQL in a Form

In this chapter, we have looked at all the tools that Acrobat provides for working with databases. What we have not yet done is seen these all work together in an actual form.

Proceed to the next chapter, where we shall put to use everything we have learned.

17

Reading and Writing a Database

In the previous chapter, we worked through an introduction to what an ODBC (Open Database Connectivity) database is and how to frame a query to such a database using SQL. We learned how to connect to a database and send it a query from within an Acrobat JavaScript using the JavaScript objects that make up ADBC, Adobe's implementation of ODBC.

In this chapter, we are going to put all that newly learned information to use. We are going to use the form in **Figure 17.1** as a user interface for browsing and searching the ADBCDemo database file we added to Microsoft Windows as a data source.

If you haven't read Chapter 16, do so right now. We are going to dive straight into our project in this chapter. If you don't have the basic knowledge of Acrobat JavaScript database usage provided by that chapter, then the following discussion will be fairly incomprehensible.

Project 1: Browsing a Database

(Files: Ch17_Example1.pdf, Ch17_Example1_raw.pdf)

Let's use the form in **Figure 17.1** as the front end to the ADBCDemo database file.

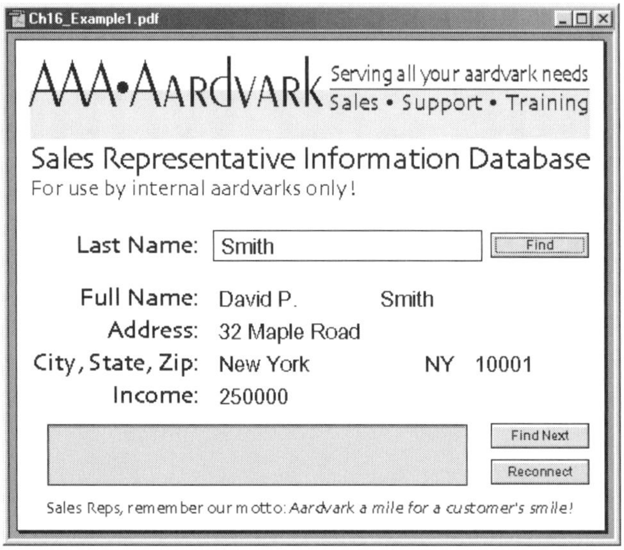

Figure 17.1 *We are going to add a series of scripts that lets the user browse a database with this Acrobat form.*

From users' standpoint, here's what happens when they use the form:

When the user first opens the document, the Acrobat page shows client information for the first person in the database. If the user clicks the Find Next button, the form displays the information for the next person in the database. The user can repeatedly click the Find Next button to step through the entire client list. When the user reaches the end of the list, the message box at the bottom of the form will display the message "No further matches."

If the user types a last name into the text field labeled Last Name and then clicks the Find button, the form will display information for the first person in the database who has that last name. Clicking the Find Next button will display information for the next person in the database who has that last name. As before, if there are no more clients with that last name, the message box will tell the user so.

Knowing the database

Before you can use an Acrobat form as a front-end to a database, you need to know two things about that database:

- The names of the tables it contains. Our ADBCDemo database file contains only one table, named ClientData.

- The names of the columns in those tables. The ClientData table has seven columns, with the following names: FirstName, LastName, Address, City, State, Zipcode, and Income.

In a real situation, you would need to get this information from whoever designed or is maintaining the database you want to use. In our case, the tables and column names for ADBCDemo.mdb are documented on the Acrobat CD-ROM.

Our form

Looking at **Figure 17.2**, you can see that this is a fairly busy form, containing nine text fields and three buttons. Seven of the text fields correspond to the columns in our database table; in fact, I gave them exactly the same names as the corresponding database columns. I shall refer to these fields in this chapter as the *client data text fields.* The other two text fields each have a special purpose: txtQuery is the text field into which the user can type a client's last name in order to search for it in the database; txtMessage displays messages (such as "Couldn't find a matching name") to the user.

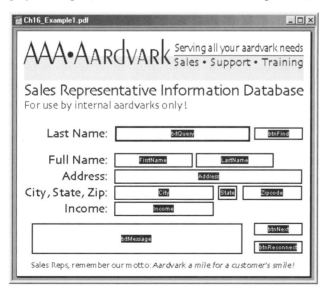

Figure 17.2 *There are a lot of form fields and a lot of scripts in this document!*

Our form will contain several JavaScripts:

- Four Document JavaScripts that define useful functions that will be used in the form

- A Page Open JavaScript that connects to the database file and displays the information for the first client, as in **Figure 17.1**

- A JavaScript attached to the Find button (which is named btnFind) that does a query on the database, looking for any fields whose LastName column matches the contents of txtQuery. If it finds a match, the script puts client data from the first matching row into the client data text fields.

- A short JavaScript attached to the Find Next button (btnNext) that displays the data in the next row in the database (that is, it displays data from the row that follows whichever row is currently being displayed)

- A very short script attached to the Reconnect button that reestablishes the connection to the database (in case the connection is broken for some reason)

All in all, this is the most complicated form in this book. Happily, it is not necessarily the most difficult to understand; there are a lot of JavaScripts here, but they aren't difficult, given what we learned in Chapter 16.

The JavaScripts

Let's look at the JavaScripts in this project. We are going to start by looking at the four Document JavaScripts and then continue on to the scripts attached to the Page Open event and the buttons.

If you wish to type these scripts into the "raw" version of the form, remember that they will work only in the Microsoft Windows version of Acrobat; the Mac version doesn't support database interaction. (Yes, this *is* irksome for those of us who do most of our work on a Mac.)

The Document JavaScripts

This form has four Document JavaScripts, each defining a single function. We are going to step through these scripts in the order they appear in the JavaScript Functions dialog box (**Figure 17.3**). The order of the JavaScripts in this dialog box is unimportant; the list is automatically alphabetized by Acrobat. Remember that you get to this dialog box by selecting Tools > JavaScript > Document JavaScripts. You add a new Document Script to this dialog box by entering a name into the Script Name text field and clicking the Add button.

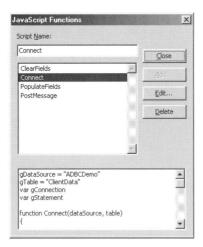

Figure 17.3 *There are four Document JavaScripts in this Acrobat file.*

ClearFields( )

The purpose of the `ClearFields` function is to empty out the value of each of the seven client data text fields (FirstName, LastName, Address, and so on). This function makes it easy to clear these fields when a search for data fails, for example.

```
function ClearFields()
{
```

Get a form field ──── `var f = this.getField("FirstName")`

Set its value to "" ──── `f.value = ""`

```
    f = this.getField("LastName")
    f.value = ""


    f = this.getField("Address")
    f.value = ""


    f = this.getField("City")
    f.value = ""
```

```
f = this.getField("State")
f.value = ""


f = this.getField("Zipcode")
f.value = ""


f = this.getField("Income")
f.value = ""
}
```

The code in detail

This function is composed entirely of JavaScript features that we've covered in earlier chapters.

```
function ClearFields()
{
```

The empty parentheses tell us that our ClearFields function will take no arguments when we use it.

```
var f = this.getField("FirstName")
f.value = ""
```

For each of the seven client data text fields, we get a reference to that field, assign the reference to a variable, f, and then set the field's value (the text it displays) to an empty string. This will make the field become blank on the Acrobat page.

ClearFields has a similar pair of lines for each of the seven client data text fields in the form.

Connect(dataSource, table)

Our Connect function connects to the ADBCDemo database and grabs the first row of data out of the ClientData table. It then displays the first row's data on the Acrobat page.

Define some global variables
```
var gDataSource = "ADBCDemo"
var gTable = "ClientData"
var gConnection
var gStatement
```

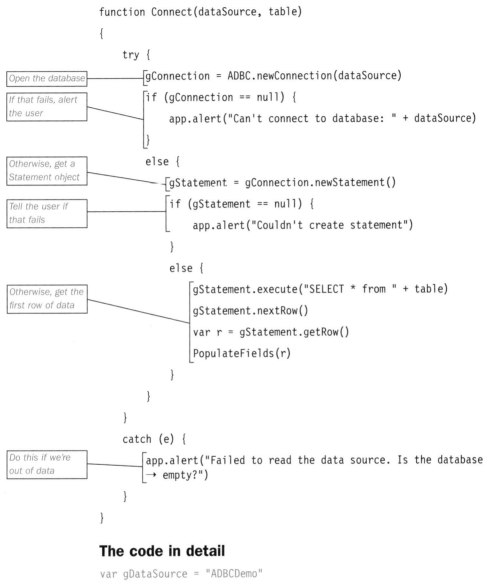

```
function Connect(dataSource, table)
{
    try {
        gConnection = ADBC.newConnection(dataSource)
        if (gConnection == null) {
            app.alert("Can't connect to database: " + dataSource)
        }
        else {
            gStatement = gConnection.newStatement()
            if (gStatement == null) {
                app.alert("Couldn't create statement")
            }
            else {
                gStatement.execute("SELECT * from " + table)
                gStatement.nextRow()
                var r = gStatement.getRow()
                PopulateFields(r)
            }
        }
    }
    catch (e) {
        app.alert("Failed to read the data source. Is the database
        → empty?")
    }
}
```

Callouts (left margin):
- Open the database
- If that fails, alert the user
- Otherwise, get a Statement object
- Tell the user if that fails
- Otherwise, get the first row of data
- Do this if we're out of data

The code in detail

```
var gDataSource = "ADBCDemo"
var gTable = "ClientData"
var gConnection
var gStatement
```

We start by defining four variables that will be available to JavaScripts throughout our Acrobat document. We assign to gDataSource and gTable the names of our data source and the table we want to read, respectively. The other two variables we leave unassigned for the moment.

Note that I start the names of globally accessible variables with a lower-case *g* so that they are instantly identifiable as being global.

```
function Connect(dataSource, table)
```

Our Connect function will take two arguments, both of them strings. The dataSource argument will be the name of the database to which we shall connect; table is the name of the table within that database that we want to use.

```
try {
```

Everything that Connect does takes place inside a try-catch pair. This is because we shall be attempting to read data from the database with the nextRow method. As we saw in the previous chapter, nextRow throws an exception if we are at the end of the database; executing our function's code in a try clause allows us to gracefully handle this situation.

```
gConnection = ADBC.newConnection(dataSource)
```

Here we attempt to connect to the database. You may recall from the previous chapter that the ADBC object's newConnection method opens a connection to an ODBC data source available to your computer. In our case, the name of the data source resides in the argument dataSource that will be passed to our function when it is called. (As we shall see, our Acrobat form executes Connect as part of a Page Open script.) Don't confuse dataSource, our function's argument variable, with gDataSource, the similarly named global variable; they are separate entities in our program.

Remember that newConnection returns a Connection object that represents the now-open data source; if it fails to connect to the named data source, it returns a null object. In our script, the return value, whether a Connection object or a null object, is assigned to our global variable, gConnection.

```
if (gConnection == null) {
    app.alert("Can't connect to database: " + dataSource)
}
```

Our JavaScript code immediately looks at gConnection to see if it is null. If so, it displays an alert, informing the user that the attempt to connect to the database failed (**Figure 17.4**).

```
else {
    gStatement = gConnection.newStatement()
```

Figure 17.4 *If* newConnection *fails to connect to the database, then our JavaScript uses* app.alert *to inform the user.*

If the gConnection variable is not null—that is, if our JavaScript successfully connected to the database—then we need to create a Statement object through which we can send SQL commands to that database. We call the Connection object's newStatement method, which returns a Statement object; our JavaScript assigns this to the variable, gStatement.

```
if (gStatement == null) {

    app.alert("Couldn't create statement")

}
```

If newStatement fails to create a Statement object, then newStatement returns a null object; so our JavaScript examines gStatement to see if it is null. If so, we inform the user of the problem with a call to app.alert. (There is no particular reason newStatement should fail, assuming we successfully connected to the data source; still, it is always wise to build in some protection from the unexpected.)

```
else {

    gStatement.execute("SELECT * from " + table)
```

If gStatement is not null, meaning we successfully created the Statement object, then we execute four JavaScript statements, of which the first is this call to execute. The Statement object's execute method sends an SQL command to the database.

In our case, we want to select all the columns from the table whose name was given to us as the Connect function's table argument. The SQL statement for this action looks like this:

```
SELECT * FROM theTable
```

The name theTable in the line above is a stand-in for the actual name of the table. In our case, the table's name is in our argument variable, table. Thus, the string we hand to the execute method, above, will be the concatenation of SELECT * FROM and the value of the variable table. (In our Acrobat form, the value of table will be ClientData.)

The database has now selected all the columns of data in the table. We haven't told it what to do with that data; that's what comes next.

```
gStatement.nextRow()

var r = gStatement.getRow()
```

Having told the data source to select all the data in the database, we now use the Statement object's nextRow method to tell the data source to prepare to send us the next row of data. (This will actually be the first row of data, since we only just connected to this database.) By the way, it is this call to nextRow that required that we execute this function's code in a try block; nextRow will throw an exception if there are no more rows to be had.

Having told the database which row we want, we now fetch the actual data with the getRow method; this method returns a Row object that represents that row of data.

A Row object has properties that correspond to the columns in the row it represents. Each property is itself an object whose value is the actual data in that column of that row in the database. Now that we've read a row of data with getRow and assigned the resulting Row object to the variable r, the first name of the current client would be in r.FirstName.value.

```
    PopulateFields(r)
}
```

We haven't yet looked at the definition of the PopulateFields function (it's next), but what it does is straightforward: It displays on our form page the information in a row retrieved from the database.

This call to PopulateFields ends our try block. If we get to this point without any exceptions, the Connect function exits. On the other hand, if there was an exception (in particular, if nextRow failed), then Connect will execute the code in the catch block.

```
catch (e) {
    app.alert("Failed to read the data source. Is the database
    → empty?")
}
```

The last thing Connect does is handle the case where try encounters an exception. If this happens, it probably will be because nextRow failed to find any rows of data, indicating we are at the end of the database. Since we just now opened this database (that's what our Connect function does), our catch block asks the user if he or she is sure it's not empty.

PopulateFields(row)

Our form (see **Figure 17.2**) has seven client data text fields with names that correspond to the names of the columns in our ClientData table (FirstName, LastName, and so on) PopulateFields sets the value of each of these seven fields to the value of the corresponding data from a Row object; the Row object is passed as an argument to the function.

```
function PopulateFields(row)
{
    var f = this.getField("FirstName")
    f.value = row.FirstName.value

    f = this.getField("LastName")
    f.value = row.LastName.value

    f = this.getField("Address")
    f.value = row.Address.value

    f = this.getField("City")
    f.value = row.City.value

    f = this.getField("State")
    f.value = row.State.value

    f = this.getField("Zipcode")
    f.value = row.Zipcode.value

    f = this.getField("Income")
    f.value = row.Income.value
}
```

Get a form field → var f = this.getField("FirstName")

Set its value to the row's data → f.value = row.FirstName.value

The code in detail

This is, again, relatively easy.

```
function PopulateFields(row)
{
```

The function takes a single argument, which will be a Row object.

```
var f = this.getField("FirstName")
f.value = row.FirstName.value
```

As we discussed earlier, the Row object has a property that corresponds to each column in the row. The name of each property in a Row object is the same as the name of the corresponding column; the value of each property is the value of the data in that column.

In our two lines of code, above, we get a reference to the form field FirstName, assigning this reference to the variable f. We then set the value of f (that is, the text that appears in the corresponding text field) to row.FirstName.value. This is odd-looking, but not hard: row.FirstName is the Property of row that corresponds to the FirstName column; row.FirstName.value is the value of that FirstName column.

Thus, we set the value (the displayed text) of the FirstName form field to the value (the text) in the FirstName column of the specified row from our database.

PopulateFields does this for all seven columns in the row and their corresponding form fields.

PostMessage(msg)

Our form uses the text field txtMessage to display messages to the user, as in **Figure 17.5**. The PostMessage function allows us to conveniently place messages in this text field. (Remember that we used this function in our Connect function to report an error message to the user.)

```
function PostMessage(msg)
{
    var fld = this.getField("txtMessage")

    fld.value = msg
}
```

The function takes a string, named msg, as its argument. It gets a reference to the field txtMessage and then sets the value of that field (in other words, the text it displays) to msg. Thus, a script that executes PostMessage("No match found for 'Gigikins'") would produce the message in **Figure 17.5**.

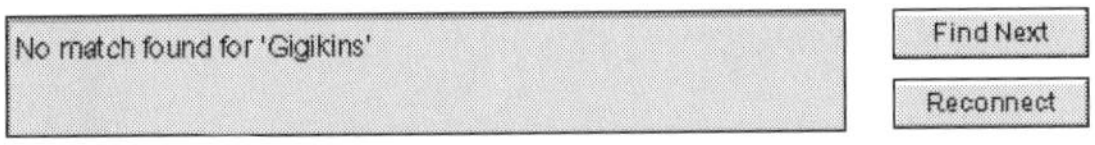

Figure 17.5 *Our* PostMessage *function uses the* txtMessage *field to display messages to the user.*

Page Open Script

Page actions are executed when Acrobat moves into or out of the page to which the script is attached. Our form's single page has a JavaScript attached to the Page Open event, so it will be executed when the document first displays the page. This script connects to the database and then displays the first client's data.

To attach the Page Open JavaScript to the form:

Start with the form open in Acrobat.

1. Select Document > Set Page Action.

   Acrobat will present you with the Page Actions dialog box (**Figure 17.6**).

2. Select the Page Open event and click the Add button.

   Acrobat will display the Add an Action dialog box.

3. Select JavaScript from the pop-up menu and click the Edit button.

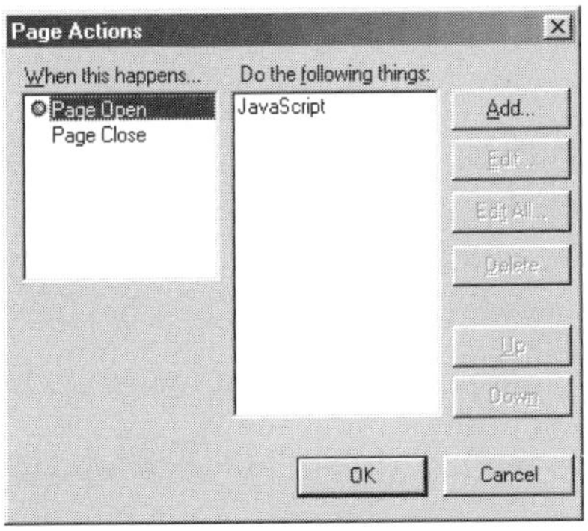

Figure 17.6 *We are going to add a JavaScript Page Action to this document's single page.*

4. In the resulting JavaScript Edit dialog box, type the following JavaScript:

```
ClearFields()

PostMessage("")

Connect(gDataSource,gTable)
```

5. Close all dialog boxes until you are once more looking at the Acrobat page.

6. Try it out: Save the form (so you don't lose your changes), then close and reopen the form. You should see the client data text fields filled out with the first client's name, address, and salary. (Don't forget that you must set up ADBCDemo.mdb as a data source on your computer; see Chapter 16 to see how to do this.)

This script makes calls to three functions we defined in the Document JavaScripts. It clears the form fields, puts a blank string into the message field (to erase any messages that might have been there already, perhaps left over from a previous use of the form), and then calls our Connect function, passing the values of gDataSource and gTable as its arguments. (Remember that the Document script that defined Connect assigned the strings ADBCDemo and ClientData to gDataSource and gTable, respectively.)

Connect connects to the ADBCDemo data source and reads the first row of data from the ClientData table, displaying that data on the Acrobat page.

Form Field Scripts

Our form has two JavaScripts that are attached to buttons, in both cases to the Mouse Up event.

btnFind

When the user types a last name into the Last Name field (whose name is txtQuery) and then clicks the Find button (btnFind), the JavaScript we shall attach to btnFind sends an SQL command to the data source that tells it to select all the rows whose LastName field matches the text in txtQuery.

To attach the JavaScript to the Mouse Up event for btnFind:

Start with the Actions panel visible in the button's Field Properties dialog box (**Figure 17.7**).

1. Select the Mouse Up event and click the Add button.

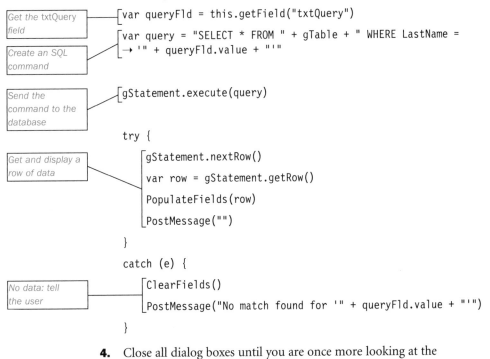

Figure 17.7 *We shall add a Mouse Up JavaScript to btnFind.*

Acrobat will display the Add an Action dialog box.

2. Select JavaScript from the pop-up menu and click the Edit button.

3. In the resulting JavaScript Edit dialog box, type the following JavaScript:

Get the txtQuery field

```
var queryFld = this.getField("txtQuery")
```

Create an SQL command

```
var query = "SELECT * FROM " + gTable + " WHERE LastName =
→ '" + queryFld.value + "'"
```

Send the command to the database

```
gStatement.execute(query)
```

```
try {
```

Get and display a row of data

```
    gStatement.nextRow()
    var row = gStatement.getRow()
    PopulateFields(row)
    PostMessage("")
}
catch (e) {
```

No data: tell the user

```
    ClearFields()
    PostMessage("No match found for '" + queryFld.value + "'")
}
```

4. Close all dialog boxes until you are once more looking at the Acrobat page.

5. Try it out: Select the Hand tool, type a name into the Last Name field (*Smith* and *Jones* both exist in the database), then click the Find button. The full name, address, and salary of the person you asked for will appear on the page.

The code in detail

Let's look at the script in some detail.

```
var queryFld = this.getField("txtQuery")
```

We start by getting a reference to the txtQuery field; we assign this reference to the variable queryFld.

```
var query = "SELECT * FROM " + gTable + " WHERE LastName = '" +
→ queryFld.value + "'"
```

Here we are assembling an SQL statement as a string to send to the data source. (Remember that the plus sign is used to concatenate strings in JavaScript.) We want the data source to select all the rows wherein the last name matches the value of txtQuery (a reference to which is stored in the variable queryFld). Remembering back to Chapter 16, such a query string should look like this:

```
Select * FROM NameOfTable WHERE LastName = 'SearchString'
```

In the line above, the two italicized names are stand-ins for the actual name of the table we want to search (ClientData, stored in the variable gTable) and the actual last name for which we want to search (which will be stored in queryFld.value).

We cobbled together this query string by concatenating the following pieces:

- The string SELECT * FROM

  Note that there is a space at the end of the string, following FROM.

- The variable gTable, which contains the name of the table

- The string WHERE LastName = '

- queryField.value, which is the name the user wants to find

- A final string holding a single quote; this terminates the query string in the SQL statement

```
gStatement.execute(query)
```

Here we send the SQL statement to the data source. The data source selects all of the rows in the table whose LastName column matches the name in txtQuery. The data source does not yet send this data back to our JavaScript.

```
try {
    gStatement.nextRow()
    var row = gStatement.getRow()
    PopulateFields(row)
    PostMessage("")
}
```

Now we have a `try` block that retrieves the data for the first matching row and displays that data on the current page. (The first three lines within this `try` block are identical to the three lines in our `Connect` function that carry out the same task.) These JavaScript statements do the following:

- Execute `nextRow` to tell the data source to select the first row of matching data in the table. This line will generate an exception if there is no row remaining—hence the use of `try` to execute this code.

- Use `getRow` to get the data in the currently selected row of data. This returns a `Row` object that is assigned to the variable `row`.

- Hand our `Row` object to the `PopulateFields` function, which displays the data on the Acrobat page.

- Finally, clear the message field by displaying a blank message.

  ```
  catch (e) {
      ClearFields()
      PostMessage("No match found for '" + queryFld.value + "'")
  }
  ```

The `catch` block will be executed if the `try` block's call to `nextRow` fails; this will happen if there were no rows that had a matching LastName column. In this case, we clear the client data text fields to make sure they are blank and then present an alert to the user, letting him or her know what happened.

Note that our alert text will incorporate the name for which we were searching (the value of the txtQuery field), as in **Figure 17.5**.

btnNext

The Next button in our form selects and displays the next person in the database whose last name matches our search string. If there are no further matches, then the button's script informs the user of that fact.

Follow the numbered steps for btnFind, above, and type in the following Mouse Up script:

```
try {
    gStatement.nextRow();
    var row = gStatement.getRow();
    PopulateFields(row);
}
catch (e) {
    PostMessage("No further matches.")
}
```

This is a simple version of the JavaScript attached to btnFind, consisting entirely of a try-catch block.

```
try {
    gStatement.nextRow();
    var row = gStatement.getRow();
    PopulateFields(row);
}
```

This try block retrieves the data for the next matching row and displays that data on the current page. These JavaScript statements do the following:

- Execute nextRow to tell the data source to select the first row of matching data in the table. This line will generate an exception if there is no row remaining—hence the use of try to execute this code.

- Use getRow to get the data in the currently selected row of data. This returns a Row object that is assigned to the variable row.

- Hand our Row object to the PopulateFields function, which displays the data on the Acrobat page.

```
catch (e) {
    PostMessage("No further matches.")
}
```

The catch block is executed if the try block's call to nextRow fails, indicating that no rows remain with a matching LastName column. In this case, we present an alert to the user, reporting what happened.

btnReconnect

Finally, the Reconnect button reconnects to the ADBCDemo data source. It is useful to provide the user with some way of reestablishing the connection to the database. In a real situation, the data source often resides on a server; if the network goes down or some other unexpected interruption occurs, your form will no longer be able to find the data source. A button such as our Reconnect gives the user some method of reestablishing the connection without closing and reopening the form.

Follow the numbered steps for btnFind, above, and type in the following Mouse Up script:

```
Connect(gDataSource, gTable)
```

All right, so it's not very complex. This script simply makes a call to the Connect function we defined in our Document JavaScripts. We are supplying as arguments the variables gDataSource and gTable, whose values are also set in the Connect Document JavaScript.

Done!

If you have now typed all of the above JavaScripts into their respective locations, you should have a functioning database browser!

Try it out: Open the Acrobat file and repeatedly click the Find Next button to see all of the clients in the database. Then type a last name into the txtQuery field and click the Find button.

Project 2: Adding New Data

Our browser example can step through the data in a database, but it can't add any new data. What if you wanted the user to be able to add new information to the database? Perhaps the company has a new client; it's reasonable to want to add that client's data to the ClientData table.

Actually, it requires little effort to take our previous browser form and give it the ability to insert new rows into a table.

Figure 17.8 shows a new version of our form, modified to allow the user to enter data into the client data text fields and save that data into the database. This new form is nearly identical to our original; it differs in just two ways:

■ The client data text fields have visible outlines. It is important to make the text fields visible if the user is expected to enter data into them. Having invisible data-entry fields is guaranteed to annoy the user. The fields are also no longer read-only; you can type data into them.

- There is a new button, labeled Add New, just above the Find Next button. The internal name of this new button is btnAdd.

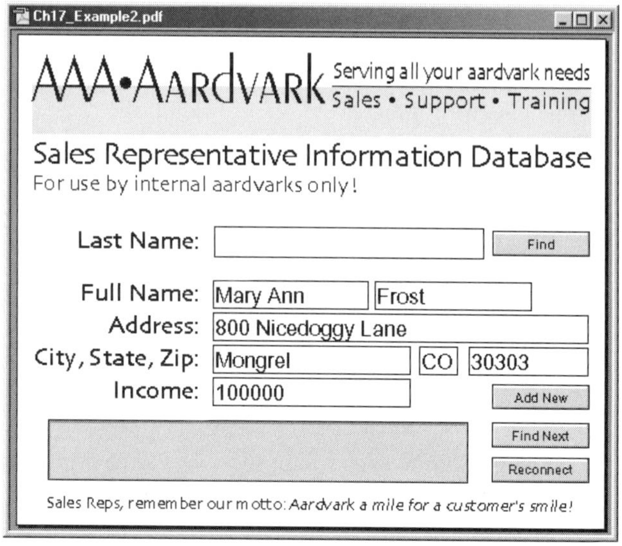

Figure 17.8 *This slightly different version of our form allows us to modify the database, adding a new row of client data.*

We are going to attach a JavaScript to the Mouse Up event for btnAdd; this JavaScript will take the data in the client data text fields and write it to the database as a new row of data.

From a user's perspective, he or she can type new client information—first name, last name, address, city, state, zip, and salary—into the form's text fields and click the Add New button, and the new client will be added to the database.

The SQL INSERT Command

The SQL command you use to insert a row of data into a database is INSERT.

```
INSERT INTO tableName (Field1, Field2, etc.) VALUES
→ (value1, value2, etc.)
```

In the above command:

- tableName is the name of the table you are altering.

- Field1, Field2, etc. are the names of the table columns for which you are supplying new data.

Note that these are in parentheses and separated by commas.

- value1, value2, and so on are the values that should be placed into each field.

The correspondence between fields and values is established by their order within the parentheses. The first value will be placed into the first field, the second into the second, and so on. Values may be strings or numbers; strings must be enclosed in single quotes, in usual SQL fashion.

Thus, if you wanted to insert the strings "Nick" and "Danger" into the FirstName and LastName fields of the table ClientData, the SQL command would be:

```
INSERT INTO ClientData (FirstName,LastName) VALUES ('Nick', 'Danger')
```

Our JavaScript for btnAdd needs to get the values of the seven client data text fields and then assemble a string containing an SQL INSERT command similar to the one above.

Let's look at the JavaScript.

The Script

We are going to attach this script to the Mouse Up action of the btnAdd button. Follow the numbered steps listed for btnFind, above, but type in this JavaScript:

Get all the fields' values

```
var firstName = this.getField("FirstName").value
var lastName = this.getField("LastName").value
var address = this.getField("Address").value
var city = this.getField("City").value
var state = this.getField("State").value
var zip = this.getField("Zipcode").value
var income = this.getField("Income").value
```

Assemble an SQL command

```
var stmt = "INSERT INTO " + table +  " (FirstName, LastName,
→ Address, City, State, Zipcode, Income) " + "VALUES ('" + firstName
→ + "', '" + lastName + "', '" + address + "', '" + city + "', '" +
→ state + "', '" + zip + "', " + income + ")"
```

Execute the command

```
try {
    gStatement.execute(stmt)}
```

```
catch (e) {

    app.alert("Action failed. The database file or ODBC datasource
    → might be read-only")

}
```

Tell the user
if it fails

In broad outline, this script does the following:

- It gets the value of each of our seven client data text fields.

- It creates a string containing a call to INSERT, put together from the values of the client data text fields.

- It executes the SQL statement in a try block.

- If the insertion fails, execute throws an exception, and the catch block displays an alert telling the user about it (**Figure 17.9**).

Figure 17.9 *If we fail to add the new row to the database, we display an alert letting the user know something is wrong.*

The code in detail

Let's look at this in detail:

```
var firstName = this.getField("FirstName").value
```

We start by getting the contents of all seven of the client data text fields. We are using an abbreviated notation to do this. In the past, we would have done this with two JavaScript statements:

```
var nameField = this.getField("FirstName")
```

```
var firstName = nameField.value
```

However, since this.getField returns a Field object, you can treat the phrase exactly as though it *were* a Field object, including using properties of the resulting Field object. this.getField("FirstName").value works as well as the two-line version and is shorter, but it's not as readable, in my opinion. Use whichever version suits you.

We have a similar line for each of the other six client data text fields, placing the text they contain into variables named firstName, lastName, address, city, state, zip, and income. The variables are not required to have these names; we could have named them after, say, days of the week. However, it makes your code much more readable if the variable names reflect what they contain.

```
var stmt = "INSERT INTO " + table +  " (FirstName, LastName,
→ Address, City, State, Zipcode, Income) " + "VALUES ('" + firstName
→ + "', '" + lastName + "', '" + address + "', '" + city + "', '" +
→ state + "', '" + zip + "', " + income + ")"
```

This rather messy single line is our assembly of the INSERT statement. We are assigning a string to variable stmt; that string is created by concatenating the following:

- The string "INSERT INTO ".

- The variable gTable, which is the name of our table.

- The names, in parentheses, of all the rows in the table.

- The String "VALUES ('". This marks the beginning of the data that should be inserted into the database.

- Alternating variables and commas, which will, when concatenated, look like: 'Mary Ann','Frost','8 Doggy Lane',... and so forth.

- A close parenthesis.

When this is all done, the string that is assigned to stmt will be a valid SQL INSERT command.

```
try {
    gStatement.execute(stmt)
}
```

Here we have a try block containing a call to execute that executes our SQL statement. This is where we actually place into the database the data that the user entered into the form.

```
catch (e) {
    app.alert("Action failed. The database file or ODBC datasource
    → might be read-only")
}
```

If INSERT fails, execute will throw an exception. In that case, our catch block will put up an alert, letting the user know that something's wrong.

Other Commands

As I said earlier, the string you hand to the execute method can be any valid SQL command. This means that there is virtually no limit to what your form can do with an ODBC database. Here we've browsed, searched, and inserted data. You can also delete data, rearrange data—anything you need to do with a database you can do from within your Acrobat form.

But to do that, you will need to learn SQL. It's not a hard language, but there is a lot to it. Happily, there are a *lot* of online resources to help you learn SQL. Chapter 19 lists some of my favorites.

18

Generating Reports

It is often useful for a form to be able to generate a new PDF file based on information the user has supplied. For example, you might want an order form to create a receipt, a faxable order page, or a summary of the order for the user to keep. Acrobat JavaScript supplies a means of doing this. The Report object allows you to create a new PDF file and print information onto the new document's pages. The results are not fancy, but this feature is *very* easy to use. This is what we shall discuss in this chapter.

The Report Object

Creating a Report

It's easy to create a report using the Acrobat Report object. This ease of use comes at a cost, however: The reports you can create using this object are pretty primitive. The methods of the Report object allow you to print lines of text from the top of the page downward, rather like a typewriter (remember typewriters?). You have no control over the font and no access to text styles, and the only graphic you can create is a horizontal divider.

But it *is* easy.

Figure 18.1 shows a typical report generated by a Report object.

Figure 18.1 *The Acrobat* Report *object lets your JavaScript program create a new Acrobat document, such as a receipt, an order summary, or some other report.*

To create a report in Acrobat JavaScript, you do the following:

- Create a Report object and assign it to a variable.

- Use a combination of Report object methods, such as writeText, indent, and outdent, to draw text onto the pages of your report.

- Finish your report by having the Report object open it in Acrobat or email it to a specified address.

Along the way, you can also specify text size and color, add a horizontal line, and specify page breaks.

Let's look in detail at the most useful properties and methods of the Report object.

Creating a Report Object

You create a `Report` object with a JavaScript line like this:

```
var rpt = new Report()
```

This line creates a new `Report` object, assigning it to the variable `rpt`. As always, there is nothing special about the variable name `rpt`; it's just something I thought was short and mnemonic.

In the discussion below, I'll use my `rpt` variable to stand in for the `report` object.

If you wish, you can specify a page size, using an array of four numbers:

```
var rpt = new Report([ 0, 0, 595, 842 ])
```

The four numbers are 0, 0, *pagewidth*, *pageheight*. (Properly, these are the PDF *x,y* coordinates of the lower-left and upper-right corners of the paper.) The above line will cause the `Report` object to create an Acrobat document using A4-size pages (210 mm by 297 mm).

Report Object Properties

Here are the most useful `Report` object properties:

- *size* is the font size that should be used to print text. Surprisingly, this is a multiplier, such as *1.3*. The `Report` object uses 12-point Helvetica for its text; the `size` multiplier changes the point size to that number times 12. For example, `rpt.size = 1.5` would change the point size to 18.

- *color* is the color that should be used for the text. You would set this to an Acrobat JavaScript color spec, such as:

  ```
  rpt.color = color.red
  ```

  See Chapter 3 for more information on Acrobat color specifications.

Report Object Methods

Drawing on the page

- *writeText("text to be printed")* prints a line of text on the Acrobat page. Each call to `writeText` will start on a new line on the page.

- *indent(numberOfPoints)* indents the text that follows by the specified number of points. You may omit the number of points, in which case, Acrobat will use a default value. The default indentation amount is not documented by Adobe, but it looks to be 18 points.

- *outdent(numberOfPoints)* moves the left margin to the left the specified number of points. You may omit the number of points, in which case Acrobat will use a default value.

- *divide(lineWidth)* draws a horizontal line across the page. The line will have the specified line width in points; if you omit the line width, Acrobat will use a default value of about 2 points.

- *breakPage* ends the current page in your Acrobat report and begins a new one.

Finishing the report

- *var doc = open("title")* ends the report, opening it in Acrobat so the user can see it. This method returns a Doc object representing the newly created Acrobat file.

- *var doc = mail(boolShowUI, "address")* ends the report, launches your email client, and emails the report to the specified email address.

  If the Boolean is true, then Acrobat will launch your email client with the "To" address set to the address you passed to the method; it is then up to the user to click the Send button in the mail client to send the message on its way. If the initial Boolean is false, you are asking that the mail client not give the user any chance to interact with the message; the mail message should immediately be sent.

  I have had spotty results with this method; it consistently launches my mail browser, but does not dependably send the message if the Boolean is false.

  There are additional arguments you can supply to this method to specify the message's subject and body text. Look at the *Acrobat JavaScript Object Specification* for more information on these.

The Project

We are going to add a "Faxable" button to the form in **Figure 18.2**. This form collects registration information from a customer. If the customer clicks the Faxable button, its Mouse Up JavaScript creates a report (see **Figure 18.1**) that the user can print and then fax to the company.

Figure 18.2 *Our project will attach a JavaScript to the Faxable button that creates a faxable registration form.*

Looking at **Figure 18.3**, there are four text fields of interest to us in this form: txtName, txtSN, txtAddress, and txtEMail. We are going to add a JavaScript to the Mouse Up event of btnFaxable that creates a report based on the contents of these fields.

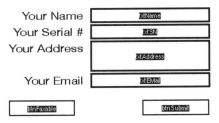

Figure 18.3 *We are going to generate a faxable registration page from the contents of the form's text fields.*

The JavaScript

To attach a JavaScript to the Mouse Up event of btnFaxable:

Start with the Actions panel visible in the button's Field Properties dialog box (**Figure 18.4**).

1. Select the Mouse Up event and click the Add button.

Acrobat will display the Add an Action dialog box.

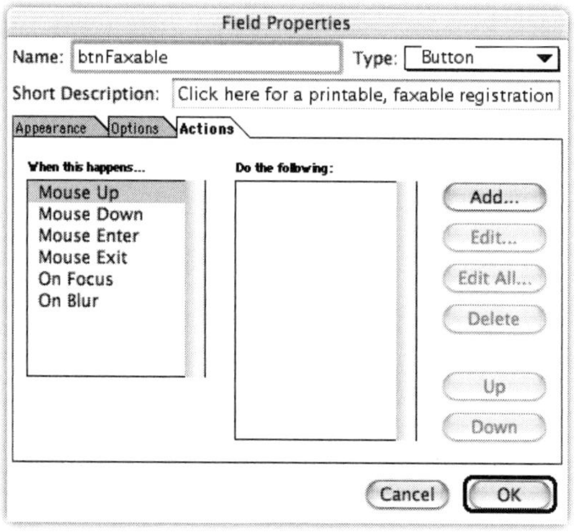

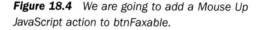

Figure 18.4 *We are going to add a Mouse Up JavaScript action to btnFaxable.*

2. Select JavaScript from the pop-up menu and click the Edit button.

3. In the resulting JavaScript Edit dialog box, type the following JavaScript:

Get references to the text fields

```
var nameFld = this.getField("txtName")
var snFld = this.getField("txtSN")
var addrFld = this.getField("txtAddress")
var emailFld = this.getField("txtEMail")
```

Create the report object

```
var rpt = new Report()
```

Text size x 2

```
rpt.size = 2
```

Text color red

```
rpt.color = color.red
```

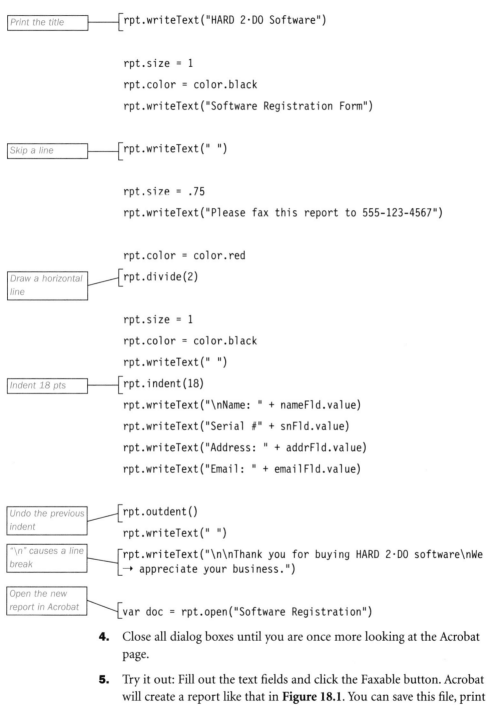

Print the title
```
rpt.writeText("HARD 2·DO Software")
```

```
rpt.size = 1
rpt.color = color.black
rpt.writeText("Software Registration Form")
```

Skip a line
```
rpt.writeText(" ")
```

```
rpt.size = .75
rpt.writeText("Please fax this report to 555-123-4567")
```

```
rpt.color = color.red
```
Draw a horizontal line
```
rpt.divide(2)
```

```
rpt.size = 1
rpt.color = color.black
rpt.writeText(" ")
```
Indent 18 pts
```
rpt.indent(18)
rpt.writeText("\nName: " + nameFld.value)
rpt.writeText("Serial #" + snFld.value)
rpt.writeText("Address: " + addrFld.value)
rpt.writeText("Email: " + emailFld.value)
```

Undo the previous indent
```
rpt.outdent()
rpt.writeText(" ")
```
"\n" causes a line break
```
rpt.writeText("\n\nThank you for buying HARD 2·DO software\nWe
→ appreciate your business.")
```
Open the new report in Acrobat
```
var doc = rpt.open("Software Registration")
```

4. Close all dialog boxes until you are once more looking at the Acrobat page.

5. Try it out: Fill out the text fields and click the Faxable button. Acrobat will create a report like that in **Figure 18.1**. You can save this file, print it, and fax it to loved ones.

The code in detail

```
var nameFld = this.getField("txtName")
var snFld = this.getField("txtSN")
var addrFld = this.getField("txtAddress")
var emailFld = this.getField("txtEMail")
```

This script starts in the common way, grabbing references to the text fields whose values we will need. We assign each reference to an appropriately named variable.

```
var rpt = new Report()
```

Here is where we create our Report object, assigning the new object to the variable rpt.

```
rpt.size = 2
rpt.color = color.red
```

We specify a text size two times the default 12 points and set the color to red.

```
rpt.writeText("HARD 2·DO Software")
```

We print the text "Hard 2·DO Software" in 24-point red type.

```
rpt.size = 1
rpt.color = color.black
rpt.writeText("Software Registration Form")
```

We set our text size back to 12 points (that is, one times the default size), our color to black, and print the text "Software Registration Form".

```
rpt.writeText(" ")
```

We skip a line, for esthetic reasons, by printing a space. Note that you need to have a space character between the quotes; if you hand an empty string ("") to writeText, it will not do anything at all, including skip to the next line.

```
rpt.size = .75
rpt.writeText("Please fax this report to 555-123-4567")
```

We set our point size to 9 (in other words, 0.75 times 12) and print text that tells the user what to do with this report.

```
rpt.color = color.red
rpt.divide(2)
```

We set the color to red again, and draw a horizontal line 2 points thick.

```
rpt.writeText(" ")

rpt.size = 1

rpt.color = color.black
```

We skip a line and then reset the text size and color.

```
rpt.indent(18)
```

We indent by 18 points. This will affect all text from this point until we change the indentation again.

```
rpt.writeText("Name: " + nameFld.value)

rpt.writeText("Serial #" + snFld.value)

rpt.writeText("Address: " + addrFld.value)

rpt.writeText("Email: " + emailFld.value)
```

We print the values of our four text fields. Note that in each case, we are printing the concatenation of a label (`"Name: "`) and the field value (`nameFld.value`).

```
rpt.outdent()
```

We undo the previous indentation.

```
rpt.writeText(" ")

rpt.writeText("Thank you for buying HARD 2·DO software\nWe
appreciate your business.")
```

We skip a line and then print a final "thank you" message. Note that we are using backslash-n (`\n`) in this string to force a line break, exactly as we sometimes do in an `app.alert` message string.

```
var doc = rpt.open("Software Registration")
```

Finally, we finish the report and open it in Acrobat for the user to see. The title of the document will be Software Registration. The open method returns a `Doc` object representing the newly made report; we don't actually do anything with it in this script. In other scripts, you could use this object to automatically print the report; see the following Customization Notes to see how to do this.

The user is now looking at the newly created report. He or she can now print it and fax it to the software company.

Customization Notes

The most useful customization of this program—aside from generating different information, of course—would be to email the form to someone or automatically print the report, rather than just opening it in Acrobat.

Printing the report

In the code above, we finished creating the report by calling the Report object's open method, which returns a Doc object representing the newly created Acrobat document. We saved a reference to that Doc object in a variable named doc:

```
var doc = rpt.open("Software Registration")
```

Something very useful we can do with that Doc object is to automatically print the report so that the user can fax it to the company. We do this by calling the Doc object's print method immediately after our call to open:

```
var doc = rpt.open("Software Registration")
doc.print(true)
```

The print method prints the document to the user's printer. If the Boolean argument is true (or omitted), then the user will be presented with a standard Print dialog box. If the Boolean is false, the document will be printed immediately, without any user interaction. (I consider using false to be impolite; you should always give the user the chance to cancel the printing or change printers, among other options.)

Emailing the report

As an alternative to finishing a report with open, you can use the Report object's mail method. This method ends report generation and then launches the user's mail client, creating a blank mail message with the newly created report file attached.

We could have added a Mail Registration button to our registration form that emails the registration report to Hard 2•Do Software. Our JavaScript program for the Mail button would be identical to our script in this chapter's example, except that we would replace the present call to rpt.open with a call to rpt.mail:

```
var doc = rpt.mail(true, "registration@hard2do.com")
```

This will launch the user's mail client and open a blank mail message with the "To" address set to `registration@hard2do.com`. The user need only click the mail client's Send button to mail the report.

In principle, passing a `false` value for the initial Boolean should cause the mail message to be sent immediately, without the user having to click a Send button. However, I have had spotty results with this, so I just always assume the user will need to explicitly send the message on its way.

Acrobat's integration with various mail clients has always been unpredictable. I recommend using the `mail` method with some caution, because it frequently will not work as you wish with certain email clients.

You should also warn the user what is about to happen. I would probably precede the call to `rpt.mail` with an alert telling the user what to do (**Figure 18.5**):

```
app.alert("We are about to launch your email software.\n\nPlease
→ click the 'Send' button to mail your registration to Hard 2·Do.")

var doc = rpt.mail(true, "registration@hard2do.com")
```

You may want to read Chapter 13 for more information on alerts.

Figure 18.5 *You should warn users before launching their email client; this tells them what to expect and keeps them calm.*

Where Now?

Congratulations!

You have made it through the entire book: You've put form fields to flight, routed regular expressions, and dabbled in databases! Now, it's time to go play. You know enough to be able to create Acrobat forms that are substantially smarter and more useful than when you started. It's time to use that new expertise.

Welcome to the JavaScript club. It's fun, interesting, and satisfying, it impresses your friends, and, best of all, there's always more to learn.

Enjoy!

What Now?

This book does not completely cover either JavaScript or Acrobat's JavaScript capabilities. So, your next assignment is to learn more about JavaScript and its Acrobat incarnation.

Your primary source for additional information on Acrobat JavaScript is the *Acrobat JavaScript Object Specification* (**Figure 19.1**); this document describes *all* of the capabilities of Acrobat JavaScript. You already own this reference, since it was installed on your hard disk when you installed Adobe Acrobat, and you can get to it conveniently within Acrobat by selecting Help > Acrobat JavaScript Guide. This document is akin to a dictionary; you likely won't read it cover to cover but rather will use it to look up specific capabilities of JavaScript objects within Acrobat. Still, I recommend at least skimming it, just to get an idea of what's in there.

After that, you should explore more about JavaScript as a language; there's much about the language that this beginning book doesn't attempt to cover. You know enough now to perform a lot of useful tasks in Acrobat, but you may eventually want to learn even more.

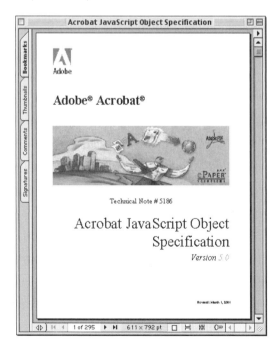

Figure 19.1
Acrobat supplies you with this comprehensive JavaScript reference. While it's not precisely light reading, it can be an invaluable resource.

The rest of this chapter lists places you can go to learn more about both JavaScript and Acrobat. Many Web sites provide everything from JavaScript tutorials to code samples to code fragments that you can cut and paste into your own scripts. Unfortunately, almost all of these resources are heavily oriented toward the Web and so are not terribly useful for Acrobat forms.

What follows are the sites and books that I have found most useful.

Acumen Training's Acrobat JavaScript Web page (www.acumentraining.com/ acrobatjs.html) has links to URLs mentioned below.

Acrobat JavaScript Resources

Books

Although most technical books on Acrobat will have at least a chapter or two on JavaScript, as of this writing there are no books devoted to JavaScript for Acrobat other than the one you hold in your hands. All the JavaScript books (and there is a boatload of them) are written for people writing scripts for Web browsers.

Internet

There are some very useful Web sites for people writing JavaScript for Acrobat. These sites supply everything from code samples to frequently asked questions (FAQs) to white papers on various JavaScript topics. These are listed in no particular order.

AcrobatJS
www.acumentraining.com/acrobatjs.html

This is my Web page for readers of this book. Here you will find the sample files for all the chapters. You'll also find a series of "E-ddenda" for *Extending Acrobat Forms with JavaScript:* changes, notes, and other tidbits that apply to sections of this book. You can download them in PDF format.

Acumen Journal

www.acumentraining.com/acjournal.asp

This is my own free monthly technical journal, distributed in PDF format. It has a monthly article on Acrobat; every second month (starting May 2003), that article will be on JavaScript, aimed specifically at readers of this book.

Planet PDF

www.planetpdf.com

This is where I go for tips and to see what other people are doing. Planet PDF has an active JavaScript Forum where you should start hanging out. You'll find a lot of people asking for help with Acrobat JavaScript problems and many other people proposing solutions. Some *very* smart people dwell therein. You'll also find a lot of code samples and some columns that are well worth reading.

PDFzone

www.pdfzone.com

Similar to Planet PDF. This site offers a lot of good information. It doesn't have a specific JavaScript forum, but the PDF Forms discussion list contains a good amount of JavaScript-related talk.

Adobe Systems' Online Tutorial

http://partners.adobe.com/asn/developer/training/acrobat/javascript/main.html

This is a very good online tutorial, though it assumes you're self-reliant. Here's how the Web page describes its audience: "You are resourceful and accustomed to learning new technologies quickly, and with minimal hand holding, if you have access to the necessary knowledge resources." If that sounds like you, there is much to be learned here.

If the URL for this site seems too long to type in, remember there's a link to it on the AcrobatJS Web site.

Google

A quick search on Google (www.google.com) for the phrase *Acrobat JavaScript* turns up 176,000 sites—and that's if you restrict it to English only! This is a good place to rummage in your idle moments. You'll find links to sites with sample code, people holding forth on what they do or don't like, FAQs, and other Web-based information sources.

Newsgroups

There are no newsgroups specifically about Acrobat JavaScript. However, the PDF newsgroup (comp.text.pdf) and the Acrobat newsgroup (list.comp.software.adobe.acrobat) have occasional discussions of JavaScript issues.

Learning JavaScript

There are zillions of resources available for learning JavaScript, pretty much all of them aimed at JavaScript for the Web. Still, these are good places to learn the language; you can then use the *Acrobat JavaScript Object Specification* to apply what you learn to Acrobat.

Books

There are far too many books on JavaScript for me to pretend I know which ones are best. However, following are the JavaScript books I have on my shelves and consider to be worth having:

JavaScript for the World Wide Web: Visual QuickStart Guide, 4th Edition
By Tom Negrino and Dori Smith
Peachpit Press (2001)

I am very fond of the Visual QuickStart series. This book is concise and complete, and is an excellent place to start your broader JavaScript education.

JavaScript Bible
By Danny Goodman
Wiley (2001)

This is a *very* comprehensive (to the tune of 1000+ pages) book on JavaScript for the Web. Probably not the book I'd want to start with, but a very good book to have on hand for reference.

Internet

Many Web sites offer JavaScript tutorials. Unfortunately, these are all tightly bound to programming for the Web. Still, I particularly like the two below.

W3Schools JavaScript Tutorial
www.w3schools.com/js/default.asp

Clear, though a bit dry in presentation.

PageResource.com
www.pageresource.com/jscript/

A couple of good tutorials here: one very basic, for beginners; another for intermediate and advanced folks.

SQL

Books

There are many good books on the market for learning SQL. (Amazon lists 842!) These are the ones I own:

SQL: Visual QuickStart Guide
By Chris Fehily
Peachpit Press (2002)

An excellent book that presents SQL in clear, bite-sized chunks.

Sams Teach Yourself SQL in 10 Minutes
Ben Forta
Sams Publishing (2003)

A very good, beginning book with an unthreatening approach.

Internet

SQLCourse.com
www.sqlcourse.com

This is an excellent beginner's tutorial. The pace is good and there's an actual SQL interpreter online so you can type in your SQL commands and see how (and if) they work. Quite cool!

W3Schools SQL Tutorial
www.w3schools.com/sql/default.asp

As with their JavaScript tutorial, this is very clear, if dry.

Regular Expressions

Regular expressions are useful, but an in-depth study of them is an acquired taste. Here are a couple of Web-based resources you might look into for samples and to further your education.

Internet

Regular Expression Library

www.regexlib.com

Bookmark this site if you use regular expressions! It contains a large collection of regular expressions suitable for pasting into your JavaScripts, searchable by topic. A stunningly useful site.

A Tao of Regular Expressions

http://sitescooper.org/tao_regexps.html

A one-Web-page introduction to regular expressions, with some good examples. The three categories of difficulty are Simple, Strange Incantations, and Magical Hieroglyphs.

Pattern Matching and Regular Expressions

www.webreference.com/js/column5/

Part of a larger tutorial, this tutorial is very good.

Form Processing

Processing form data was not among this book's topics, but we did mention it in a few places, so I thought it would be useful to point you to a source of free or inexpensive processing scripts.

When you submit form data, you send that data to a program or a script residing on a remote server; your form's Submit action must provide the URL of that remote script. That script must be written in a language known to the server, such as ASP, PHP, or Java. Happily, if your form submits its data in HTML format, you can use any number of already-written scripts that are available on the Web for free.

The CGI Resource Index

www.cgi-resources.com

This is probably the largest, best-organized source of free server-side programs for processing HTML form data.

Note that even using free programs for processing form data takes some technical skill and is not something you would usually do as a form designer. In most cases, a system administrator would set this up.

Object Reference

This appendix supplies a brief description of every object, property, and method used in this book. Look here for a reminder of how a particular method works or what a property means. This is *not* a complete reference of all objects available in Acrobat; for that you must look to the *Acrobat JavaScript Object Specification*, which is installed on your computer along with Adobe Acrobat. In Acrobat, select Help > Acrobat JavaScript Guide.

The descriptions here are intentionally brief; extensive descriptions are in the body of the book. Where appropriate, there are references to the chapter that covers a particular item in detail.

Within this appendix, each variable and argument name is given a suffix that indicates the data type of each item. These suffixes are listed in table A.1.

Table A.1 *Data Type Suffixes*

SUFFIX	TYPE	EXAMPLE
a	Array	aMenuItems
b	Boolean	bSaveFirst
n	Number	nPageNumber
o	Object	oRow
s	String	sMessage

In addition, method arguments that are listed in square brackets are optional. Thus, the following line:

```
app.alert(sMessage, [nIconCode], [nButtons])
```

tells us that the *app.alert* method takes as arguments a string and two optional numbers.

ADBC Object

This object represents a connection to an ODBC database.

Methods

newConnection

```
ADBC.newConnection(sDataSource)
```

Opens a connection to the specified ODBC data source. See Chapters 16 and 17 for more information.

Returns: A Connection object or a null object if the connection failed.

App Object

The App object represents the application that is displaying the current Acrobat document.

Properties

viewerVersion   (Number) The version of the user's Acrobat viewer.

Methods

alert

```
alert(sMessage, [nIcon], [nButtons])
```

Puts up an alert with the specified message. nIcon is a code that indicates what kind of icon should be displayed in the alert; nButtons indicates what set of buttons should be presented. See Chapter 13 for a list of icon and button codes.

Returns: Button code

beep

```
beep([nType])
```

Causes the computer to play a sound. The argument, nType, indicates what kind of sound to play. Valid codes are listed in Table A.2. The Beep code only has meaning on Windows systems; it is ignored on the Macintosh.

Table A.1   *Beep Codes*

BEEP TYPE	CODE
Error	0
Warning	1
Question	2
Status	3
Default	4

popUpMenu

popUpMenu(item1, item2, ...)

Displays a pop-up menu at the mouse pointer's position. Each item among the arguments is a string, indicating the text of a menu item, or an array of strings, indicating a submenu. See Chapter 15 for more details.

Returns: The text of the selected item or a null object if no item was selected.

response

response(sQuestion, [sTitle], [sDefault], bIsPassword)

Presents an alert to the user that contains a text field into which the user can type the response to a question, sQuestion.

sTitle is the title of the alert; sDefault is the text that should be placed into the text field as the default response; bIsPassword, if true, indicates that characters typed by the user should be displayed as bullets. See Chapter 13 for more detail.

Returns: The text typed by the user or a null object if the Cancel button was clicked.

Connection Object

This object represents an open connection to an ODBC database.

Methods

newStatement

newStatement()

Creates a statement object through which SQL messages may be sent to an ODBC database. See Chapters 16 and 17 for details on how to use newStatement as part of an SQL query.

Returns: A Statement object or a null object if the action fails.

Doc Object

The Doc Object represents an Acrobat document. The most commonly used Doc object is the `this` object, which, within Field and Document JavaScripts, refers to the currently displayed document.

Properties

author	(String) The author of the document.
fileSize	(Number) The size of the document, in bytes.
numPages	(Number) The number of pages in the document.
pageNum	(Number) The page number of the currently visible page.
title	(String) The title of the document.

Methods

closeDoc

`closeDoc([bDontSave])`

Closes the document. If `bDontSave` is true, the document will not be saved. If the Boolean is false or omitted, then the user is given the chance to save the document.

getField

`getField(sFieldName)`

Gets a reference to the named field.

Returns*:* A Field object representing the named field.

getTemplate

`getTemplate(sTemplateName)`

Gets the named template from the document. See Chapter 9 for details.

Returns*:* A Template object or a null object if no template with the specified name exists.

submitForm

`submitForm(sURL, [bFDF], [bEmpty])`

Submits the form to the specified URL. If `bFDF` is true or omitted from the code, then the form data is submitted in FDF format; if `bFDF` is false, the data is submitted as HTML. If `bEmpty` is true, then all fields, including empty fields, are submitted; if it's false or missing from the code, then only fields with a value are submitted. See Chapter 13 for more information.

This method has a large number of optional arguments that are not mentioned in this book. See the *Acrobat JavaScript Object Specification* for a complete list.

Event Object

The Event object contains information about the event that triggered a JavaScript. These objects are used throughout the book; Chapter 8 gives the most complete description of the Event object's properties.

Properties

change	The new value of the field that triggered the event.
changeEx	(String) The new export value of the field that triggered the event.
target	(Field object) A Field object representing the form field that triggered the event.
value	(String) The value of the form field that triggered the event.

Field Object

The Field object represents a form field. It has a *lot* of properties beyond those we have used in the book; every control in the Field Properties dialog box has a corresponding property in a Field object. See the *Acrobat JavaScript Object Specification* for a complete list.

Properties

borderColor	(Color Spec) The color of the field's border.
fillColor	(Color Spec) The color of the field's interior. (The "Background Color" in the *Field Properties* dialog box.) See Chapter 3 for a discussion of specifying color in JavaScript.
hidden	(Boolean) If true, the field is not visible to the user.
textColor	(Color Spec) The color of the text within the field. See Chapter 3 for a discussion of specifying color in JavaScript.
value	(Various) The value of the form field.

RegExp Object

A RegExp object encapsulates a regular expression that may be used for matching strings with a specified pattern. See Chapters 10 through 12 for a discussion of regular expressions.

Properties

RegExp.$1... RegExp.$9   (String) These nine properties contain the text that matches any parenthetical phrases in the regular expression.

Methods

test

`test`(String)

This method tests the supplied string against the pattern described by the regular expression.

Returns*:* A Boolean true if the string matches the expression.

Report Object

The Report object creates a new Acrobat document whose contents are generated by the JavaScript using the Report object. See Chapter 18 for a full description.

Properties

color   (Color) The color that should be used for text and lines. See Chapter 3 for details on specifying color in Acrobat JavaScript.

size   (Number) Specifies the point size of printed text. This is a multiplier; the actual point size will be this number times the default point size of 12.

Methods

breakPage

`breakPage`()

Ends the current page and starts a new page in the report document.

divide

`divide([nWidth])`

Draws a horizontal line from the current left margin (including indentation) to the right margin. The optional line width is measured in points; if this term is missing, Acrobat uses a linewidth of 2 points.

indent

`indent([nDistance])`

Moves the left margin to the right by the specified distance in points. If the distance is omitted, an indentation of 18 points is used.

mail

`mail([bShowUI], [sAddr])`

Ends report generation, launches the user's mail client, and mails the report to the specified address. If `bShowUI` is false, the user is not shown the mail message; the message is just sent directly to the specified address. If `bShowUI` is true or omitted, the blank mail form is displayed in the mail client; the user must click the mail client's Send button to send the message on its way.

The `mail` method can take several additional, optional arguments; these are documented in the *Acrobat JavaScript Object Specification.*

open

`open(sDocName)`

Ends report generation and opens the new Acrobat Report file in the viewer. The user can print, save, or otherwise treat this file like any other Acrobat file.

Returns*:* Doc object representing the Report file.

outdent

`outdent([nDistance])`

Moves the left margin to the left by the specified distance or by the default amount (18 points).

writeText

`writeText(sText)`

Prints the specified text. Each call to `writeText` starts on a new line.

Statement Object

The Statement object is a conduit through which SQL commands can be sent to an ODBC data source. See Chapters 16 and 17 for detailed information.

Methods

execute

`execute(sSQLStatement)`

The execute method sends the specified statement to the ODBC data source. If the command fails, execute throws an exception. (Note: the *Acrobat JavaScript Object Specification* incorrectly says that execute returns a Boolean false if the statement fails; this is wrong.)

getRow

`getRow()`

Gets the current row of information from the ODBC datasource. Must be preceded by a call to nextRow.

Returns*:* Row object representing the retrieved row of information.

nextRow

`nextRow()`

This method points the ODBC database to the next row of selected data. This command does not actually retrieve the information; that is done by getRow.

Template Object

This object represents a template in an Acrobat document.

Methods

spawn

`spawn([nPageNum], [bRenameVars], [bOverlay])`

Creates a new set of PDF page elements based on the contents of the template.

If bOverlay is true or omitted, the new elements will be added to page nPageNum in the Acrobat document; if bOverlay is false, the new elements will be added to a new page inserted into the document in front of page nPageNum. If bRemameVars is true or omitted, form fields in the Template will be renamed. The default value for nPageNum is 0.

See Chapter 9 for a complete description of how Template objects work.

Regular Expression Metacharacters

This appendix presents a table of all the metacharacters that have meaning within a regular expression.

Table B.1   *Regular Expression Metacharacters*

CODE	MEANING
\	Indicates the next character should be taken literally, that is, a character to be matched, even if that character is normally a metacharacter. For example, /F+/ will match one or more "F" characters; on the other hand, /F\+/ will match "F" followed by a plus sign.
^	Matches the beginning of the string. Thus, /^A/ will match the "A" in "An excess of buffalo", but not in "The Abacus".
$	Matches the end of the string. Thus, /help$/ will match "Please help", but not "Please help me".
\w	Matches a single alphanumeric character. Thus, /\w/ will be a match if the test string were "X", but not if it were "™".
\W	Matches a single *non-* alphanumeric character.

Table B.1   *Regular Expression Metacharacters (continued)*

CODE	MEANING
[xyz]	Matches any one of the characters in the brackets. You can use a hyphen to indicate a range of characters. Thus, /[afbt]/ would match "a", "f", "b", or "t", but not "m". Similarly, /[a-c]/ would match "a", "b", or "c".
[^xyz]	Matches any character *except* those in the brackets. Thus, /[^afbt]/ would match "m", but not "a", "f", "b", or "t". Note that this is a different use of the carat character than that used above.
\d	Matches a single-digit character, 0 through 9.
\D	Matches any non-digit character.
\s	Matches a single whitespace character, that is, a single space, tab, Return, or linefeed character.
\S	Matches a single non-whitespace character, that is, any character except space, tab, Return, or linefeed character.
*	Must follow a character specification; indicates 0 or more instances of that specification. Thus, /ba*d/ would match "bd", "bad", "baaad", etc.
+	Matches the preceding character specification 1 or more time. Thus, /ba+d/ would match "bad" or "baad", but not "bd".
?	Matches the preceding character 0 or 1 time. Thus, /ba?d/ would match "bd" and "bad", but not "baaad".
{n}	Where *n* is a number: matches exactly *n* instances of the preceding specification. Thus, /Du{3}de/ would match only "Duuude".
{n,m}	Where *n* and *m* are numbers: matches at least *n* but not more than *m* instances of the preceding specification. /Du{1,3}de/ will match "Dude", "Duude", and "Duuude".
\b	Matches any word boundary, including the beginning of the string, a space character, a tab, or a newline.
\B	Matches a non-word boundary. Thus /\Bx/ would find a match in "box", but not in "my xylophone."
[\b]	Matches a backspace character (character code 8). Note this is different from \b (without the brackets).
.	(Period) Matches any single character except newline or the beginning of the string. Thus, \.B\ will match "A Boy", but not "Boy".
(X)	(Parentheses) Matches the expression *X* and remembers the match. The matching text can later be retrieved in the JavaScript with the RegExp properties $1 through $9. See Chapter 12 for a lengthy description.

Table B.1   *Regular Expression Metacharacters (continued)*

CODE	MEANING
x|y	Matches either expression *x* or *y*. Thus, /bad|good/ would match both "bad dog" and "good dog".
\cX	Matches a Control character in a string. Thus, /\cZ/ matches Control-Z (character code 26) in a string.
\f	Matches a form feed character (character code 12).
\n	Matches a line-feed character (character code 10).
\r	Matches a character return character (character code 13).
\t	Matches a tab character (character code 9).
\v	Matches a vertical tab character (character code 11).
\n	(Where *n* is an integer) Matches the text that matched the *nth* parenthetical expression in the regular expression. Thus, /(w+), \1/ would match "House, House" but not "House, Mouse"
\oXXX	(Where each X is a numeral 0 through 7) Matches the specified octal character code. Thus /\o062/ would match "2"; octal 062 is the character code for the numeral 2.
\xXX	(Where each X is a numeral 0 through 7 or a character a through f or A through F) Matches the specified hexadecimal character code. Thus /\x44/ would match "D", hex 44 being the character code for "D".

Index

Z